SECURITY & CRIME

Sara Miller McCune founded SAGE Publishing in 1965 to support the dissemination of usable knowledge and educate a global community. SAGE publishes more than 1000 journals and over 800 new books each year, spanning a wide range of subject areas. Our growing selection of library products includes archives, data, case studies and video. SAGE remains majority owned by our founder and after her lifetime will become owned by a charitable trust that secures the company's continued independence.

Los Angeles | London | New Delhi | Singapore | Washington DC | Melbourne

SECURITY & CRIME

CONVERGING PERSPECTIVES ON A COMPLEX WORLD

ALISON WAKEFIELD

Los Angeles | London | New Delhi
Singapore | Washington DC | Melbourne

Los Angeles | London | New Delhi
Singapore | Washington DC | Melbourne

SAGE Publications Ltd
1 Oliver's Yard
55 City Road
London EC1Y 1SP

SAGE Publications Inc.
2455 Teller Road
Thousand Oaks, California 91320

SAGE Publications India Pvt Ltd
B 1/I 1 Mohan Cooperative Industrial Area
Mathura Road
New Delhi 110 044

SAGE Publications Asia-Pacific Pte Ltd
3 Church Street
#10-04 Samsung Hub
Singapore 049483

Editor: Natalie Aguilera
Assistant editor: Ozlem Merakli
Production editor: Jessica Masih
Copyeditor: Elaine Leek
Proofreader: Caroline Hallworth
Indexer: Paula Clarke Bain
Marketing manager: George Kimble
Cover design: Wendy Scott

Typeset by KnowledgeWorks Global Ltd.
Printed in the UK

Library of Congress Control Number: 2020949213

British Library Cataloguing in Publication data

A catalogue record for this book is available from the
British Library

ISBN 978-1-4129-3100-7
ISBN 978-1-4129-3101-4 (Pbk)

eISBN 978-1-5264-5367-9

At SAGE we take sustainability seriously. Most of our products are printed in the UK using FSC papers and
boards. When we print overseas we ensure sustainable papers are used as measured by the PREPS grading
system. We undertake an annual audit to monitor our sustainability.

For Danielle and Sophie

Contents

List of figures and tables

Figures

Tables

About the author

Alison Wakefield is Professor of Criminology and Security Studies and Co-Director of the Cybersecurity and Criminology Centre at the University of West London. She is also an Associate Fellow of the Royal United Services Institute and was Chair of the Security Institute, the UK's largest member association for security professionals, from 2018 to 2020.

Alison's recent honours and awards include ranking third in the thought leadership category of IFSEC Global's Top Influencers in Security and Fire for 2020, featuring in IT Security Guru's Most Inspiring Women in Cyber 2020 and SC Media UK's 50 Women of Influence in Cyber Security 2019, earning an Emerald Outstanding Paper 2018 award for the co-authored paper 'Confronting the "fraud bottleneck"' in the *Journal of Criminological Research, Policy and Practice*, and receiving the Association of Security Consultants Imbert Prize 2017 for her contribution to the security profession.

Her other publications include *The Sage Dictionary of Policing* (Sage, 2009, edited with Jenny Fleming), *Selling Security: The Private Policing of Public Space* (Willan Publishing, 2003) and *Ethical and Social Perspectives on Situational Crime Prevention* (Hart Publishing, 2000, edited with Andrew von Hirsch and David Garland).

Acknowledgements

In the course of writing this book I have benefitted from the support and encouragement of many people. I am grateful to family members and friends for putting up with my long disappearances, including colleagues at the University of West London and the Security Institute who allowed me space for intense periods of writing. I would particularly like to thank the numerous people who spared time to offer their insights on aspects of the book, or introduced me to new issues and ideas, including Andrea Birdsall, Andrew Glazzard, David Brooks, Donna Peacock, Hamish Cameron, James Banks, Jenny Fleming, Karim Murji, Keith Ditcham, Mahesh Nalla, Martin Gill, Mike Gips, Nigel Rourke, Paul Martin, Peter Squires, Phil Wane, Robert Hall and Toby Harris. I am grateful to Yvonne Jewkes for giving me the opportunity to contribute to the excellent Key Approaches to Criminology book series, and Paula Clarke Bain for her most comprehensive and thorough index. Finally, I am hugely appreciative to the team at Sage for their faith in me and considerable help throughout the writing process, including Caroline Porter, Eve Williams, John Nightingale, Ozlem Merakli, Jessica Masih and especially Natalie Aguilera, whose encouragement, patience and guidance played no small part in getting me to the finish line.

List of abbreviations

4IR	fourth industrial revolution
9/11	11 September 2001, the date of four coordinated terrorist attacks against the United States
ACT	Action Counters Terrorism
BCM	business continuity management
BID	business improvement district
CCTV	closed circuit television
CNI	critical national infrastructure
COVID-19	coronavirus disease 2019
CPTED	crime prevention through environmental design
DHS	Department of Homeland Security
EEZ	exclusive economic zone
EU	European Union
FAO	Food and Agriculture Organization of the United Nations
GCR	global catastrophic risk
ICT	information and communications technology
IGO	inter-governmental organization
ILP	intelligence-led policing
IMF	International Monetary Fund
IMO	International Maritime Organization
IOM	International Organization for Migration
IoT	internet of things
ISO	International Standards Organization
IUU	illegal, unreported and unregulated fishing
IWF	Internet Watch Foundation
JRF	Joseph Rowntree Foundation
LGBT	lesbian, gay, bisexual and transgender
MDGs	Millennium Development Goals
MoD	Ministry of Defence
NAFTA	North American Free Trade Agreement
NATO	North Atlantic Treaty Organization
NCIS	National Criminal Intelligence Service
NCMEC	National Center for Missing and Exploited Children

NCS	National Crime Squad
NCSC	National Cyber Security Centre
NGO	non-governmental organization
NIC	National Intelligence Council
NIM	National Intelligence Model
NSA	National Security Agency
NSS/SDSR	National Security Strategy and Strategic Defence and Security Review
OECD	Organisation for Security Co-operation and Development
ONS	Office for National Statistics
OSCE	Organization for Security and Co-operation in Europe
PCSO	police community support officer
PSPO	public spaces protection order
SDGs	Sustainable Development Goals
SIPRI	Stockholm International Peace Research Institute
SOCA	Serious Organized Crime Agency
SPR	Strategic Policing Requirement
Tor	The Onion Router
UK	United Kingdom
UN	United Nations
UNCTAD	United Nations Conference on Trade and Development
UNDP	United Nations Development Programme
UNHCR	United Nations High Commissioner for Refugees
UNODC	UN Office on Drugs and Crime
UNODRR	UN Office for Disaster Risk Reduction
US	United States
WMD	weapon of mass destruction

Table of legislation, conventions and treaties

International

Budapest Convention on Cybercrime, 2001
Convention on International Civil Aviation, 1944
Convention on the International Maritime Organization, 1948
Geneva Convention on the High Seas, 1958
International Opium Convention, 1912
International Opium Convention, 1925
Peace Treaties of Westphalia and Osnabrück, 1648
Safety of Life at Sea Convention, 1974
Treaty on the Non-Proliferation of Nuclear Weapons, 1968
United Nations Convention on the Law of the Sea, 1982
United Nations Convention against Transnational Organized Crime, 2001
United Nations Framework Convention on Climate Change, 1992

European

Directive (EU) 2016/1148 (Security of Network and Information Systems), 2016
European Convention on Human Rights, 1953
Europol Convention, 1995
Regulation (EU) 2016/679 (General Data Protection Regulation), 2016
Schengen Convention, 1990

National
United Kingdom

Anti-Terrorism Crime and Security Act 2001
Bribery Act 2010
Civil Contingencies Act 2004
Climate Change Act 2008
Computer Misuse Act 1990
Crime and Disorder Act 1998
Criminal Justice and Courts Act 2015
Human Rights Act 1998
Immigration Act 1971
Intelligence Services Act 1994
Metropolitan Police Act 1829
Modern Slavery Act 2015
Official Secrets Act 1911
Official Secrets Act 1920
Police and Criminal Evidence Act 1984
Police Reform Act 2002
Police Reform and Social Responsibility Act 2011
Proceeds of Crime Act 2002
Private Security Industry Act 2001
Regulation of Investigatory Powers Act 2000
Security Service Act 1989
Security Service Act 1996
Terrorism Act 2000
Vagrancy Act 1824

United States

Coal and Iron Police Act 1867
Espionage Act 1917
Foreign Corrupt Practices Act 1977
Homeland Security Act 2002
National Security Act 1947
Uniting and Strengthening America by Providing Appropriate Tools Required
to Restrict, Intercept and Obstruct Terrorism (USA PATRIOT) Act 2001

1

Introduction: Navigating a complex world

Chapter overview

This chapter provides:

- A discussion of the drivers of change and future security trends that are expected to shape our world over the coming decades.
- An appraisal of the contested concept of security and its multiple applications and meanings.
- An assessment of the relationship between the two concepts of security and crime, and the capacity of a crime-focused criminology discipline to adapt to the increasingly security-focused agendas of politicians and policy-makers.
- An outline of the aims of the book and the dimensions of security to be addressed in each of the ensuing chapters.

Key terms

- Cold War
- Foresight studies
- Globalization
- Human security
- International relations
- Risk
- Securitization
- Security
- Security governance
- Security studies

Exploring global complexity

Our world today is characterized by rapid change, interconnectedness, complexity and uncertainty. The acceleration of **globalization** and technological advancement have revolutionized international trade, communication and travel, and average standards of living are higher than they have ever been. At the same time, the continuing advancement in the speed of change across multiple areas of human activity, and our reliance on interdependent systems, leave us exposed to innumerable and uncertain threats, as demonstrated so profoundly by the cascade of health, economic, social and political effects of the coronavirus (COVID-19) global pandemic.

Insights into the extent of the challenges confronting national governments as they plan for the future are provided by **security** and defence **foresight studies**, particularly those published periodically by government **national security** agencies. Such analyses, which employ a variety of methodologies, are military in origin and can be traced back to the period between the First and Second World Wars (Dreyer and Stang, 2013). They examine the major political and social trends likely to impact on the future of global security, providing strategic **intelligence** to inform governments' long-term strategic planning, policy-making and capability-building. They also serve to 'alert readers to changes that are likely to become threats but may, if addressed promptly, provide opportunities' (Ministry of Defence, 2018: 11). Foresight research projects may be privately or publicly funded, and national or international in focus (Jordan, 2017), examples including the *Global Trends* reports of the United States National Intelligence Council (NIC) and the *Global Strategic Trends* publications of the United Kingdom Ministry of Defence (MoD). Both series are in their sixth edition at the time of writing, with the next US edition due out in 2021, the US analyses having been launched in 1997 and the UK's in 2001. Others that are publicly available include those of the North Atlantic Treaty Organization (NATO), the European Union and the governments of Canada, France, Germany, Italy and Spain, which are discussed and compared by Jordan (2017) in a review of foresight studies produced by official defence and security bodies in North America and Western Europe between 2007 and 2017.

For the purpose of this book, the latest NIC and MoD reports have been the main focus. A central theme is the changing balance of power in the world, with the dominance of the West now being challenged, politically and economically, and power shifting eastwards. The international system of institutions, regulations and mechanisms that developed after the end of the Second World War in 1945, shaped by the victorious powers, must adapt significantly to accommodate these shifts. Global **risks** and threats on the horizon are becoming more complex and difficult to predict, and the relative power of states is reducing in parallel with the expansion in number and influence of non-state transnational actors, such as inter-governmental organizations (IGOs), non-governmental organizations, multinational companies, media organizations, and criminal, ethnic and religious groupings.

While both reports observe that inequality between countries has reduced, largely due to rapid economic growth in Asian countries, they highlight the problems of rising inequality within countries, particularly in central Asia, Europe and North America. This is seen to be eroding social cohesion and fuelling political populism and nationalist sentiment, particularly in states where there is a lack of trust in government institutions or economic instability, with signs that many governments are becoming more authoritarian. The reports highlight the challenges facing national economies, which need to manage the costs of technological advancement while confronting budgetary pressures in key areas of public spending like defence, health and welfare, as well as trying to manage the expectations of citizens who have become accustomed to a continuing rise in living standards. The implications of the ongoing shift towards a more automated world, encapsulated in the concept of the 'fourth industrial revolution' (4IR) (Schwab, 2017, 2018b), are explored, and the automation of work, the expanding information space and challenges in its regulation, human enhancement technologies, and **artificial intelligence** (the capability of machines to perform human-like tasks such as learning, problem-solving and decision-making) are identified as being among the technological trends presenting the greatest future implications.

Demographic change is a central theme of both reports, with the global population projected to reach 8.5 billion in 2030, 9.7 billion in 2050 and 10.9 billion in 2100 (United Nations Department of Economic and Social Affairs, 2019: 5). Rapid population growth is expected in many developing countries, where populations are becoming younger and more male due to female infanticide, child neglect and sex-selective abortion. In such countries, investment in education and employment, as well as measures to address gender imbalances, are deemed essential to mitigate consequential rises in crime and violence, including **human rights** violations against women and girls. In the developed world, as the reports note, very different demographic challenges apply: the population is ageing and will require much greater spending on health and social care. Both reports note the risks of pandemics and epidemics and the factors that heighten those risks, including a greater propensity for the transfer of zoonotic diseases (those transferred from animals to humans), associated with increasing global connectivity and changing environmental conditions; growing population density in urban areas; and unaddressed deficiencies in national and global health systems for disease control. They predict increasing migration flows within and between countries, motivated by economic opportunity and flight from conflict or worsening economic conditions, and driving rapid urban expansion, particularly in developing countries where it will be more difficult to manage. Continuing and growing pressures on the environment are expected, with the growing world population increasing the demand for resources including water, food and energy, raising the costs to governments of climate change and mitigation measures. The governance of the **global commons** – the management of areas and resources beyond sovereign jurisdiction, specifically the oceans, polar regions, air space, outer space and **cyberspace** – is an increasingly pressing concern as competition grows for access to natural resources, and rivalry intensifies between the US and other major powers, particularly China.

The two analyses anticipate increasing risk of conflict as the global balance of power changes and the interests of major powers diverge, the threat of terrorism grows, weak states remain unstable, and weapons of mass destruction proliferate. While recognizing that countries' economic interdependence provides a check on intra-state aggression, the reports predict that many of the issues and trends identified in the reports and the interplay between them will raise tensions within and between countries. Weak and fragile states are presented as a significant concern, being viewed as potential breeding grounds for terrorism, organized crime, pandemics or mass movements of people, while global interconnectedness and the cumulative effect of these threats create vulnerabilities for others who are thousands of miles away. Rising inequality and unemployment within countries, along with social fragmentation and the weakening of communal values, amplified and exacerbated by social media, are expected to increase the risk of disorder, crime and extremism.

With longstanding vulnerabilities as well as new, complex and cascading threats on the horizon, we have reached an 'inflection point', according to the MoD (2018: 3), and face an 'unsettled geopolitical landscape' (World Economic Forum, 2020: 6). The NIC declares that the characteristic feature of our era is that we are 'living in a paradox', with a future being shaped that is 'both more dangerous and richer with opportunity than ever before' (2017: ix). For today's governments to address the strategic challenges for defence and security that confront them, it is argued that they need to make fundamental changes in approach, to one that is 'permanently innovative, adaptable, responsive and proactive' (MoD, 2018: 3). The NIC (2017) emphasizes the importance of 'long-term thinking', based on the likely future consequences of actions, and the fact that major concerns like terrorism, cyber attack and climate change can only be addressed through multi-stakeholder dialogue and sustained collaboration. Their report implies that it is states' capacity to do this effectively that will separate the winners and losers in the decades to come, observing that 'the most powerful actors of the future will draw on networks, relationships, and information to compete and cooperate' (p. ix).

Conceptions of security

Such challenges can be placed under the broad heading of 'security', which is a universal concern and one of the major challenges facing humanity. Indeed, Crawford and Hutchinson argue that it may now be '*the* key problematic of our time' (2016: 1050, emphasis in original). While it has no obvious disciplinary home, as a theme that has relevance to many, if not most, academic fields, it is a foundational concept of **international relations** and, as the discipline expanded and broadened, became the central concern of its 'most prestigious sub-field' (McSweeney, 1999: 25), **security studies**. The term is derived from the Latin word *securus*, meaning 'free from care', yet it serves as a versatile and 'essentially contested' concept (Buzan, 1983: 6; Smith, 2005: 27) – one that defies precise definition and means different things to different people – being an area of particular contention within international relations scholarship.

Booth (2007) observes that security is an instrumental value: not an end in itself, but a means towards living a fulfilling life beyond basic survival. Alluding to Maslow's (1970) well-known 'hierarchy of needs' psychological theory, Martin similarly describes it as 'a basic human need', allowing us to go about our lives 'freely and without harm', liberating us 'from the disruptive fear of harm', and building 'confidence to invest in the future' (2019: 1). Booth (2007) illustrates his point using three distinctions: between survival and security, as already implied; absolute and relative security; and objective and subjective threats. Security is a relative concept, in that it is difficult to envisage in absolute terms, and likely to be undesirable if such an end-state could be reached. This means that, in practice, it is based on calculations of the likelihood and consequences of undesirable events taking place, and trade-offs being made between security and competing factors such as cost, convenience and personal privacy or liberty.

Objective and subjective conceptions of security reflect a distinction between an 'absence of threats' and an 'absence of fears' (Wolfers, 1962: 149), expressed in the primary definition of the concept in the *Oxford English Dictionary* (2011): 'The state or condition of *being* or *feeling* secure' (emphasis added). Objectively, security is the relative certainty that one is safe from certain threats, the level of threat is minimal, or the necessary precautions are in place to mitigate any discernible risks. This perspective carries the presumption that security can be measured and quantified. By contrast, subjective considerations relate to a sense of security, absence of fear, or level of confidence that one is secure. Efforts to pursue objective security can be symbolic and enhance subjective perceptions of security, speaking to people's 'ontological insecurities' (Giddens, 1991) or fears of uncertainty. However, Valverde questions whether it is possible to measure security objectively, in the way that lawbreaking can be measured, arguing that insecurity 'is not a series of objectively measurable events, but rather a tendency, or what would soon come to be called a probability (and much later, a risk)' (2014: 383).

These considerations bring to light a further distinction, as to whether security is a passive condition or an active process. Security may be conceived simply as a state of being, but the term is also used to *describe* activities undertaken to enhance that state. The actions that we take, or products and services that we purchase to protect ourselves or others, serve not only as means of protection, but as enablers of risk-taking. They allow people or organizations to undertake activities that would otherwise expose them to hazards or liabilities, the focus of Ulrich Beck's (1992) influential 'risk society' thesis on human adaptations to living in a highly developed, more complex and less controllable world. Security 'actors' or 'providers' can put processes in place to identify, analyse, evaluate and manage security risk, requiring an awareness and understanding of both the threats being confronted and the vulnerabilities that are present. Such processes will often address both objective indicators and subjective perceptions of security, since stakeholders will not necessarily have informed understandings of threat levels, and certain measures may serve to be primarily symbolic, providing reassurance that 'something is being done'.

The rhetorical power of the concept of security is exemplified in the advertising of security products and services, politicians' promises to address voters' personal or community safety concerns, and security awareness campaigns employed by **police** forces, governments and employers to influence individual behaviour and reassure people that their concerns are being taken seriously (Zedner, 2009). Security has become a 'buzzword' (see Cornwall, 2007), with an 'allure' that 'has seen it attached to a long line of neologisms ... that deliberately use the term to mobilize political support and economic resources' (Zedner, 2009: 22). There is ample room for unscrupulous security providers to take advantage of people's fears, profiting from unassuaged demands for security products and services: the 'commodification of security' (Spitzer, 1987; Loader, 1999; Neocleous, 2007). On the other hand, the 'right kind of security', according to Martin (2019: 2), is 'a basic building block of civil society', 'intelligent and proportionate to the risks', and 'concerned with **safeguarding** lives, property, information, wealth, reputations, and societal wellbeing'.

Two further dimensions of security that have been heavily debated in international relations relate to its referent object – the question as to whose security is the focus of concern – and what constitutes a security issue. The discipline's traditional focus has been the state and its security from external threats, thus placing a primary emphasis on 'national security'. This perspective has been increasingly challenged since the early 1990s, however, in growing calls for a shift from a state-centred to a human-centred approach ('**human security**'), particularly within United Nations (UN) development circles. State-centred conceptions of security have traditionally prioritized military threats to a nation's territories, people and government, and reflected the primary threats to the major powers through the World War and **Cold War** decades when the international relations discipline emerged and developed. Following the collapse of the Soviet Union – officially the Union of Soviet Socialist Republics (USSR) – in late 1991, what soon came to be distinctive about the post-Cold War world was the broader set of issues coming to be conceived as **international security** threats, which could be military, economic, political, societal or environmental in nature (Buzan, 1983), a political process described by Wæver (1995) as '**securitization**'. The human security perspective takes account of a still wider range of issues, an influential UN report breaking the concept down into the sub-categories of economic, food, health, environmental, personal, community and **political security** (UN Development Programme [UNDP], 1994).

Tadjbakhsh (2013) adds to the fundamental questions of 'whose security?' and 'security from what?' a third question of 'security by what means?', inferring that the causes of human security challenges can be complex and require long-term and multi-faceted solutions – not just narrow, military interventions, for example. The 'human security approach' therefore lies at the heart of the UN development agenda, informing the **Sustainable Development** Goals (UN General Assembly, 2015; UN News, 2017), and illustrating the increasingly blurred lines between security and development in the post-Cold War world. The competing frameworks in international relations for interpreting the scope of the concept of security and the means of delivering it are explored in more depth in the next chapter, and the development and application of the human security perspective is a recurring theme of the book.

The intersection of security and crime

While security studies first emerged as a sub-field of the international relations discipline, analyses of security problems and strategies and mechanisms for their mitigation are now an interdisciplinary enterprise. In common with other texts in Sage's 'Key Approaches to Criminology' series, this book adopts such an approach to the study of security, with an analysis that is situated at the intersection of criminology, international relations and numerous other fields including development studies, economics, history, political science, postcolonial studies, sociology and the STEM (scientific, technological, engineering and mathematical) disciplines, as reflected in the book's subtitle 'Converging Perspectives on a Complex World'. The subject of security has been slow to gain the full attention of criminology and many other disciplines, and the term 'has, for the most part, been eschewed' within the criminology discipline (Froestad, Shearing and van der Merwe, 2015: 177–178). Yet its profile within the subject has grown in the new millennium in accordance with widening conceptions of security concerns and new forms of regulation (Crawford and Hutchinson, 2016), which Zedner (2009) was early in beginning to detail, and Froestad et al. (2015: 177) now describe security as 'criminology's most fundamental topic'.

Shearing (2015) builds on the work of Valverde (2013, 2014) to argue that a 'security-ology' and a 'risk-ology' is now taking shape within criminology, pursuing four principal directions. These are (1) a concern with a broader set of 'harms' beyond simply crime, (2) a shifting of focus beyond the state to take account of a broader range of actors, (3) risk-focused and forward-looking means of mitigating the realization of harms, and (4) explorations of the normative implications of these developments. The former of these, the idea that social harm matters more than crime and is a more meaningful focus of criminological attention, derives from the work of Hillyard and colleagues (Hillyard, Pantazis, Tombs and Gordon, 2004; Hillyard and Tombs, 2007) and is now a key dimension of a growing 'green criminology' movement within the discipline, concerned with environmental harms impacting on humans, other species and the natural environment (see White and Heckenberg, 2014; Brisman and South, 2020). The social harm perspective brings criminology closer to international relations, and specifically to its schools of thought that challenge state-centric security frameworks and promote an agenda for human security, a concept that has become a recurrent area of attention in Shearing's work (see Wood and Shearing, 2007; Leman-Langlois and Shearing, 2009; Froestad and Shearing, 2012; Harrington and Shearing, 2017).

Shearing's (2015) second theme, a broadening of the focus of criminology beyond the state, particularly within police studies, has been the central theme of his scholarship over more than four decades, observing the contributions of a widening set of 'auspices' (governing entities or users) and 'providers' to social control in Western democratic countries, alongside police forces (Bayley and Shearing, 2001). Preferring the term **'security governance'** to policing as a description of the collective activities of 'diversified networks of security and justice' (Johnston and Shearing, 2003: 10), and the varying configurations of security actors from one jurisdiction to the next, Shearing has long challenged criminology's disproportionate focus on the police when compared with other state, private and voluntary providers of security, drawing instead on ideas from sociology and political science about the broader administration of 'governance'. Notably, as Shearing's ideas about security governance were introduced and gained currency within criminology early in the new millennium, the concept emerged and evolved in parallel within the international relations discipline, where it is used to describe the pluralization of actors engaged in international affairs in response to a widening security agenda following the end of the Cold War, as will be discussed in the next chapter.

The idea of 'governance' as distinct from 'government' can be summarized as 'the deployment of multiple forms of regulation ... involving a wide range of actors and stakeholders' (Webber, 2014: 18). It is informed by perspectives such as Foucault's (1991 [1978]) concepts of governmentality and the disciplinary society, which reflect the dispersal of social control mechanisms beyond the state and through networks of actors; Castells' (1996) conception of the contemporary world as the 'network society', based on the sharing of authority among nodes of the network; and Rhodes' (1996, 1997) observations of an ongoing shift in British public administration away from 'government' through hierarchical bureaucracies, as states looked for more efficient ways of meeting the rising demands of their citizens, to 'governance' through 'self-organizing, interorganizational networks' that are more adaptable to the more difficult policy problems of the modern era.

Shearing's (2015) third theme is the refocusing of criminological attention from past-focused governance processes (criminal justice systems that deal with crimes that have already occurred), to more forward-looking, pre-emptive approaches to the minimization of harms that are a distinctive feature of social control within the risk society (Beck, 1992). Such an approach is characteristic of **private security**, as exemplified in a vivid ethnographic account by Shearing and Stenning (1985) of a trip to Disney World and the subtle disciplinary controls designed to regulate and optimize the visitor experience (see also Wakefield, 2003); the regulation of cyberspace, much of which is reliant on public–private partnerships and market-driven strategies (see Chapter 7); and the practices of the insurance industry (see Ericson, 1994). A related concept is that of '**resilience**', which features in Shearing's more recent work with respect to 'urban resilience', 'climate resilience' and 'water resilience' (Simpson, Simpson, Shearing and Cirolia, 2019); 'community resilience' (Hamann, Makaula, Ziervogel, Shearing and Zhang, 2019); and 'resilience policing' (Mutongwizo, Holley, Shearing and Simpson, 2019). Applicable to a wide range of risks and harms and a recurring theme of the book, resilience is defined by the UN International Strategy for Disaster Reduction (2009: 4) as 'the ability of a system, community or society exposed to hazards to resist, absorb, accommodate to and recover from the effects of a hazard in a timely and efficient manner, including through the preservation and restoration of its essential basic structures and functions'. With early applications to ecological systems (Holling, 1973) and psychological wellbeing (Kagan, 1975), the concept has gained prominence in the new millennium across multiple spheres of policy, to become 'a quasi-universal answer to problems of security and governance, from climate change to children's education, from indigenous history to disaster response, and from development to terrorism' (Aradau, 2014: 73).

Shearing (2015) credits criminology's exploration of the normative implications of these developments, his fourth theme, to a body of scholars including Dupont, Ericson, Haggerty, Johnston, O'Malley, Simon, Wood and Zedner whose work, along with that of Shearing and others, has come to constitute a sizeable body of literature on what Shearing terms 'the governance of security through risk' or 'governing through (in)security'. He sees this work as forming a useful basis to an evolving criminology that is redefining understandings of security and its governance. In a separate article, Shearing looks further at the ways in which the themes of risk and security are moving closer to the 'center of the criminological stage' (Froestad et al., 2015: 178), presenting the emergence of green criminology as a key example, with its focus on the security and preservation of ecosystems to maintain a safe space for human existence, mirroring the growing attention to '**environmental security**' within the international relations literature (see Hough, 2014), and encompassing such dimensions as '**food security**', 'water security' and '**energy security**'. A second example given is criminology's growing engagement with **cyber security** as an area of practice reliant on forward-looking approaches based on minimizing risks and mitigating their realization as harms. In arguing for a shift from criminalities to securities, Froestad et al. caution that, 'if criminology remains within its established crime-focused framings it will not be in a position to recognize, let alone respond to the shifting landscape of insecurities, and their associated securities, that emerged in the 20th century and are defining the current century' (2015: 183).

One could go further than Shearing's (2015) argument and assert that most (if not all) topics of criminological research could be placed under a 'security' heading. Crawford and Hutchinson (2016) observe how the blurring of established distinctions that have shaped the boundaries of criminology – between, for example, war and crime, the military and the police, the domestic and the international, and the public and the private – has widened the scope of the field and challenged disciplinary boundaries, as have popular cross-disciplinary concepts like 'risk', 'resilience', 'globalization' and 'governance'. They also note the influence of the concept of security across a wide range of domestic and international policy realms, from housing and health care to global conflict, environmental sustainability and the multiple dimensions of human security, as well as the explosion in the new millennium of related scholarly literature across multiple disciplines, and emphasize the need for cross-disciplinary engagement around its many applications. Loader and Percy (2012) note the absurdity of the enduring disciplinary separation of criminology and international relations on issues that sit at the frontier of the two, like **maritime piracy**, terrorism, narco-terrorism, and the activities of private military and security companies, while Bigo (2016) details some of the challenges to be overcome as well as some of the key ideas and contributions occurring at the boundary of the two disciplines.

It is the contention of this book that the flexibility of the concept of security, in the ways highlighted by Buzan (1983), Booth (2007), Zedner (2009), Shearing (2015) and others, makes it a much more useful organizing concept than crime, both in analyses of threats and mitigation strategies at the global level, and in the micro-managing of risk in the most specific of contexts. Today, priority areas for security research and innovation funding by government and industry cut across the STEM disciplines, social sciences, humanities and business studies, including the need to understand human behaviour better, the intersection of security with development as well as other areas of public policy, scientific and technological security solutions, the interactions of humans with such solutions, and the development of the risk management-based approaches that often underpin these. All are common threads in funding calls by such initiatives as the UK government-sponsored Partnership for Conflict, Crime and Security Research programme and the Centre for Research and Evidence on Security Threats, as well as the European Commission's Horizon 2020 Secure Societies Challenge. Such fields of study frequently require interdisciplinary teams and perspectives that are equipped to address the multiple facets of complex security problems. Many disciplinary groupings and the learned societies that represent them, not only those of criminology, would benefit from making their contributions to the analysis of security challenges more explicit and better understood, with 'security' – as opposed to 'crime' – certain to be an increasingly central theme of research and innovation funding for the foreseeable future. As 'an umbrella term that both enables and conceals a very diverse array of governing practices, budgetary practices, political and legal practices, and social and cultural values and habits' (Valverde, 2001: 90), some of security's many 'auspices' and applications are implicit in the respective chapter topics making up this book, which provides a structure for an inter-disciplinary analysis of the concept and its applications.

Dimensions of security and the plan for the book

This chapter has explored the nature, meaning and implications of security threats and mitigation strategies with reference to three themes:

- The first was the strategic security challenges that confront governments today and over the coming decades due to the interconnectedness of the contemporary world, from the perspective of national security agencies in the UK and US. These reflect longstanding vulnerabilities as well as new, complex and cascading threats to the extent that an 'inflection point' is said to have been reached (MoD, 2018: 3), requiring a fundamental change of approach to a much more agile and adaptable way of working.
- Second was the amorphous nature of 'security' which, although a public policy priority for governments and a significant research theme across a wide range of academic disciplines, remains a contested term and therefore conceptually, analytically and practically challenging.
- The third theme was the intersection of the concepts of security and crime, and the advantages for criminologists of employing a wider 'security' lens on the world.

The broad subject of security presents a bewildering array of issues. In delivering the 'converging perspectives on a complex world' promised in the title, the objectives of this book are to present a holistic framework in which to consider a diversity of security challenges, actors and strategies, drawing on a variety of disciplinary perspectives. The book is structured around different spatial dimensions or units of analysis, moving from the international to the regional, national, local and individual levels, as well as extending into the cyber, corporate and maritime spheres. Characteristic of criminology as a 'rendezvous subject' (Downes, 1988), a wide range of disciplinary perspectives inform the analysis, bringing criminological concerns together with themes and contributions from international relations in particular, but also a host of other academic fields. Many of the recurring topics of the book are interdisciplinary, including globalization, security governance, resilience and complexity. It is laid out as follows.

Chapters 2 to 4 provide accounts of the global political and economic transformations of the 20th century and thereafter, and how these have shaped the security landscape at the global, regional and national levels. Chapter 2 presents a primarily Western/'**Global North**' perspective on recent history that moves through three phases. It discusses how the post-Cold War era has seen a significant widening of the range of issues deemed to be matters of international security, but a continuing prioritization by the international community of interventions to address deliberate, violent threats to states and their people – regarded as being predominantly located in the regions of the **Global South**. The acceleration of globalization is discussed as a significant dimension of the story and the international security challenges of the future, with the COVID-19 crisis having highlighted the vulnerabilities of the contemporary international order.

Chapter 3 provides an alternative view of the world with a focus on the Global South which, until recently, has been almost invisible in international relations scholarship and remains considerably under-represented in criminology. It discusses the ways in which countries and regions of the South have been constructed in Western thought and literature, and explores the impact of colonization and **decolonization**, including the '**neocolonialism**' of the Cold War and thereafter and the movement to 'decolonize knowledge' by challenging established, Western-centric mechanisms of knowledge production. It goes on to detail how, as the security challenges confronting the South have gained more priority on the international stage, international security and development agendas have converged and the themes of human security and resilience have become prominent. The chapter also discusses the growing agency of the South in the international security architecture through **regional security** organizations and regional peacekeeping interventions.

Chapter 4 explores the ways in which states' national security priorities have evolved to encompass a broadening range of global threats, with a focus on developments in the UK and the US. It begins with a discussion of the distinctive features of the two nations' 'national security cultures', including self-identities as a 'force for good' in the world (UK) and 'global custodian of order' (US), and national narratives that place an emphasis on military and economic prowess. The chapter then documents the development of the UK and US national security architectures since the early 20th century, driven by different phases and priorities in international security and the changing profile of threats at home. It is argued that one of the most significant changes to both countries' national security arrangements in the new millennium has been a growing focus on resilience, mirroring developments in international security and development interventions, and centred around the establishment of the civil contingencies system in the UK and the Department of **Homeland Security** in the US.

In *Chapter 5*, attention turns to the delivery of security at the local or community level, predominantly from a UK perspective, beginning with the introduction of formal policing in London in 1829 by Sir Robert Peel, and then exploring the evolution of UK policing from the end of the Second World War to meet the demands of a changing world. It details how, over the past few decades, police forces have had to adapt to the needs of an increasingly diverse society, the changing profile of crime, growing demands for service and accompanying financial pressures. The chapter also notes how the appetite for security from organizations, communities and citizens has ensured an increasing role for other actors and initiatives at the local level, including both private sector and community-driven solutions, and discusses how the growing application of resilience thinking to urban design and management is further influencing the way in which security is delivered.

The relationship between the concept of security and the individual is the subject of *Chapter 6*, which is structured around the seven dimensions of human security identified by the UNDP (1994) in order to consider the major threats to human survival and wellbeing both globally and nationally, in the UK. Social inequality is a major recurring theme of the chapter, which demonstrates the pervasive inequalities in access to income, food and health care (economic, food and **health security**), the human impact of environmental degradation (environmental security), and experiences of deliberate threats against the person, collective identities and human rights (personal, community and political security). Among the many issues raised in the chapter are the major global environmental challenges that have become pressing human security concerns, but are not being treated by the international community with the degree of urgency that is necessary to ensure the sustainability of the natural environment.

The focus of *Chapter 7* is the dilemmas associated with the securing of cyberspace, the virtual space that exists within the scope of the internet, and a dimension of the global commons. It first examines the ways in which the development of the internet and the World Wide Web have profoundly changed and are changing the world. The aforementioned concept of 4IR is introduced as a framework in which to consider the cumulative societal effects of rapid technological advancement and the possibilities as well as the challenges that these present. The chapter then discusses the main features of internet-based security threats and their implications for individuals, states and corporations; as well as the governance of the internet and of cyber security, which may be conceived as competing models for internet regulation. It is argued that, while an increasing sense of the risks of cyber attack and disinformation, much of which is perpetrated by other states, is driving an increased focus on cyber security, in Western democracies the approach to internet regulation remains primarily forward-looking, risk management-based and market-driven, due to the commitment to an open internet and the challenges of policing a vast, open, multi-jurisdictional environment.

Chapter 8 considers the substantial private sector contribution to the delivery of security, through organizations' **corporate security** management arrangements, and the **commercial security** industry that supplies services to corporate, governmental, third sector and individual clients. Whether their reach is global, national or local, corporations need to protect themselves from a range of security risks, the profiles of which vary according to their market sectors and geographical locations. The chapter explores how the corporate security sector has developed and continues to evolve, having gradually moved up the corporate hierarchy to protect both tangible and intangible assets and taking an increasingly global outlook, and then discusses the varying security threats faced by organizations and the strategies being employed to mitigate them. Given the extent of societal dependence on the corporate sector, and the scale of the activity undertaken by such organizations to secure their assets, corporations are held to be key players in the international security complex. The final section of the chapter details the main sectors making up a vast, global commercial security industry to serve the needs of corporate, government and other major clients.

The distinctive features of the **maritime security** environment, a further domain of the global commons, are the concern of *Chapter 9*. The chapter seeks to convey the complex and challenging nature of the marine environment, involving multiple jurisdictions, multiple stakeholders and multiple security actors facing a diverse and evolving range of security challenges. After providing an overview of the governing framework for the oceans, the chapter discusses the diverse range of threats to the maritime space, including military conflict, terrorism, multiple forms of organized crime, piracy and environmental crimes, and explores the definition and scope of maritime security. It is observed that one of the success stories of maritime security interventions has been the effectiveness of multi-sector, multi-agency collaboration, which is becoming increasingly common by necessity. One of the most negative aspects concerns the fortification and militarization of borders, as regional instability and strife lead increasing numbers of people to seek better lives elsewhere, often at considerable personal risk, serving as a further reminder of the stark inequalities that characterize our world.

The concluding chapter centres on the 'complexity' theme of the book's title and opening section, with a focus on how the effective governance of complexity is necessary to build a resilient future. It notes how global risks and threats on the horizon are becoming more complex and difficult to predict, manifesting within an equally complex global system in which connections are tightly coupled, so that something that affects one part of the global system may cause cascading effects throughout (as exemplified in the case of the COVID-19 pandemic). It revisits the above arguments by the UK and US governments that fundamental changes in approach are necessary if the challenges of the future are to be mitigated. The growing prevalence and impact of resilience-based approaches to international development, national security policy and the design and management of cities are discussed, as well as the potential for a growing inter-disciplinary body of work centred on complexity to help mitigate global catastrophic risks and other complex security challenges across all policy areas. The applications of such thinking to criminology are explored, as well as the need for the discipline to recognize the challenges and opportunities that complexity presents. The chapter finishes with an outline of the main aspirations underpinning the book, that it will help inform a variety of audiences of the importance of flexible and networked approaches for the effective governance of complexity, and the implications of an increasingly complex world for their own professional development and practice.

Study questions

- Undertake a 'PESTLE' and/or 'SWOT' analysis of the major political, economic, social, technological, legal and environmental factors likely to have an impact on your country in the coming years; or the strengths and weaknesses in your country's current position, along with the major opportunities and threats in the external environment. See the website of the Chartered Institute of Personnel and Development (www.cipd.co.uk) for online resources on these analytical tools (you will need to register for a free account), and research your country using foresight studies; country profiles published by government departments, IGOs and private intelligence companies; and other reputable and verifiable online resources.

- Why is the era we are entering described by the US National Intelligence Council as 'both more dangerous and richer with opportunity than ever before' (2017: ix)?

- What is 'security'? Taking account of the range of considerations discussed in this chapter, identify its main features and construct your own definition.

- What are the strengths and limitations of the criminology discipline in its capacity to contribute to appraisals of contemporary security challenges and the development of solutions?

Further reading

Jordan's (2017) review of foresight studies produced by official defence and security bodies in North America and Western Europe between 2007 and 2017 provides a useful synthesis of projected security trends for the coming decades according to those agencies, while the latest versions of the two reports introduced in this chapter (NIC, 2017 and MoD, 2018) offer fascinating US and UK government perspectives on key trends and strategic priorities. The article 'Between "muddling through" and "grand design": regaining political initiative – the role of strategic foresight' (Burrows and Gnad, 2018), offers an insight into the role and application of foresight studies in national security decision-making, while its practice can be explored via the website of the UK Government Office for Science's Futures, Foresight and Horizon Scanning programme, which provides a useful overview of the Office's work, and includes a blog and 'Futures Toolkit' for policy-makers and analysts (see www.gov.uk/government/groups/futures-and-foresight). For appraisals of criminology's relationship to the study of security, *Security* (Zedner, 2009) and 'The future(s) of security studies' (Crawford and Hutchinson, 2016) are recommended. These are usefully supplemented by *Security: Dialogue across Disciplines* (edited by Bourbeau, 2015), which encourages scholars of security to break out of their disciplinary silos and explore how the concept is theorized and studied across other disciplines.

2

Securing the globe

Chapter overview

This chapter provides:

- A review of the key events, security challenges and developments in the international order that characterized the period from the end of the First World War to the end of the Cold War, a period of ideological confrontation between the Soviet-led communist world and the US-led capitalist world that began after the Second World War.
- A discussion of the global ramifications of the abrupt end of the Cold War in late 1991 when the Soviet Union collapsed, removing the uneasy equilibrium of political and economic power resulting from the 'balance of terror' and the 'iron curtain' that had blocked the former Soviet states from open contact with the rest of the world.
- An analysis of the benefits and challenges presented by the acceleration of globalization after the Cold War, and the key characteristics of international security threats and mitigation strategies in the new millennium, beginning with the terrorist attacks of 11 September 2001 and the launch of the global 'war on terror'.
- A review of the international relations schools of thought that emerged in each of these phases, being very much products of their time, and their distinctive features and contributions.

Key terms

- Cold War
- Collective security
- Global governance
- Globalization
- Global North
- Global South
- Human security
- International relations
- International security
- Liberalism
- Realism
- Securitization
- Security governance

Introduction

International security is, in many respects, national security on the global stage. The founding member states of the United Nations (UN) were concerned with protecting state security, and creating a system in which aggression against one state would be regarded as aggression against all, with members pledging to commit to a collective response should such an event occur (UN General Assembly, 2004). In the decades since the UN's establishment, the threats to the international order have come to extend much more widely, and international security arrangements have evolved significantly. Early in the new millennium, an expert panel convened by then UN Secretary-General Kofi Annan identified the primary global security issues as being 'poverty, infectious disease and environmental degradation; war and violence within States; the spread and possible use of nuclear, radiological, chemical and biological weapons; terrorism; and transnational organized crime', encompassing threats from non-state actors as well as states, and **human security** as well as state security concerns (UN General Assembly, 2004: 11). Given the differing agendas of different member states and power imbalances within the UN structure, the panel saw the major challenge for the international community as being its capacity to reach consensus about priorities and mutual responsibilities, such as whether threats such as poverty and HIV/AIDS constitute security or development concerns, or civil wars in Africa are matters for international involvement.

This is the first of two chapters examining security from a global perspective. It presents a view of the world through a primarily Western or **'Global North'** lens, and with a predominant focus on deliberate, violent threats to the **physical security** of states and their people, while the next chapter gives more focus to perspectives from the formerly colonized regions of the **'Global South'** and wider human security concerns. This chapter explores three distinct phases of the 20th and 21st centuries in turn, covering the periods spanning the end of the First World War to the end of the **Cold War** in late 1991, the first 10 years following the Cold War, and the terrorist attacks of 11 September 2001 (9/11) up to the present day. Each section reviews the key international security events, adaptations of the international community, and emerging **international relations** schools of thought that characterized each of those phases, and the implications of the intensification of **globalization** from the early 1990s are also examined in the course of the discussion.

The balance of power in international security

The 20th century has often been described as the bloodiest of centuries, the first half of which was dominated by the First and Second World Wars.

The two World Wars reflected the culmination of a process of 'totalization' observed from the mid-19th century, whereby wars increasingly involved the mobilization of nations' entire military, economic, industrial and human resources (see Imlay, 2007). The First World War lasted from 1914 to 1918 and produced one of the highest death tolls of war that the world had ever seen, estimated at over 14 million combatants and civilians (Gilbert, 2004). The Paris Peace Conference of 1919–20 brought the victorious powers together to establish the terms of peace in Europe, and a framework for a peaceful and enduring world order based on a set of unanimously accepted principles put forward by US President Woodrow Wilson. This included the formation of a League of Nations, offering 'mutual guarantees of political independence and territorial integrity to great and small States alike' (cited in Temperley, 1920: 435), and marked the beginnings of the idea of '**collective security**'. This 'rests on the notion of all against one' through participation in an inter-governmental security alliance, which 'entails a commitment by each member to join a coalition to confront any aggressor with opposing preponderant strength' (Kupchan and Kupchan, 1991: 118).

The League of Nations was ultimately remembered for its failure to prevent the Second World War, but its efforts were hindered by considerable international instability following the First World War, and the failure of the US and the Soviet Union to endorse the peace settlement or join the League. While Wilson was awarded the Nobel Peace Prize in 1919 for his role as its leading architect, he was unable to secure a mutually satisfactory compromise with opponents in the Republican Party. However, as Henig (2019) details, the League had some significant achievements that established a lasting legacy for modern international relations. As the first permanent and multilateral platform for diplomacy, it peacefully resolved a number of international disagreements, and laid the groundwork for the system of rules, norms and standards that are today generally accepted in relations between states, including the frameworks for the safeguarding of minority rights and human rights. The League's activities in the fields of humanitarian relief, repatriation of prisoners of war and refugees, the establishment of an international court, financial and economic cooperation, international labour organization, the prevention and control of epidemics, the countering of the international drugs trade, and numerous other humanitarian activities were the precursors to many of today's UN agencies and other global bodies. The 1920s also saw the establishment of the International Criminal Police Commission, which brought together law enforcement agencies from around the world in response to rising transnational crime, and in 1956 became the International Criminal Police Organization, abbreviated to ICPO-Interpol or just Interpol, as it is known today.

The Second World War ran from 1939 to 1945 and was the deadliest conflict in world history, with over 46 million casualties (Gilbert, 2009). The war prompted the dissolution of the League, and the formation of the UN in 1945 attempted to address its predecessor's limitations and make a stronger commitment to collective security. Member states had to commit not to use or threaten force against each other, except in self-defence, and the Security Council was established as the organ through which military force could be authorized in order to preserve peace and security. The UN also retained the League's specialized agencies. At its founding, the UN had 51 member states and it is now made up of 193 (UN, 2021). A major in-built weakness of the UN was the power imbalance in the structure of the Security Council, comprising five permanent members with veto powers (the US, the Soviet Union – later succeeded by the Russian Federation, China, the UK and France) and 10 further members on a rotating basis.

The aspirations behind the UN's creation were, however, greatly constrained by two significant events – the Cold War and **decolonization** – which dominated the period from the end of the Second World War to the early 1990s and significantly shaped the world we inhabit today. The former is a focus of this chapter, while the latter is a major theme of the next. The Cold War was a global conflict between the communist world, led by the Soviet Union, and the capitalist nations, led by the US, that formed the North Atlantic Treaty Organization (NATO) military alliance in 1949. It spanned almost half a century, consumed vast resources and threatened nuclear anarchy due to the intensifying arms race between the two sides. In contrast with the first half of the 20th century, the Cold War period was one of 'limited' wars in which military force occurred through proxies and allies, such as the wars in Korea (1950–53) and Vietnam (1959–75) as well as the Arab–Israeli War, with the two 'superpowers' seeking to prevent escalation. Cold War hostilities between the two sides affected most areas of the globe, directly or indirectly, and increased and diminished through several distinct phases, but they also contained conflict by organizing the world into two separate blocs, a stand-off that became known as the 'balance of terror'.

International relations began to emerge as a field of academic study following the devastation of the First World War, as scholars sought to explain the causes of war and conditions for peace. As a discipline that seeks to understand the nature of the international order, its agenda has evolved through the decades in accordance with the changing dynamics of political and economic power. The longer-established, 'traditional' schools of international relations regard the origins of the modern states system as being the Peace Treaties of Westphalia and Osnabrück (1648), which marked the end of decades of conflict and destruction in Europe and established the legal basis of statehood, by means of an agreement by Europe's rulers to recognize each other's right to rule their own territories.

Following the failure of idealists in politics and scholarship to establish an effective framework for a peaceful world order and prevent the Second World War, a realist school of international relations that viewed states as the central actors in international politics rose to prominence. The aim of 'classical **realism**', associated with the ideas of Hans Morgenthau (1948), was to explain the behaviour of states in international politics, based on the principle that, like humans, they were primarily motivated by self-interest and the pursuit of power, and therefore conflict was a result of human nature. Realists made a distinction between what they termed 'high' and 'low' politics, denoting the relative importance attributed to key areas of politics and policy. 'High politics' refers to matters of state sovereignty and military power, whereas 'low politics' covers the internal, domestic matters of a state, including economics, the environment, health, social security and criminal justice (see Keohane and Nye, 2011, which links realist analysis to the authors' liberal concerns). The effectiveness of the latter was held to be contingent on the former, with individuals' interests seen to be best served by states pursuing the maximization of their power. As Burchill observes of the realist school, 'The relevance of an approach which accords priority to military power, perceptions of vulnerability, superpowers, wars and the perpetuation of a system which seems chronically troubled by conflict, was obvious to all in the most violent of all centuries – the twentieth' (2005: 32).

The scope of international politics began to broaden in the 1960s and 1970s due to the nature and impact of the superpower rivalries of the Cold War, the growing role of inter-governmental organizations (IGOs) (NATO, the International Monetary Fund and the World Bank as well as the UN) on the global stage, and its expansion beyond matters of military authority to encompass issues of economic power and influence. A new branch of realism known as 'structural realism' or 'neorealism', established by Waltz (1979), evolved out of this new phase in world affairs. This perspective disregarded human behavioural explanations for the actions of states, and instead examined the ways in which the international 'system' conditioned these, centred on the relationship between the two superpowers and their similar behaviours, despite their diametrically opposed ideological and political orientations.

Second in prominence to the realist school among the international relations schools of thought is **liberalism**, emerging in the same period with well-established roots in philosophical, economics and political science scholarship, and informed by such thinkers as Adam Smith and Immanuel Kant. Liberals favoured cooperation and collective action over the dominance of states, underpinned by the belief that individuals' rights and freedoms are better served through cooperative patterns of behaviour. It took a broader perspective than neorealism to recognize the increasing influence of IGOs; a widening range of actors on the world stage, including non-governmental organizations (NGOs) undertaking advocacy and humanitarian aid roles, and multinational corporations (MNCs); and the expanding range of concerns that were driving these developments. Matters of low politics such as protection of the environment and human rights were becoming global as well as domestic issues. Key texts included Cooper's (1968) *The Economics of Interdependence*, which discussed the influence of post-war growth of trade among the advanced countries on the logic of cooperation in international affairs, and an edited volume by Keohane and Nye (1972) on *Transnational Relations and World Politics*, which provided a framework for examining the role of non-state actors in the global system. The liberal agenda of international relations was expanding, driven by efforts to make sense of the growing density and complexity of post-war political and economic relations. Yet both the realist and liberal schools failed to account for the end of the Cold War in 1991.

International security in the 'new world disorder'

One of the most striking features of the collapse of Soviet communism was its suddenness. In the 1980s, the Soviet economy was stagnating. Mikhail Gorbachev, who took up the Soviet Presidency in 1985, set out to liberalize the Soviet Union's command economy by introducing many market-like reforms to keep up with thriving capitalist economies like the US, Germany and Japan. Gorbachev set out his political doctrine in a book called *Perestroika* (1987), meaning 'restructuring'. He also advocated a policy of *glasnost*, or 'openness', loosening controls on the media, allowing freedom of worship and promoting a freedom of expression that had long been suppressed in the Soviet Union. However, by finally giving citizens a voice, and introducing limited free market principles into what had been a highly controlled economic system, Gorbachev set off a process of change that became difficult to control, beginning in the countries of Eastern Europe where communism had been imposed after the Second World War. In a chain of events beginning in the summer of 1989, communist regimes across the region collapsed like dominoes, the most memorable moment being the collapse of the Berlin Wall in November 1989, which paved the way for the reunification of Germany in October 1990. On 8 December, the Soviet Union was dissolved and replaced by a Confederation of Independent States, and Gorbachev resigned as Soviet President on 25 December 1991.

Shortly before the Cold War formally came to an end, an influential article of the period by Francis Fukuyama, an American political scientist, declared its conclusion to be the 'triumph ... of the Western *idea*' (1989: 3, emphasis in original). He proclaimed 'not just ... the passing of a particular period of post-war history, but the end of history as such' (p. 4) based on the elimination of ideological alternatives to liberal democracies and free trade, and the universalization of Western liberalism. The immediate post-Cold War period was indeed a time of optimism in international relations: a new phase of international security cooperation was now conceivable, with the end of East–West rivalries making it possible among the permanent members of the UN Security Council, and revitalizing the Council's role. Former US President George H.W. Bush (1991) is credited with popularizing the term 'new world order' to describe the new global arrangements in a series of speeches, including his State of the Union Address in January 1991, in which he pronounced:

What is at stake is more than one small country, it is a big idea – a new world order, where diverse nations are drawn together in common cause to achieve the universal aspirations of mankind: peace and security, freedom, and the rule of law.

Another feature of the post-Cold War world was the intensification of globalization. After the fall of the so-called 'iron curtain', the ideological and physical barriers that had sealed off communist Eastern Europe from open contact with the West and other non-Soviet-controlled states, the former Soviet states began to reintegrate into the global economy. As globalization was no longer limited to the West and the world quickly became more interconnected, the threats facing the international community were distinctive in their multiplicity, and globally significant since security challenges in one part of the world had consequences for many others. At the UN, the definition of 'a threat to international peace and security' – the threshold for Security Council enforcement actions – widened and the Council declared at its January 1992 Summit that 'non-military sources of instability in the economic, social, humanitarian, and ecological fields have become threats to peace and security' (UN Security Council, 1992: 3).

The era of peace that had been hoped for proved elusive, however, and instead there was a flourishing of conflicts in the immediate post-Cold War period, including the 1991 Persian Gulf War, the break-up of Yugoslavia, the Rwandan genocide in 1994 in which an estimated 800,000 people were murdered, the persistence of the Israeli–Palestinian conflict, and the emerging nuclear rivalry between India and Pakistan. In contrast with the two World Wars and the Cold War, characterized by confrontations between nation states, most of the subsequent conflicts involved ethnic groups seeking to control existing states or establish new ones. UN operations became more enforcement-oriented, and the Security Council also began to make more use of economic sanctions, as well as establishing international criminal tribunals and, in 1998, an International Criminal Court to enable prosecutions for war crimes. Even before the world was shaken by the attacks of 11 September 2001, one might have asked whether 'new world disorder' was a more appropriate description. Bauman (1998: 57–59) observed how during the Cold War period every 'nook and cranny of the globe' had been assigned a 'significance in the "global order of things"' and 'meticulously guarded, though forever precarious, equilibrium'. By contrast, the post-Cold War world appeared not like a totality but rather 'a field of scattered and disparate forces'. He saw the concepts of 'new world disorder' and 'globalization' as being intimately connected, and argued that the deepest meaning conveyed by the idea of globalization was that of the indeterminate, unruly and self-propelled character of world affairs.

In international security, the lines between domestic and international agendas became increasingly blurred. Regional security organizations expanded in number, membership and remit, as will be discussed in the next chapter, with those that undertook peacekeeping missions often authorized by the UN Security Council to assume command, while the international framework for transnational policing cooperation expanded beyond Interpol to include Europol, the European Union (EU) police agency; the UN Office on Drugs and Crime; and a variety of other international, regional and national actors in the public and private sectors (see Bowling, 2009). The notion of 'global governance' became popular in international relations scholarship, stimulated by observations of 'governance without government' (Rosenau and Czempiel, 1992) and 'governance on a global scale' (Rosenau, 1992: 1) occurring in response to transnational developments and challenges associated with rapid and extensive global change 'crowding the global agenda', and necessitating responses by 'sub-national collectivities' (p. 3). Defined by Young (1999: 11) as the 'combined efforts of international and transnational regimes', it reflects the way in which governments became increasingly engaged in alliances and networks with a growing number of IGOs, NGOs, multinational corporations and other actors as they recognized the limitations in their capabilities and resources to deal with the widening range of global issues (Krahmann, 2003b).

The changing character of international security inevitably generated fresh thinking in international relations scholarship and, as the post-Cold War era began to take shape, a number of new perspectives challenged the discipline's prevailing assumptions. In the ensuing years, a constructivist paradigm emerged, viewing world affairs as being socially constructed; continually shaped by international actors' identities, values, cultures and practices; and influenced by constantly evolving regional and international orders. Onuf (1989) is often credited with introducing the term 'constructivism' in international relations theory, while other leading proponents include Finnemore (1996), Katzenstein (1996), Ruggie (1998) and Wendt (1999). While sharing with realism and liberalism a state-centred focus and conception of security, it offered a new way of looking at the world at a time of great uncertainty and change, taking account of the contributions of a wider range of actors, including NGOs and transnational activist networks, and became one of the leading schools in international relations.

Another set of viewpoints, collectively described as 'critical security studies', questioned how the international order had come about as well as the interests it served, and sought to conceptualize security in a different way. When interpreted in broad terms – as critical of all mainstream approaches (see Krause and Williams, 1997) – the many dimensions of critical security studies include critical theory, feminism, postcolonialism, poststructuralism, **securitization** theory and green theory, although the critical theorists of the 'Welsh School' (e.g. Booth, 2005) adopt a narrower definition and claim the label as their own. These various approaches challenge dominant associations of the concept of security with threats to states ('national security'); address areas that were formerly overlooked in the study of security such as environmental degradation, health, migration and international terrorism; and see varying representations of threat and security as having significant implications for the international political agenda.

The idea of a 'new security agenda' gained currency in the 1990s in recognition of changing international security priorities, with many threats requiring solutions beyond traditional military capabilities and interventions. Accordingly, arguments were put forward by critical scholars for the 'widening' and 'deepening' of the concept of security. The focus of the 'wideners' was a greatly expanded range of security concerns, while the 'deepeners' looked beyond the state as the main referent object, also taking account of the individual people who belong to those nations. 'Wideners' such as Wæver (1995) and Ayoob (1997) challenged traditional realist perspectives while retaining their focus on state sovereignty as the central ordering concept in international relations. They believed that national security concerns extended beyond military threats to a variety of other internal and external issues, including the depletion of energy resources, food scarcity, environmental harm, demographic pressures, virulent nationalism and domestic economic instability. For Wæver (1995), the threshold for an issue to be considered a security threat was that it was 'securitized', describing the rhetorical processes by which issues come to be identified as matters of security, and the responses that are triggered by such processes; in other words, their social construction as security threats. Such thinking was opposed by some 'traditionalists', such as Walt (1991), who were concerned that it diluted the concept of security so much as to make it redundant (Hough, 2005), but it was not intended to undermine the realists' state centrism, and merely drew attention to a wider range of areas of concern to states.

The work of the 'Copenhagen School' of Buzan, Wæver and others (Buzan, 1983; Buzan, Wæver and de Wilde, 1998) through the 1990s took this thinking further and formed the basis of 'securitization theory'. They viewed securitization as a political process that enables issues to receive disproportionate attention and resources, as in the case of terrorism, which came to be reformulated by the UN Security Council (2001) as a 'threat to international peace and security', or migration, which has been constructed as a high priority political concern that requires action, such as the securing of borders (Bigo, 2002) (discussed further in Chapter 9). Their more profound widening of security allowed for the consideration of non-military issues providing they represented 'existential threats', as well as 'deepening' its meaning to encompass issues that may not directly threaten a state but could still be considered to be security concerns. Thus, Buzan et al. (1998) identified five dimensions of security: military security, **economic security**, **political security** (relating primarily to states' political stability), societal security (the sustainability of collective identity and customs) and **environmental security** (the maintenance of the biosphere).

The 'deepeners' introduced different dimensions of analysis, with Buzan et al. (1998) identifying five levels of depth to security: international systems, international subsystems, units, subunits and individuals. Associated with critical security studies and the variety of approaches it encompasses, this perspective focuses on *whose* security is being threatened, with some critical scholars challenging the 'fetishization of the state' (Wyn-Jones, 1999: 96) and arguing that the protection of individuals should be the primary focus of international security (Booth, 1991). Many deepeners (e.g. Thomas and Tow, 2002; Dunne and Wheeler, 2004) embraced the idea of 'human security', a concept that gained traction in UN development circles in the 1990s and makes the individual rather than the state the referent object of security. This approach, discussed further in the next chapter, recognized that the causes of human insecurity extend well beyond war, conflict and violent crime, and can more often be attributed to other challenging social conditions such as poverty, disease and displacement of populations. It also acknowledged that states do not necessarily deliver protection to their citizens and can be the perpetrators of human rights abuses and even genocide (see UN Development Programme, 1994). Yet despite its growing influence in international development policy and international relations scholarship, just 10 years into the post-Cold War era, global events ensured that traditional, state-based security concerns remained at the forefront of the international security agenda.

International security since 9/11 and the acceleration of globalization

The four coordinated suicide attacks on US landmarks of 11 September 2001, killing nearly 3000 people, marked another historic global turning point, and the beginning of a new geopolitical phase shaped by the US-led global **counter-terrorism** campaign in response to the attacks. The 9/11 attacks and the 'war on terror' reflect the way in which the intensification of globalization has profoundly changed the security landscape, enabling terrorist groups to recruit, raise funding, transport arms and communicate internationally, and leading the 'failed' or 'fragile' states that can serve as operational bases and safe havens for terrorist groups to be viewed as an international security concern (Toft and Duursma, 2018). Jackson, Jarvis, Gunning and Breen-Smyth observe that, 'in its scope, expenditure and pervasive impact on social and political life, the war on terrorism is comparable to the decades of the cold war' (2011: 249). This section examines the key features of the post-9/11 era, with a focus on the effects of the acceleration of globalization on international security threats and structures.

Globalization and its impact

Before examining the connections between globalization and security, it is useful to clarify the meaning of this expansive concept. In simple terms, 'globalization' refers to a process of increasing global interconnectedness and interdependence between societies, although interpretations vary markedly. As Nederveen Pieterse (2019) demonstrates through a comparison of disciplinary perspectives, from the viewpoint of economists, it represents the accelerated movement of goods and services across national and regional boundaries (Oman, 1994: 56), and the growing similarity of economic conditions and policies (Gray, 1993: 38), resulting in a deepening integration of national economies through the movement of goods, services, capital and labour across borders. For sociologists, it refers to receding geographical constraints on social and cultural arrangements (Waters, 1995: 3), and might be interpreted as 'the compression of the world and the intensification of consciousness of the world as a whole' (Robertson, 1992: 8). Historians remind us that such increasing interconnectedness is a long-term historical process (Nederveen Pieterse, 1995: 45) that has merely accelerated in recent decades.

The speed and scope of contemporary globalization is captured in the terms 'hyperglobalization' and 'globalization 4.0'. The economists Rodrik (2011) and Subramanian and Kessler (2013) employ the former concept to refer to the dramatic increase in the speed and scope of economic globalization from the late 1990s, following the establishment of the World Trade Organization in 1995 and its work to liberalize international trade. Inoue (2018: 12) presents a broader interpretation through his 'three forces' of 'economic force', 'human communications via the Internet force', and 'technological disruptive force'. Respectively, these refer to the extensive growth in global trade and consequential expansion of cross-border economic integration; changing norms of human communication and reduction of sociocultural barriers facilitated by social media and the internet; and rapid socioeconomic changes driven by technological innovations such as the **internet of things**, big data and **artificial intelligence**, concepts that are discussed in Chapter 7. For Baldwin (2018), these two perspectives represent consecutive phases that he labels 'globalization 3.0' and 'globalization 4.0', arguing that the latter phase, associated with the increasing velocity of the **fourth industrial revolution** (Schwab, 2018a), is only just beginning (phases 1.0 and 2.0 are attributed to the development of large steam vessels before the First World War, and domestic and international strategies to support the post-Second World War economic recovery in Europe and promote trade).

The acceleration of globalization has brought many benefits, including the ease of international communication and travel, increased exposure to cultural influences from around the world, and decreasing costs of goods and services due to reductions in trade restrictions and economies of scale. Economic integration potentially reduces the prospect of intra-state conflict by increasing interdependence between states and promoting the spread of democracy. Globally, average living standards have improved significantly, and the most substantial increase has occurred in developing nations. Between 1990 and 2015, the percentage of the global population living in extreme poverty (living on less than $1.90 per day) fell from nearly 36% to 10% (World Bank, 2018). Developing countries have had access to major technological improvements without the need for the costly infrastructure investments that have preceded these in developed countries. For example, mobile phone technology has enhanced the lives of millions in the developing world, providing access to goods and services that were previously out of reach, particularly to people in remote, rural areas. Technological advancement is closely linked to globalization as it is both an enabler of, and enabled by, increasing global interconnectedness. By making foreign knowledge more accessible and fostering competition and innovation, it will continue to enhance sustainable development by facilitating the better management of the environment and natural resources, advances in health care, and greater resilience in transport systems, information systems and other infrastructure sectors.

Significant disadvantages and challenges have also accompanied the acceleration of globalization, however, relating to inequalities in the distribution of its benefits and more direct international security challenges characteristic of a 'runaway world' (Giddens, 1999). We now have a global economy that is beyond the control of individual governments. A growing divide is occurring globally between wealthier, better educated urban residents and rural populations (MoD, 2018). Poverty reduction in sub-Saharan Africa is progressing much more slowly than in the rest of the world, with extreme poverty becoming more rather than less concentrated (World Bank, 2018). Opponents of globalization argue that it promotes a 'race to the bottom' whereby, as states are forced to compete with one another, they are tempted to reduce labour, environmental and tax regulations to lower costs, promoting a downward spiral of weakening standards (see McKenzie and Lee, 1991; Rodrik, 1997). Since the 1990s, a substantial international 'anti-globalization' or 'global justice' movement, concerned about vast inequalities in the distribution of the economic benefits of globalization associated with Western dominance of the international order and capital flows, has contested 'neoliberal' economic integration associated with unfettered markets and free trade. Mostly left-leaning, it is motivated by a variety of human security concerns primarily associated with the Global South, ranging from environmental degradation to labour exploitation, indigenous land rights and gender inequalities, and calls for a more participative, democratic and sustainable form of globalization.

More recently, the backlash against globalization has also encompassed discontent from the right of the political spectrum about economic conditions in the Global North (see Stiglitz, 2017; Horner, Schindler, Haberly and Aoyama, 2018).

A YouGov study in 2016 found that in the 19 countries surveyed, many more people agreed than disagreed that the wealthy have benefitted more from globalization than ordinary citizens. The countries in which the fewest participants believed that 'globalization has been a force for good' were France, the US and the UK, where the changing political tide has manifested respectively in the *gilets jaunes* movement, the presidential election of Donald Trump on an 'America First' platform, and the referendum vote to leave the EU. Horner et al. (2018) attribute such developments in those and other Global North countries to the uneven impacts of globalization on different social groups: while many people in the Global South have seen improved living standards, albeit often from a very low starting point, many of those in the Global North have experienced relative stagnation (see also Cox, 2017).

Globalization has also played a significant role in the international security agenda of the new millennium, which has seen a reaffirmation of traditional, state-based security concerns associated with deliberate, violent threats to the physical security of states and their people, as well as a focus on regions of the Global South as the locus of those threats. Terrorism is now well recognized as a major international security problem, and the activities of al-Qaeda and Islamic State, as well as related groups Boko Haram in Nigeria and al-Shabaab in Somalia, are strongly linked to globalization. Such groups are now commonly referred to as 'new-style' or 'international' terrorism by commentators and security agencies. They are characterized by loose, disparate, multinational networks and cells, held together by a strong commitment to a puritanical form of Islam and a loathing of modernity and the West; the use of innovative communication systems to coordinate actions and propaganda strategies to promote the cause; the establishment of home bases in so-called 'fragile states' that they can effectively take over; and much greater ruthlessness in their tactics than the developed states of the Global North had previously experienced (see Giddens, 2005; Neumann, 2009). While presenting a significant threat to Northern powers, terrorism bears far more heavily on Global South regions and countries. According to the Global Terrorism Index 2019, the 10 countries most impacted by terrorism in 2018, by number of deaths, were Afghanistan (accounting for 46% of global deaths), Nigeria (13%), Iraq (7%), Syria, Somalia, Pakistan, Mali, the Democratic Republic of Congo, India and Yemen, collectively accounting for 87% of deaths. The four deadliest terrorist groups in that year were the Taliban, ISIL, the Khorasan Chapter of the Islamic State, and Boko Haram (Institute for Economics and Peace, 2019).

Following 9/11, fragile states in the Global South quickly came to be seen by politicians, policy-makers and academics of the Global North as being the origins of conflict, terrorism, transnational crime and human security threats, and significant sources of vulnerability in an increasingly interconnected world. One year on from 9/11, US President George W. Bush stated at the beginning of the latest *National Security Strategy for the United States of America* that,

'America is now threatened less by conquering states than we are by failing ones' (White House, 2002: 1). The broader and less controversial concept of 'fragile' states was subsequently promoted by IGOs to encompass a range of notions, including 'weak', 'failing' and 'failed', describing countries in which states institutions' legitimacy, authority or capacity are dramatically diminishing, precarious or broken down (Nay, 2013), so that they are unable to deliver the basic functions necessary for poverty reduction, development and the safeguarding of their populations' security and human rights (Organisation for Economic Co-operation and Development, 2007: 2). The marked shift in the focus of international security from some of the biggest economies in the world to some of the smallest has led to a convergence in the politics of development and security, discussed in the next chapter.

The nature of contemporary wars has also been associated with globalization. While inter-state wars were the predominant form of warfare for most of the 20th century, wars within states, encompassing civil war, genocide and other mass atrocities, have been more characteristic of the post-Cold War period. Kaldor's (2012) 'new wars' thesis observes that most contemporary warfare takes place in regions in which authoritarian states have been weakened as a result of opening up to the rest of the world. She argues that it is typically conducted in the name of identity (ethnic, religious or tribal), driven by the advancement of communications technologies, and migration both from rural to urban areas and internationally, in contrast with the 'old' inter-state war of the 20th century typically motivated by geopolitical interests or ideology. Rather than being fought by state armed forces, such wars are attributed to networks of state and non-state actors who normally direct their violence towards civilians rather than militaries, using such techniques as the forced displacement of those with different identities, while their financing is decentralized and globalized through means like loot and pillage, hostage-taking, protection rackets, illegal trading and donations from diasporas and other external actors.

Other dimensions of contemporary conflict that can be linked to globalization include technological advancement, such as the increasing use of precision-guided munitions or so-called 'smart weapons' like unmanned aerial vehicles (UAVs) or 'drones', and hybrid warfare. The latter term refers to the use of varied methods to destabilize adversaries through both military and non-military means and overt and covert methods, such as the disinformation and cyber attacks being employed among Russia's current arsenal against the West to erode US hegemony, and which rely on the exploitation of vulnerabilities in information technology and information ecosystems. On the positive side, the proportion of lives lost globally due to armed conflict is believed to be at the lowest level since at least the end of the Middle Ages (Roser, 2020): the trend since the early 1990s has been towards a greater number of smaller and less violent conflicts (Pettersson, Högbladh and Öberg, 2019).

The global proliferation of weapons of mass destruction (WMDs) became another significant area of international concern after the end of the Cold War and particularly after 9/11, and is the subject of numerous multilateral treaties, conventions and resolutions. There are five recognized 'nuclear weapon states' under the terms of the 1968 Treaty on the Non-Proliferation of Nuclear Weapons: the US, Russia, the UK, France and China, while India, Pakistan, Israel and North Korea also have nuclear arsenals (Stockholm International Peace Research Institute, 2019). Non-adherence to international commitments to arms control, disarmament and non-proliferation, and programmes to develop WMD, are seen to undermine global norms and international security, while the illicit trafficking and further diffusion of chemical, biological, radiological and nuclear weapons to rogue states, organized criminal enterprises and terrorists have become a matter of global priority. The pace of technological change in this arena presents a further challenge, in that advancements in weaponry may outpace the establishment of international regulations to govern their use.

A related issue is the substantially enhanced opportunities for criminal enterprise associated with globalization, to the extent that illicit networks now form a significant dimension of the international order. The collapse of the Soviet Union created an unprecedented threat from organized crime, causing a massive power vacuum ready to be filled by whoever seized the opportunity. Criminal syndicates – whose ranks were swelled by countless former KGB agents, soldiers, police and customs officers who had been left unemployed – flourished (see Volkov, 1999; Gerber, 2000), with the fall of the iron curtain allowing the threat to expand across Europe, and organized crime groups to develop transnational alliances (see Allum and Gilmour, 2019; Natarajan, 2019). Organized crime has also become a major source of revenue for terrorist groups worldwide, as part of a blurring of the distinction between political and criminally motivated violence often described as the 'crime–terror nexus' (Makarenko, 2004). The development of container shipping has transformed the scale and speed of cargo transportation, including that of illicit goods, while maritime piracy has re-emerged in the new millennium as a significant threat to major shipping routes (see Chapter 9). Advancements in information and communications technologies have allowed international criminal networks to communicate and coordinate their activities more easily, enabled traditional crimes to be committed on much grander scales (e.g. forms of internet-based fraud and the exchange of child sex abuse images), and facilitated new forms of internet-enabled crime (e.g. cyber attacks).

Globalization and international security structures

While international relations scholarship saw relatively little attention to the links between globalization and the structure of international security in the first decade or so after the Cold War (Cha, 2000; Buzan and Wæver,

2003; Bilgin, 2012), perhaps due to the difficulties in distinguishing the security effects of globalization from the more dramatic effects of the Cold War's end (Buzan and Wæver, 2003), this began to change after the 9/11 attacks. One of the common themes in the literature concerns the extent to which state power has diminished in accordance with the increasing prominence of IGOs, NGOs and the multitude of other actors on the international stage. Ayoob (1997) asserted that a realist Global North was overstating the impact of globalization to justify increasing its dominance over the South. Ripsman and Paul (2005, 2010) argued that the decline in inter-state warfare was primarily the result of the end of the Cold War rather than globalization, major powers (in particular, the US, Russia and China) were still pursuing traditional 'balance of power' competitive strategies, regional security structures like the EU had not achieved much, and globalization had not altered states' primary emphasis on security matters nor dramatically changed their security architectures. Buzan and Wæver (2003) and Ripsman and Paul (2005, 2010) contrasted such viewpoints with those that they attributed to 'globalists' or 'globalization theorists' – the collective of scholars coming from 'the new interdisciplinary field of Global Studies' (Barrow and Keck, 2017: 177) – which saw the significance of the state as being challenged or at least diminished.

To these perspectives Buzan and Wæver (2003) added their 'regionalist' approach, which addresses the growing autonomy and prominence of the regional level of security in international politics, accelerated by the end of the Cold War. It views the regional level as the major focal point for contemporary conflict and security cooperation, recognizing that most security analyses focus on the national or the global but not the dimension in between, 'where most of the action occurs' (p. 43). This perspective is articulated in their regional security complex theory, centred on the idea that, 'since most threats travel more easily over short distances than over long ones, security interdependence is normally patterned into regionally based clusters' (p. 4), a position that takes account of the emergence of regional security bodies since the establishment of the UN, and their increasing significance and contribution as discussed in the next chapter.

Also closely linked to the transformations brought about by globalization is the '**security governance**' concept, introduced in Chapter 1, employed by international relations scholars in analyses of 'the development from the centralized security system of the Cold War era to the increasingly fragmented and complex security structures of today' (Krahmann, 2003a: 5), as governments became more willing to cooperate with non-state actors, such as IGOs, NGOs and private security companies. Krahmann (2003a) attributes the shift from 'government' to 'governance' in the responses to security challenges to increased budgetary pressures and the bid for improved efficiency, leading to the outsourcing and privatization of public policy functions; growing awareness of new global security challenges such as transnational crime, terrorism and mass migration which require international cooperation for their mitigation; and globalization as a driver of such problems. Having developed as an alternative to, and sub-category of, the idea of global governance, which has been criticized for being so broad that it is hard to know what to exclude (Finkelstein, 1995; Kavalski, 2008), the notion of security governance came to be promoted by a growing body of scholars in the new millennium (see Kavalski, 2008; Sperling and Webber, 2014) and it is now the subject of a sizeable body of work.

The concept's impact is exemplified in Sperling's (2014) edited collection, the *Handbook of Governance and Security*. In his introduction to the handbook, he presents security governance both as a significant contemporary phenomenon, and as a framework for understanding the security challenges of the new millennium as well as the international system's evolutionary trajectory, while recognizing that certain limitations seem to be limiting its influence. Elsewhere, he observes that security governance 'has still some way to go before it obtains clear definitional precision, conceptual clarity and a standing that is distinct from other more time-honored concepts in the Security Studies lexicon' (Sperling and Webber, 2014: 127), and in both publications he notes the lack of engagement with the security governance literature in prominent overviews of the security studies field by Buzan and Hansen (2009) and Cavalty and Mauer (2010). However, the usefulness of the concept and the extent of academic engagement with it across a range of contexts and theoretical positions is evident in the breadth of Sperling's (2014) 37-chapter handbook, which sees it being applied to the international level; the major regions of the world; dimensions of the **global commons**; policy areas such as conflict management, **counter-terrorism**, **energy security** and **health security**; and specific institutions operating at international and regional levels or in particular issue areas.

The COVID-19 pandemic has brought into sharp focus many of the negative dimensions of globalization: its facilitation of the rapid spread of infectious disease, and the cascading effects of the closure of borders, lockdown of populations, disruption of supply chains and resultant economic uncertainty on national economies, businesses and individual workers. It follows the 9/11 terrorist attacks of 2001, and the global financial crisis of 2008 to 2009, as one of the major crises of globalization of the new millennium, and has given further fuel to the backlash against free trade and open borders (Goodman, 2020). The barriers put in place to reduce the spread of COVID-19 effectively represent an experiment in deglobalization, and may mark a turning point in this direction for the longer term, if companies decide to reduce their dependence on fragmented international supply chains and seek to produce goods closer to home. The pandemic may mark the beginning of a new phase in global security governance, such is the scale of the threat to human security, national security and international security being presented by the global spread of infectious disease. It remains to be seen whether it serves to reinforce the sovereignty of national governments in the international system or, conversely, gives impetus to new forms of collaboration.

Summary

This chapter introduced the concept of international security, providing an overview of changing threats on the global stage and the development of measures by states and IGOs to mitigate them, starting from the early 20th century when the League of Nations laid the foundations for the IGOs of today. The range of security issues deemed to be matters of international concern was shown to have significantly widened since the end of the Cold War, although deliberate, violent threats to states and their people – seen as being predominantly located in the regions of the Global South – continue to have been prioritized by the international community. The acceleration of globalization has been a critical dimension of the story, bringing about great benefits to global society as well as significant challenges, and the chapter introduced the notion of 'hyperglobalization' to reflect the momentum of the changes now occurring today and their implications for the future. The various international relations schools of thought, providing insights into the changing relationships between states and non-state actors, have been presented as products of their time, which help advance understanding of the evolving geopolitical environment. The concept of security governance, while lacking the status and influence of these more established schools, nonetheless provides a useful framework within which to consider the multiplicity of bodies in the international system coming together to address the diverse, complex and interconnecting security challenges of the present era and foreseeable future. The global COVID-19 crisis has exposed the vulnerabilities within existing security governance frameworks, but may also provide impetus for the fundamental changes in approaches that will be needed over the coming decades.

Study questions

- In what ways has the structure of global security governance evolved since the end of the First World War, and why?
- What were the causes and consequences for international security of the Cold War?
- How significant is the idea of human security to the development of solutions for today's global security challenges?
- What is globalization, and is it a force for good or bad?

Further reading

There are numerous comprehensive security studies textbooks offering overviews of the major themes and trends in international security, with the most recent publications inevitably encompassing the newest developments and issues on the horizon. *International Security Studies: Theory and Practice* (edited by Hough, Moran, Pilbeam and Stokes, 2020), for example, encompasses chapters on theoretical and conceptual dimensions of security studies, different forms of military and non-military security, global and regional security institutions, the security of different domains of the global commons, and issues and perspectives from different powers and regions. *The Making of Global International Relations* (Acharya and Buzan, 2019) provides a comprehensive chronological account of the development of the international relations discipline in accordance with a changing world, as well as an important critical appraisal, giving equal weight to the neglected perspectives of the Global South and the dominant Western viewpoints. *Globalization and Crime* (Franko, 2020) offers an insightful analysis of the ways in which globalization shapes crime and crime control, and an invaluable review of criminology's contribution to its analysis.

For further web-based resources and perspectives from around the globe on the diversity of contemporary security threats, as well as the global security governance structures and programmes to address them, an international array of think tanks with a focus on foreign policy and international relations supply a great deal of free access material. The Global Go To Think Tank Index (www.gotothinktank.com/) maintained by the University of Pennsylvania provides an annual international ranking that, while being US-centric, serves as a useful listing. The highest-ranked British think tanks for 2020 are Chatham House (www.chathamhouse.org/) and the International Institute for Strategic Studies (www.iiss.org), respectively placed sixth and twelfth in the world, while the Royal United Services Institute (www.rusi.org) and RAND (www.rand.org) are also recommended for their extensive resources relevant to the themes of this and other chapters of the book.

3

Regional security

CHAPTER OUTLINE

Chapter overview

This chapter provides:

- A critical discussion of the ways in which countries and regions of the Global South have been constructed in Western thought and literature.
- An examination of the demise of European colonial empires and its aftermath, including the 'neocolonialism' of the Cold War and thereafter, and the movement to 'decolonize knowledge' by challenging the established, Western-centric mechanisms of knowledge production.
- An exploration of the convergence of security and development agendas, in international politics and policy, commonly described as the 'security–development nexus', in response to the security challenges in many of the states and regions of the Global South.
- An investigation of the growing engagement of Southern states in collective security through the development of regional security organizations and participation in international peacekeeping missions.

Key terms

- Cold War
- Colonization
- Decolonization
- Global North
- Global South
- Neocolonialism
- Postcolonial studies
- Regional security
- Resilience
- Security–development nexus
- Sustainable development

Introduction

The previous chapter presented international security from a primarily Global North perspective, reflecting the relative absence of the Global South in analyses of international security before the intensification of **globalization** and expansion of regional integration after the end of the Cold War. Adopting a '**regional security**' lens, this chapter aims to redress the imbalance and examine the differing experiences and interests of the developing world or '**Global South**' countries, most of which are former European colonies, recognizing that recent history looks very different from such a perspective. There is an ongoing shift in the global balance of power to a multipolar world in which the rising powers are predominantly Southern nations, and the chapter begins by exploring the economic and cultural elements of this shift. It then examines the impact on the Global South of **colonization**, **decolonization**, the **Cold War**, the end of the Cold War, and the economic agendas of the global financial institutions, regarded by many as a form of **'neocolonialism'**. The chapter also touches on the movement to 'decolonize knowledge', which has gained particular prominence in recent years.

The focus then turns to the contemporary security challenges for regions of the Global South and the steps being taken to address them, with the international security agenda having seen an increasing post-Cold War shift in attention from an East–West axis to one of North and South. The chapter discusses how the casting of many Global South countries as weak states presenting security threats to the North has led to a convergence in security and development agendas, often described as the **'security–development nexus'**. Yet, as the final section of the chapter details, other states have established a presence and more unified voice through regional organizations and gained greater political agency and bargaining power through participation in regional peacekeeping interventions.

The West versus the rest?

Western literature has long conveyed a sense of superiority over the less powerful regions of the world and placed an emphasis on cultural as well as geographical distance, with an enduring impact on the way in which the non-Western world is constructed in Western thought. The 'West' or 'Western world', also sometimes referred to as the 'Occident', are terms that have long been used – particularly by Westerners themselves – to describe the historically Christian countries whose populations originate from Europe, as compared with nations of the 'East', 'Eastern World' or 'Orient'. Cultural theorist Stuart Hall (1992) argued in an influential paper called 'West and the rest' that conceptions of both were central to the Enlightenment, the intellectual and philosophical movement of 18th-century Europe that established the foundations of contemporary liberal thought, observing:

> In Enlightenment discourse, the West was the model, the prototype and the measure of social progress. It was *western* progress, civilization, rationality and development that were celebrated. And yet, all this depended on the discursive figures of the 'noble vs ignoble savage', and of 'rude and refined nations' which had been formulated in the discourse of 'the West and the Rest' ... Without the Rest ... the West would not have been able to recognize and represent itself as the summit of human history. (pp. 313–314, emphasis in original)

The distinction is cultural as much as it is geographical, although the 'West' now embraces North America and Australasia, while the 'East' refers predominantly to Asia. One of the best-known critiques of such constructions of non-Western cultures was the 1978 book *Orientalism* by Edward Said, who coined the term of the book's title to refer to romanticized Western cultural representations of the East that asserted the West's superiority in European centres of learning and their colonial outposts. Said associated these biases with the rise in the 18th century of what is now referred to as the Second British Empire, built around the East India Company's trading networks in Asia, and Britain's exploitation of territories 'discovered' by Captain James Cook. He saw Orientalism as continuing into the Cold War period, when the US became the hegemonic power of the non-Soviet world.

Not all countries aligned with the capitalist nations of the North Atlantic Treaty Organization (NATO) nor the communist Soviet bloc during the Cold War, and Sauvy (1952), an economist, coined the term 'Third World' ('Tiers Monde') to refer to these other nations. 'First World' and 'Second World' became widely used alternatives for 'West' and 'East' until the collapse of the Soviet Union, when the Second World label became less relevant, some of its former states being more appropriately categorized as First World. As the typology became outdated, it was increasingly replaced by designations such as 'developed' and 'developing' countries, while the terms 'Global North' and 'Global South' have also been increasingly used to distinguish between the developed and developing worlds, having first been coined in a 1980 report by a World Bank Independent Commission on International Development Issues. The Commission, chaired by former German Chancellor Willy Brandt, depicted the boundary between the wealthy North and poorer South, which came to be known as the 'Brandt Line', dividing North and Central America, passing north of Africa and India, and lowering to place Australia and New Zealand above the line.

Today, the distinction between North and South is less straightforward: as noted in the first chapter, many poorer countries have experienced significant economic and social development, while inequality within countries is growing, with the rich becoming richer as the 'precariat' (the poorest citizens), working and middle classes experience much slower economic growth (MoD, 2018). The acronym 'BRIC' was coined by O'Neill (2001) to refer to the four rapidly developing countries of Brazil, Russia, India and China that have come to rival Western economies in their revenue, depicting an ongoing shift in economic and political power away from the developed G7 economies (Canada, France, Germany, Italy, Japan, the UK and the US). Sometimes the term 'BRICS' is used, adding South Africa, and there are further variations including 'BRICSAM', encompassing the 'ASEAN4' states (Indonesia, Malaysia, Philippines, and Thailand, the four largest economies of the Association of Southeast Asian Nations) and Mexico.

The shifts in the balance of power in the post-Cold War world are important culturally as well as economically and politically. At the end of the Cold War, the

West's triumph was accelerated by the technological revolution and the world entered a new era of globalized capitalism and consumerism. As many countries were thrust into the world market economy and democratization, these processes were accompanied by a profound cultural penetration, of famous brands like McDonald's, Disney, Coca-Cola and Sony, and new sites of leisure like shopping malls, multiplex cinemas, chain restaurants and sports stadia. The evolving 'global culture' was dominated by the West but also multicultural, absorbing images and styles from around the world in film, fashion, literature and music, for example. The impact of such trends was explored in a number of influential Western articles that each became books, including Fukuyama's (1989, 1992) conception of 'the end of history', Huntington's (1993, 1996) notion of the 'clash of civilizations' and Barber's (1992, 2001) metaphor of 'Jihad vs McWorld'. Huntington's (1993, 1996) heavily cited but greatly contested thesis divided the world's people into eight 'major civilizations' and attributed global conflicts in the 1990s to such cultural divisions, including a Western–Islamic clash over perceived Western cultural imperialism. While the attacks of 11 September 2001 (9/11) played into his argument and bolstered its influence in policy circles, one of his many critics was Said (2004), who denounced it not only as 'a reductive and vulgar notion' (p. 226) but also 'the purest invidious racism, a sort of parody of Hitlerian science directed today against Arabs and Muslims' (p. 293).

Said was one of the founding voices of **postcolonial studies**, an interdisciplinary field that observes how Western traditions of thought with their roots in the Enlightenment period have become the hegemonic values within the world system, not only in formerly colonized societies. Postcolonial perspectives challenge the theories and stereotypes through which imperialist powers have perceived and constructed the world, and seek to represent and give voice to colonized peoples. Emerging within international relations after the end of the Cold War alongside other dimensions of 'critical security studies', they challenge the discipline's framing of Europe as the main actor in the history of the international system, and the systematic understating and misrepresentation of the Global South, leading Saurin (2006) to recast international relations as 'imperial relations'. As they have gained influence, international relations as an area of study has followed international relations as an area of political activity in becoming more globalized, yet postcolonial studies remains at the fringes of the discipline (Acharya and Buzan, 2019).

Decolonization and its aftermath

Colonization and decolonization have had a profound effect on the regions of the Global South and significantly shaped the world we inhabit today. By the 1930s, colonies and ex-colonies of Europe made up 84.6% of the land surface of the globe, and the only regions that had never been under formal European government were parts of Arabia, Persia, Afghanistan, Mongolia, Tibet, China, Siam and Japan (Fieldhouse, 1989). In general terms, decolonization refers to the undoing of colonization – the process in which one country imposes and maintains control over other peoples or territories – but it typically refers to the period following the Second World War when European colonial empires, ruling over approximately 750 million people and nearly a third of the world's population at that time, were removed from Asia and Africa. Jansen and Oster-hammel describe the concept as 'a technical and rather undramatic term for one of the most dramatic processes in modern history: the disappearance of empire as a political form, and the end of racial hierarchy as a widely accepted political ideology and structuring principle of world order' (2017: 1).

Colonization had come to be regarded with increasing hostility, and con-flicted with the founding principles of the United Nations (UN) laid out in its Charter in 1945, including those of equal rights and self-determination of peoples, and the sovereign equality of all of its members. Decolonization was made legally binding in 1960 under UN General Assembly Resolution 1514, which declared that, 'The subjection of peoples to alien subjugation, domi-nation and exploitation constitutes a denial of fundamental human rights, is contrary to the Charter of the United Nations and is an impediment to the promotion of world peace and co-operation', and that, 'All peoples have the right to self-determination; by virtue of that right they freely determine their political status and freely pursue their economic, social and cultural develop-ment'. More than 80 former colonies gained independence in the post-Second World War decades, and the UN has grown from its 51 founding member states to 193.

While experiences of decolonization varied considerably between regions, colonial powers and colonies, and in some cases the transfer of power was relatively peaceful, it was a violent process. The partition of India in 1947 brought about the forced migration of about 15 million refugees and displaced persons. Among the bloodiest conflicts were the wars of independence in Indo-nesia (1945–49), Indochina (1946–54) and Algeria (1954–62); those in Korea (1950–53) and Vietnam (1964–73) driven by tensions over postcolonial polit-ical solutions to decolonization and complicated by the superpower rivalry and international allegiances; the civil wars that followed decolonization in a number of newly independent states including the Congo, Nigeria, Angola and Mozambique; and the confrontations between rebels and colonial powers that tried to hang onto control (Jansen and Osterhammel, 2017). As Hough (2020d) observes in a chapter on security in Africa, it is now better appreciated that democracy takes time to bed in, and can be vulnerable to collapse if ushered in too quickly, with many of the new democracies swiftly turning authoritar-ian under the tyranny of strongman leaders who remain a significant feature across the continent.

Britain and France sought to grant independence on terms that were advantageous to their own longer-term economic and political interests, establishing the British Commonwealth and the French Union in Africa as the primary instruments for doing so. European policies to maintain control of former colonies soon came to be referred to as 'neocolonialism', a concept that is attributed to the former Prime Minister and President of a newly independent Ghana, Kwame Nkrumah. In 1957, he hosted the first of three All African People's Conferences (AAPC), attended by delegates representing independence movements in colonized countries, and independent states that supported independence for the colonies, strengthening of the independent states and resistance to neocolonialism. The term was first officially used in the 1950s and 1960s at these events (Mentan, 2018), and formally defined in the AAPC's 1961 Resolution on Neocolonialism as, 'The survival of the colonial system in spite of formal recognition of political independence in emerging countries, which become victims of an indirect and subtle form of domination by political, economic, social, military, or technical means' (cited in Martin, 1985: 190–191). It came to international attention on the publication of Nkrumah's book *Neo-Colonialism, the Last Stage of Imperialism* (1965: 1), in which he argued that neocolonialism had replaced colonialism as the 'main instrument of imperialism', whereby the state appears independent and sovereign, yet 'In reality its economic system and thus its political policy is directed from outside', most typically 'through economic or monetary means'. 'The result', Nkrumah asserted, 'is that foreign capital is used for the exploitation rather than for the development of the less developed parts of the world.'

The conditional aid packages, loans and foreign investment provided to African governments from the early 1980s, initially associated with the so-called 'Washington Consensus' (Williamson, 2009) of the advanced industrialized countries and the global financial institutions, are widely criticized today. The 'structural adjustment programmes' of the World Bank and the International Monetary Fund (IMF) – known as the Bretton Woods Institutions, and established by 43 countries in 1944 to help rebuild the international economic system after the Second World War – imposed 10 strict economic policy conditions on the usage of the loans, such as privatization of state enterprises, deregulation and the reduction of trade barriers. One critic observed that, by the end of the 1980s, 'the only development policy that was officially approved was not having one – leaving it to the market to allocate resources, not the state' (Leys, 1996: 42). Subsequent foreign investment, aid and loans have frequently occurred against the best interests of receiving countries. Accompanying conditions for economic policy, democracy and respect for human rights have contributed in some poorer countries to the weakening of the state and conflicts over decreasing state resources (Siitonen, 2010). They have also contributed to unsustainable development: exploitation of resources that puts pressure on the natural environment so that, in the longer term, it is unable to provide the natural resources or maintain properly functioning ecosystems on which the economy and society depend (see Elliott, 2012).

A further dimension of decolonization that has recently gained prominence in Northern academia, although its roots in Southern scholarship go back some decades (see Moosavi, 2020), is that of intellectual decolonization. It came to global attention through the student-driven 'Rhodes Must Fall' movement, which began with a protest action at the University of Cape Town on 9 March 2015 when a student defaced a statue of the imperialist Cecil Rhodes, and spread to other campuses around the world. The movement gained renewed attention through the global protests following the death of George Floyd at the hands of police in Minneapolis, Missouri in the US in 2020, and recently led the authorities at Oriel College, Oxford University, to agree to remove its own monument to Rhodes (Coughlan, 2020). An accompanying global movement to 'decolonize the curriculum' asks scholars to look critically at their shared assumptions about how the world works and should be studied; consider more carefully the identities of the authors they cite, how those identities shape what they write and whether other perspectives are being missed; and take account of the implications of the perspectives being taught for student learning, including the sense of belonging of black and ethnic minority students.

In criminology, decades have passed since Cohen (1982: 85) observed that 'criminologists have either ignored the Third World completely or treated it in a most theoretically primitive fashion', yet little has changed, with criminological journals being dominated by the Anglophone countries, and the discipline remaining weak in regions of the Global South such as Latin America, and the African continent beyond South Africa (Bosworth and Hoyle, 2011). Enterprises in the new millennium to 'decolonize' the criminology discipline include 'counter-colonial' (Agozino, 2003), 'postcolonial' (Cunneen, 2011), 'Asian' (Liu, 2009) and 'Southern' (Carrington, Hogg, Scott, Sozzo and Walters, 2018) criminologies. Amid the 'current decolonization hype' (Behari-Leak, 2019: 58), Moosavi (2020) puts forward a set of principles to guide Northern academics embarking on intellectual decolonization and argues that, while the surge of interest is to be celebrated, it should be pursued in a reflexive manner, giving due recognition to the ways in which we have benefitted from coloniality and may even help perpetuate its enduring inequalities.

The convergence of security and development

For most of the 20th century, not only were the ideas of Southern thinkers under-represented: the regions of the Global South were largely absent from both academic and policy debates in international relations (Abrahamsen and Sandor, 2018). Its main cooperative institution during the Cold War period, the

Non-Aligned Movement, received little attention from international relations scholars other than Willetts in 1978 (Acharya and Buzan, 2003). Despite the violence that accompanied decolonization, since this mainly took the form of civil wars or proxy wars involving the two superpowers, it was not until the end of the Cold War that the wider world beyond the US, the Soviet Union and their allies began to receive more attention. This section examines three significant dimensions of international engagement in the Global South in the dual areas of development and security: the emergence of a **human security** agenda, an evolving security–development nexus, and the rise of resilience thinking, policies and practices.

The human security agenda

A growing consensus that poverty and conflict are linked, and that conflict bears more heavily on poor countries than richer ones, led to increasing concern by wealthier countries about limiting the international diffusion of threats as the world became more interconnected. Even during the tensest phases of the Cold War, in Africa, for example, the most pressing security problems were not nuclear annihilation but famine, hunger and disease, and today they remain much greater threats to the continent than war and terrorism (Hough, 2020d). As the African Leadership Forum, representing public, private and civil society organizations and actors from across Africa, observed as the Cold War drew to a close:

> The concept of security goes beyond military considerations; it embraces all aspects of the society including economic, political and social dimensions of individual, family, and community, local and national life. The security of a nation must be construed in terms of the security of the individual citizen to live in peace with access to basic necessities of life while fully participating in the affairs of his/her society in freedom and enjoying all fundamental human rights. (1991: 2)

Such a philosophy was also gaining traction in UN development circles, coming to wider attention in the 1994 Human Development Report of the UN Development Programme (UNDP), which promoted human security as a new perspective challenging state-centric, military-focused conceptions of security. The report combined the aspirations of 'freedom from fear' and 'freedom from want', deriving from the 'four freedoms' articulated by US President Roosevelt (1941) in his 1941 State of the Union address, advocating a holistic approach that takes account of all issues with potentially life-threatening consequences for individuals, and identifying seven dimensions of security (explored more fully in Chapter 6):

1.   Economic security: an assured basic income;
2.   Food security: physical and economic access to food at all times;

3. Health security: good nutrition, clean water, a safe environment, access to healthcare, safe and affordable contraception, and support during pregnancy;
4. Environmental security: a healthy physical environment, e.g. clean water, productive land, clean air;
5. Personal security: security from physical harm arising from violent crime, conflict, rape, child abuse, industrial and traffic accidents, and threats to the self, such as suicide and drug use;
6. Community security: security of communities and their members from marginalization and division; and
7. Political security: living in a society that honours one's basic human rights.

This approach provided a way of framing and bringing coherence to disparate UN policy initiatives (Krause, 1994), and the human security concept attracted considerable interest in international political, policy and academic circles. A human security agenda informed the UN's Millennium Declaration (UN General Assembly, 2000), and its Millennium Development Goals (MDGs) for the year 2015, which targeted eight areas – poverty, education, gender equality, child mortality, maternal health, disease, the environment and global partnership.

The security–development nexus

While the Millennium Declaration omitted to translate the themes of peace and security into explicit goals, the marked shift in the focus of international security from some of the biggest economies in the world to some of the smallest led to a convergence in the global politics of development and security. Through the 1990s, rather than focusing on economic growth on the assumption that development would follow, development policies became increasingly preoccupied with under-development as a cause of conflict (Duffield, 2014). The 'security–development nexus' is a phrase that has become well used to describe the dual processes of the 'securitization of development' and the 'humanization of security' (Tadjbakhsh and Chenoy, 2007: 146) taking place in the post-Cold War period (see Chandler, 2007; Stern and Öjendal, 2010). Duffield (2014) observes how the view that 'underdevelopment has become dangerous' (p. 1) has come to be generally accepted, and the 'reinvention of development ... as conflict resolution and societal reconstruction' (p. 135) has been widely endorsed by an expanding network of global governance actors made up of leading inter-governmental organizations, international financial institutions, donor governments, UN agencies, think tanks, NGOs and private companies. Having first made these observations in the 2001 edition of his book, Duffield's analysis proved prescient in anticipating the increasingly interventionist and militarized operations that would characterize the subsequent decades.

The 9/11 attacks placed military rather than development missions back at the top of the international security agenda, with interventions prioritized in states considered to present the greatest threats to international security. The human security concept remained influential, but also came to mean different things to different people (see Liotta and Owen, 2006; Gasper, 2010). Some favoured the UNDP's (1994) broad definition, and others preferred a narrower, more protection-based approach, concentrating solely on deliberate, violent threats to the physical security of states and their people associated with intra-state war, weapons proliferation, terrorism, fragile states and transnational crime, which are often interlinked (see Makarenko, 2004 on the 'crime–terror nexus' and de Boer and Bosetti, 2015 on the 'crime–conflict nexus'). The narrower interpretation is reflected in the emphasis of UN Security Council debates and actions, although even these have widened in scope and included references to 'the impact of HIV/AIDS on peace and security in Africa, food security, climate change, children in armed conflict, women and peace and security, and the protection of civilians more generally' (Nasu, 2013: 96). In the ensuing years, human security thinking informed the development of a doctrine adopted by the UN in 2005 called the 'responsibility to protect' (R2P) (Axworthy, 2013). This is based on 'the obligation of states toward their populations and toward all populations at risk of genocide and other mass atrocity crimes' (Global Centre for the Responsibility to Protect, 2019), and serves as a framework to guide UN Security Council decision-making on humanitarian interventions.

While any hopes for a paradigm shift in the international community from a traditional security approach to a more human-centred one are largely unrealized (Malik, 2020), the human security 'approach' (UN General Assembly, 2012) remains at the centre of the UN development agenda. The final report on the MDGs reports its successes as including helping to lift more than a billion people out of extreme poverty, reducing undernourishment in the developing regions by almost half, and enabling more girls to attend school than ever before, and its main challenge as having been uneven progress and persistent inequalities between countries, rural and urban areas, and the factors of gender, age, disability and ethnicity (UN, 2015a). The MDGs were succeeded by the Sustainable Development Goals: 17 goals to be achieved by 2030 that were agreed in a 2015 Resolution by the UN General Assembly, following a series of global consultations involving a range of stakeholder organizations and specialists from around the world (Kumar, Kumar and Vivekadhish, 2016).

One of the most profound critiques of the human security paradigm in international relations and international development is that it has reinforced, rather than challenged, traditional frameworks for global policy-making. Despite its emphasis on a broader set of policies, such as poverty-reduction, **sustainable development** and climate change adaptation, Chandler (2008) argues that, based on how these have predominantly been applied in practice, human security approaches appear to share with realism the post-9/11 assumptions that the biggest security threats lie in the world's poorest countries. Martin (2014: 7) makes similar arguments, that 'humans in human security are more usually conceived as "others" in relation to Western, developed societies', and this understanding is evident within policy agendas where human security terminology is excluded from domestic reforms. The fact that the MDGs were focused on developing countries with funding from rich countries supports these assertions. Tadjbakhsh contends that the concept is universally applicable, however, and that perceptions and experiences of insecurity persist as much in the developed as the developing world, arguing:

> Urban violence, job insecurities, health epidemics, privatization of social delivery, militarization of societies, etc. that plague industrialized societies of the North are as much human insecurities as famine, wars, poverty and genocides that characterize extreme situations of some countries, notably in the postcolonial world. (2013: 48)

This principle is a central theme of the SDGs, which are declared to be 'universal goals and targets' that apply to 'developed and developing countries alike' (UN General Assembly, 2015: 3). The SDGs retained and extended the first seven MDGs and added goals to address work and economic growth, infrastructure development, inequality, several dimensions of sustainable development, and peace and justice. They are broken down and discussed more fully in Chapter 6, where the Goals are listed in full in Table 6.1. As noted by Kumar et al. (2016), in contrast with the MDGs, the SDGs place an emphasis on human development, human rights and equity that had been missing previously, and all countries are expected to work towards achieving them. Major challenges to doing so are identified, however, including the significant cost, such as in the area of infrastructure investment; threats to peace and stability, which displace populations and undermine development; the challenges in measuring progress; lack of accountability at all levels for meeting the targets; and lack of international commitment to the UN target adopted in 1970 for donor countries to contribute at least 0.7% of their Gross National Income (GNI) as Overseas Development Assistance (ODA) (UN General Assembly, 1970).

The rise of resilience

The renegotiation of the global goals and other dimensions of the global development agenda around or after 2015 has seen the embedding of discourses and practices of '**resilience**' both explicitly and implicitly, as detailed by Coaffee and Chandler (2017), marking a further dimension of the security–development nexus. As defined in Chapter 1, resilience relates to the ability of an individual, system, community or society to recover from an adverse event. Resilience thinking, which emphasizes the complexity and interconnectedness of security challenges, has influenced a shift towards 'more holistic and systemic approaches' to their mitigation informed by disaster risk reduction strategies, whereby 'interventions do not bring security in "from the outside" but enable its internal and "bottom-up" development' (Chandler, 2016: 268). Aradau (2014) observed the shifting development priorities within the UK's Department for International Development between 2006 and 2011, which sought to reduce dependency on humanitarian aid and help recipient communities become more self-sufficient, as articulated in a report outlining its humanitarian policy:

> Humanitarian assistance should be delivered in a way that does not undermine existing coping mechanisms and helps a community build its own resilience for the future. National governments in at-risk countries can ensure that disaster risk management policies and strategies are linked to community-level action. (Department for International Development, 2011: 10)

Such an approach is not without its critics. Duffield (2016: 57) argues that the vulnerable are being 'politically exposed to disaster in order to become resilient', while Evans and Reid assert that:

> Rather than enabling the development of peoples and individuals so that they can aspire to secure themselves from whatever they find threatening and dangerous in worldly living, the *liberal* discourse of resilience functions to convince peoples and individuals that the dream of lasting security is impossible. (2014: 68)

Such criticisms reflect wider concerns about austerity budgets and the permeation of neoliberal ideologies of individual responsibility (Duffield, 2012). While these are legitimate considerations, there has also been a growing scepticism of earlier models related to concerns about Western paternalism, with resilience-based models reflecting a preference for cultivating more organic interventions alongside communities that are treated as equals in the process (Chandler, 2016).

The Hyogo Framework for Action, an initiative of the UN International Strategy for Disaster Reduction (2005), had placed resilience on the international agenda, aiming to build nations' and communities' resilience to disaster. Since then, it has become a key concept in international development policy and scholarship, employed by the UN, EU, World Bank, IMF, governments, NGOs and community groups, and applicable to a range of policy areas including conflict management, mitigation of climate change, response to economic crisis, mitigation of urban poverty or disaster risk management (Chandler and Coaffee, 2017). The *Sendai Framework for Disaster Risk Reduction 2015–30* (UN, 2015b) is a further international framework promoting resilience as a central dimension of all development plans, policies and procedures in order to support sustainable development. Later the same year the SDGs were released, employing a resilience discourse, as in goals 9: 'Build resilient infrastructure, promote inclusive and sustainable industrialization and foster innovation', Goal 11: 'Make cities and human settlements inclusive, safe, resilient and sustainable', target 1.5 to 'build the resilience of the poor and those in vulnerable situations ... to ... economic, social and environmental shocks and disasters', and target 13.1: 'Strengthen resilience and adaptive capacity to climate-related hazards and natural disasters in all countries' (UN General Assembly, 2015). Resilience was also a significant theme of the UN Climate Change Conference (COP21) in December 2015, where the Paris Agreement on climate change was signed, and the UN Conference on Housing and Sustainable Urban Development (Habitat III), where Resolution 71/256 for a New Urban Agenda (UN General Assembly, 2017) for pursuing the SDGs was adopted.

These post-2015 agendas, observe Coaffee and Chandler (2017), demonstrate the significance and value of resilience ideas and practices in protecting people, communities and countries whose security is at most at risk, and advancing sustainable development. There is still a long way to go, however. With respect to climate change, for example, since developed states historically bear most responsibility for its manifestation, and developing countries are most vulnerable to its effects, wealthier signatories to the Paris Agreement pledged to contribute $100 billion a year in aid to developing countries by 2020 to support climate change adaptation and mitigation. Yet environmental security threats, discussed further in Chapters 6 and 9, present an ongoing political challenge, with issues like climate change being commonly perceived 'as longer-term creeping emergencies rather than imminent disasters', and a sovereign state system set up to prioritize national over global or human security interests being poorly served to address issues that do not represent an imminent crisis (Hough, 2014: 32).

Regional security governance

While many countries of the Global South have been cast as weak states presenting security threats to states of the North, others have increased their authority in the international system as their economies and populations have grown, they have established a presence and more unified voice through regional organizations, and their contributions to international peacekeeping missions have increased their political agency and bargaining power (Abrahamsen and Sandor, 2018). Since the myriad of security threats and challenges that confront the international system typically fall beyond state boundaries but are not global either (Tavares, 2009), regional organizations have come to play an increasingly important role in global security governance, enabling localized interventions without the need to rely on the largesse of the five permanent members of the UN Security Council (Hough, 2020c). The development of regional cooperation is described as 'regionalism' in international relations scholarship, defined by Nye as 'the formation of interstate associations or groupings on the basis of regions' (1968: vii), or more broadly in terms of common identity and norms as articulated by Habib (1995: 305), who conceived it as 'the expression of regional consciousness that develops from a sense of identity among states situated in geographical proximity which motivates them to mutually cooperate in one or another mode to attain common goals, satisfy common needs, or to solve political, military, economic and other practical problems'.

Having grown in number and scope since the Second World War and especially after the end of the Cold War, regional organizations are usually made up of neighbouring countries in a geographically delimited area, but may cover two or more regions, as in the case of NATO, the Association of Southeast Asian Nations (ASEAN), the Commonwealth, and the Organisation Internationale de la Francophonie. Virtually all countries belong to at least one regional organization (Tavares, 2009), but their distribution is uneven: some parts of the world are covered by multiple bodies, whereas others have no regional organization or no organization with a security mandate. Tavares (2009) counted 38 regional institutions that declare a peace and security mandate, a selection of which are listed in Table 3.1.

Table 3.1 Selected regional organizations with a peace and security mandate

Region	Year founded	Organization
Africa (sub-Saharan)	1975	Economic Community of West African States (ECOWAS)
	1992	Southern African Development Community (SADC)
	2001	African Union (AU)
Americas	1948	Organization of American States (OAS)
	1969	Andean Community (CAN)
	1973	Caribbean Community (CARICOM)
	1991	Common Market of the Southern Cone (MERCOSUR)
	2008	Union of South American Nations (UNASUR)
	2011	Economic Community of Latin American and Caribbean States (CELAC)
Asia	1967	Association of Southeast Asian Nations (ASEAN)
	1985	South Asian Association for Regional Cooperation (SAARC)
	2005	East Asia Summit (EAS)

(Continued)

Table 3.1 (*Continued*)

Region	Year founded	Organization
Europe	1949	North Atlantic Treaty Organization (NATO)
	1992	European Union (EU)
	1995	Organization for Security and Cooperation in Europe (OSCE)
Eurasia	2001	Shanghai Cooperation Organisation (SCO)
	2003	Collective Security Treaty Organisation (CSTO)
Middle East	1945	League of Arab States (LAS)
	1981	Gulf Cooperation Council (GCC)

Fawcett (2018) identifies three early types of regional organization: 'multi-purpose' organizations with security, economic and political functions, including the League of Arab States, the Organization of American States, and the Organization of African Unity, which was replaced by the African Union; those with a primarily economic focus such as the European Community, the precursor to the European Union; and security alliances such as NATO. She argues that three broad waves of institutional growth since 1945 can be identified. The first phase, the post-Second World War and early Cold War period, saw states forming groupings after 1945 to prevent the conditions that led to war in 1939 happening again, and to protect their own interests. However, the onset of the Cold War meant that the authority of the new regional organizations was subordinated to that of the two superpowers.

The second phase, the mid- to late Cold War period, was marked by endeavours to improve regional self-sufficiency and build a stronger security remit, partly in response to superpower dominance and particularly among developing countries. Early efforts by newly independent states to come together and speak with a common voice were pursued at the Bandung Conference, a meeting of Asian and African states, in 1955, which led to the establishment of the Non-Aligned Movement in 1961, made up of countries that were not aligned with any major power bloc seeking to pursue a collective agenda. Acharya and Buzan (2019) contrast the motivations in pursuing regionalism of post-Second World War Western European leaders, who sought means of curbing the nationalism that was blamed for the two World Wars, with those of non-Western heads of state who viewed regionalism as a means for attaining national independence and sovereignty that had been lost to the West, and advancing decolonization in their own nations as well as in general.

The third – and still ongoing – post-Cold War phase left many countries more vulnerable, but also able to exert more autonomy, and more favourable to regional cooperation in response to the waves of democratization and trade liberalization that occurred during this period. There was room for alternative approaches to order and security and, as Fawcett observes, expressions by regional elites of the 'Asian Way' or 'African solutions to African problems' that explicitly challenged Western-dominated international agendas 'foreshadowed what has become a new "southern" agenda for regional organization' (p. 289). While the UN was also taking on a much expanded security role, it lacked both the resources and the commitment of the most powerful states to become the sole provider of global security. As it became more involved in peacekeeping missions, it also became more engaged in empowering regional institutions to fulfil a more active security role, through capacity-building and political support, and thus supporting their expansion and influence.

Regional bodies, as Tavares (2009) points out, may better understand the conflict at hand, can often respond more quickly, may be able to act more cost-effectively because they are closer to it, may have more of a stake in maintaining regional stability, may be better welcomed in the conflicted state, and can give a voice to less influential countries in the world system. On the other hand, they may lack the capacity to intervene, are less likely to be impartial, and may be dominated by the more powerful countries in the region. The relationship between the UN and regional bodies is described by Hough as being 'symbiotic', since 'the UN cannot police the globe without them, and ... most of the regional organizations cannot police their regions without the UN' (2020c: 334). Hampson (2004) discusses more fully the reasons why the UN may or may not be the 'mediator of choice' in a conflict, and the advantages that regional organizations can have.

The UN has deployed peacekeeping operations under the authority of the UN Security Council since 1948, when it sent observers to the Middle East to mediate conflict between Israel and its neighbours during and after the 1948 Arab–Israeli war. There have been over 70 such operations since 1948, of which the majority were deployed after the end of the Cold War (UN Peacekeeping, 2020). Initially, they had the limited goals of supporting peace-making in inter-state conflict, supporting political efforts to resolve conflicts peacefully. Such missions tended to be instigated with the consent of the states to which they were deployed, and conducted with strict impartiality and neutrality. Post-Cold War, however, interventions increasingly addressed intra-state conflicts and civil wars, widened in scope to include the deployment of military force without consent in humanitarian interventions, and employed increasingly standardized strategies. The two main approaches of UN peacekeeping are disarmament, demobilization and reintegration (DDR) of ex-combatants, and longer-term processes of security sector reform (SSR) which seek to establish accountable public security architectures according to Western models of democratic accountability (see von Dyck, 2016).

By 2018, over half of the 60 peacekeeping operations deployed worldwide in that year were conducted by regional organizations. According to the Stockholm International Peace Research Institute (SIPRI) (2019), regional organizations and alliances led 33 operations, the UN conducted 21, and six were carried out by *ad hoc* coalitions of states. Geographically, 24 were deployed in Africa, 18 in Europe, 10 in the Middle East, five in Asia and Oceania and three in the Americas. Regional organizations also undertake political missions, such as conflict prevention, peace-making, crisis management and post-conflict peacebuilding. The world's largest regional security organization is the Organization for Security and Co-operation in Europe (OSCE), with 57 member states in 2019, which conducted 16 peacekeeping operations and political missions in 2019 (OSCE, 2020). The second largest is the African Union, with 55 member states.

The regionalization of security governance is a process that is still ongoing. In an increasingly multipolar world, Fawcett (2018) anticipates that regional collective security will become increasingly sophisticated and engaged in regional conflict management, with the UN's encouragement and in response to demand for alternatives to US-led intervention as seen in the Middle East, as well as to changing US security priorities. Financial limitations are one of the biggest constraints on the effectiveness and autonomy of regional organizations in the Global South, some of which still rely heavily on external support from states of the Global North, while other challenges for regional bodies include political divisions, poor coordination mechanisms, lack of military capability and/or unresolved ethnic and territorial disputes (Bujun, Foucault and Mérand, 2014). However, Hough (2020c) observes that, while the coverage of regional security organizations is uneven, with some regions of the world much better policed than others, and national security concerns are generally better addressed than non-military threats to human security, enhancements in regional security provision are certain to be among the factors behind falling numbers of conflict-related deaths across the globe, and better global provision for human security than at any time in the past.

Summary

This chapter built on Chapter 2's Western-centric analysis of international security challenges in an evolving world order, presenting a contrasting view of the world that gives prominence to perspectives and issues of the Global South that have been neglected in mainstream scholarship. It sought to emphasize the profound effect of colonization and decolonization on the regions of the Global South and the world we inhabit today, with the demise of European colonial empires after the Second World War marking the beginning of the South's challenge to Western dominance of the international order. That challenge was shown to be economic, political and cultural, with most of the world's fastest-growing economies being located in the Global South, many Southern states now able to exert increasing political authority through regional organizations, and an international movement to 'decolonize knowledge' bringing to mainstream attention the undue dominance of Western worldviews.

As emphasized in this and the previous chapter, the acceleration of globalization has meant that the most powerful countries on the world stage are no longer insulated from the impact of strife elsewhere, and see the most critical international security challenges as residing in the Global South. This chapter showed how a growing recognition of the interrelationship between poverty and conflict has led to the convergence of international security and development agendas, conceived by many Southern thinkers and Northern critics as forms of neocolonialism. Dimensions of the so-called 'security–development nexus' include the embedding of the human security approach in international development through the SDGs, and the rise of resilience ideas and practices in the Goals and other significant global initiatives for sustainable development in the latter half of the 2020s. The pressing issues of climate change and environmental degradation highlight the extent of the challenges still needing to be adequately addressed by the global community.

Study questions

- What has been the impact of colonization and decolonization on our world today?
- Where do the main similarities and differences lie in the security challenges facing the Global North and Global South?
- What is the significance of regional organizations in international security?
- What is the relationship between colonial history and criminology?

Further reading

For a fuller account of the history of colonization, challenges to colonization and the development of postcolonial histories and perspectives, *Colonialism/Postcolonialism* (Loomba, 2015) is a thorough, engaging guide, while a useful critique of the Eurocentric character of security studies is offered by Barkawi and Laffey in their 2006 paper 'The postcolonial moment in security studies'. *Globalization and Postcolonialism: Hegemony and Resistance in the Twenty-First Century* (Krishna, 2008) offers a lucid examination of the impact of colonialist legacies on the post-9/11 world and the relationship between postcolonialism and globalization. The controversial 'clash of civilizations' thesis is an interesting area for discussion and debate, and two interviews of under 30 minutes with the late Samuel Huntington can be found on YouTube, as can Edward Said's acerbic critique of the thesis in a 1996 lecture at the University of Massachusetts on 'The myth of the clash of civilizations' (www.youtube.com). *Human Security: Concepts and Implications* (Tadjbakhsh and Chenoy, 2007) offers a thorough examination of the human security approach, which can be supplemented by the reading recommendations for Chapter 6 on its seven dimensions. For a critical examination of the security–development nexus, *Global Governance and the New Wars: The Merging of Development and Security* (Duffield, 2014) is recommended. Among a growing literature on regional security governance, *The Governance, Security and Development Nexus: Africa Rising* (edited by Omeje, 2021) is distinctive in offering a Global South perspective.

4

Securing the nation

CHAPTER OUTLINE

Chapter overview

This chapter provides:

- An exploration of the distinct 'national security cultures' of the United Kingdom (UK) and the United States (US), the two nations that are the focus of this chapter, which help explain their responses to significant international events.
- An overview of the origins and development of the national security architectures of the UK and the US, through the decades of the two World Wars and the Cold War.
- An appraisal of the major national security challenges to both nations in the immediate post-Cold War period, in which the proliferation of threats began to blur the operational boundaries between military, intelligence and policing agencies and required national and international agencies to work much more closely together.
- An examination of the impact of the 9/11 terrorist attacks and the rise of international terrorism, as well as the new frameworks and structures for national security governance that have evolved in the UK and the US in the new millennium, including a growing emphasis on the ideas and practices associated with the concept of 'resilience'.

Key terms

- Biosecurity
- Counter-terrorism
- Critical national infrastructure
- Energy security
- Homeland security
- Intelligence
- Intelligence agency
- National security
- Resilience
- Space security

Introduction

Early conceptions of **national security** were typically associated with protection from military attack. One influential explanation stated: 'A nation has security when it does not have to sacrifice its legitimate interests to avoid war, and is able, if challenged, to maintain them by war' (Lippmann, 1943: 32), while another described national security as 'freedom from foreign dictation' (Lasswell, 1950: 51). However, even amid the Cold War, a widely cited article by Ullman (1983: 129) criticized the 'excessively narrow' and 'excessively military' conception of 'every administration in Washington' since the late 1940s, arguing that it led states to ignore other and perhaps more harmful dangers, and contributed to a 'pervasive militarization of international relations that in the long run can only increase global insecurity'. Today, the concept is commonly seen to encompass a much broader range of issues in accordance with the broadening scope of international and regional security since the end of the Cold War, one contemporary definition referring to 'public policies that protect the safety or welfare of a nation's citizens from substantial threats' (Murphy and Topel, 2013: 508).

The focus of this chapter is the evolution of national security agendas and arrangements in the UK and the US. It begins with a discussion of the distinctive national security cultures of those nations, and then examines the changing threat landscape and evolving security architectures of each through distinct chronological phases, in common with Chapter 1. These cover the period from the early 20th century to the end of the Cold War; the ensuing decade, when national governments adjusted to the end of a bipolar world, and the distinctions between domestic and foreign policy and the functions of the different government security agencies became increasingly blurred; and the new millennium, from the terrorist attacks of 11 September 2001 (9/11) onwards, in which **resilience** has become a significant theme of the two countries' national security agendas.

National security cultures of the UK and the US

The study of state cultures in an international relations context dates back to the Second World War, when the American government sought operational insight on the 'national character' of its German and Japanese enemies (Haglund, 2011). In an edited collection of papers on national security cultures, Kirchner and Sperling (2010) observe how states' different responses to significant international events such as the end of the Cold War, the 9/11 attacks and wars in Afghanistan, Iraq and elsewhere that have threatened regional or global order, reflect not only different resourcing capacities, but also different national security cultures. Four criteria by which to evaluate national security cultures are proposed by Sperling (2010a): the 'worldview' of the external environment, relating to perceptions of the major threats, the importance of state sovereignty and the dynamics of the international system; 'national identity', in terms of the commitment to autonomy and independence versus the values shared with neighbours and allies; 'instrumental preferences' for the exertion of 'hard' power (military and economic instruments) or the 'soft' power of diplomatic relations, humanitarian assistance and cultural exchange; and 'interaction preferences' along the continuum from unilateral to multilateral.

Sperling (2010b: 19) identifies a 'common core' in the 'worldviews' of the UK and the US, sharing close bonds in their histories, cultures and common language; a common view of the threat from Islamist terrorism; and a similar position on the global role and responsibilities of each state in the international system. The most recent national security strategies of both nations (at the time of writing) present similar perspectives on the major threats, describing an increasingly complex global security environment and growing competition between major states, with the UK referring in particular to increasing Russian aggression, and the US to the actions of both Russia and China as 'revisionist powers' seeking to challenge the *status quo* in a Western-centric international order (HM Government, 2015; White House, 2017). On their respective roles in the world, the UK has reiterated a wish to be a 'force for good' (Ministry of Defence, 1998: 4, 2008: 2; Conservative and Unionist Party, 2019: 51) in the international system, and the US is described by Sperling (2010b: 20) as viewing itself as 'the global custodian of order spreading the benefits of democracy and capitalism', given its capacity to act unilaterally, although Trump's presidency has marked a shift away from these values.

Sperling's (2010a) second criterion of 'national identity' has become a contentious topic in both the UK and the US in recent years, the *Washington Post* noting just after the UK's Brexit vote and prior to Trump's election on an 'America First' platform that, 'We are in the midst of a worldwide sea change regarding how people view themselves, their government and their countries. The Brexit referendum and the rise of Trump – while separated by thousands of miles and an ocean – are both manifestations of that change' (Cillizza, 2016). Fukuyama (2016) points to an increasing cultural divide between residents of urban centres and those in smaller cities, towns and rural areas as having driven political events in both the UK and the US, while the Ministry of Defence (2018: 12) observes a broader pattern of 'growing division within many countries between those with liberal and those with traditional views', which demonstrably includes different stances on liberal multilateralism, such as European Union (EU) membership. Such divisions are arguably not new, but have been brought to the surface through the increasing power of digital communications for contemporary political mobilization. Trump's presidency has marked a departure from established American foreign policy values: Mead (2017) observes that, 'For the first time in 70 years, the American people have elected a president who disparages the policies, ideas, and institutions at the heart of post-war U.S. foreign policy'. The national security strategy of the Trump Administration (White House, 2017) is declared to be one of 'principled realism', prioritizing 'American sovereignty' in a 'competitive world', contrasting with his predecessor Obama's vision of 'a rules-based international order advanced by US leadership that promotes peace, security, and opportunity through stronger cooperation to meet global challenges' (White House, 2015: 2).

UK and US 'instrumental preferences' for hard or soft power are articulated in both countries' national security strategies. In the 2015 edition of the UK strategy, the preface by then Prime Minister David Cameron emphasizes Britain's military prowess, as well as its ability to honour its commitments to the international community on defence spending (the North Atlantic Treaty Organization [NATO] target of 2% of gross domestic product) and international aid (the United Nations [UN] target of 0.7% of gross national income) (HM Government, 2015). Declarations of defence and security capability in the main body of the document include references to the UK's defence budget 'the second largest in NATO after the US, and the largest in the EU' (p. 13), and its investment in prestige assets such as the Trident nuclear defence system and new aircraft carriers. Rogers (2018: 3) echoes many liberal critics in questioning the UK's 'national narrative based on an enduring cultural belief in great power status, with emphasis on the "great"', expressed through the use of military power including its position as one of few states retaining nuclear weapons, and which he links to the UK's former imperial 'greatness'. The UK strategy also emphasizes the UK's status at the time as the world's fifth biggest economy, and claims the position of 'the world's leading soft power' (HM Government, 2015: 13) (runner-up in 2019, according to Portland's 2019 Soft Power 30 rankings).

On America's 'instrumental preferences', Sperling (2010c: 172) describes the country as 'singular in its possession of a military capable of global power projection and simultaneous multi-theatre combat' with 'similarly unparalleled' economic capacity, while having lost power and influence in the international system following the Bush administration's wars in Afghanistan and Iraq. The 2017 US national security strategy (White House, 2017) gives more priority to 'hard power' than versions published under Obama's presidency, and declares that the US will respond to challenges by China, Russia and others to US influence and interests, modernize its military and maintain its military superiority. Its enduring global leadership in outer space, another theme of the latest strategy, is a further expression of hard power, both military and economic. Although this is balanced with the soft power of diplomacy and development to project US influence, US soft power is judged in the *Soft Power 30* global rankings to have declined each year since 2016 (Portland, 2019). This is attributed to Trump's 'America First' messages, reliance on the hard power of trade tariffs, abandonment of its traditional role as the guarantor of the rules-based system, and the declining performance of government at home (for example, following the longest federal government shutdown in history at the end of 2018). However, as Portland acknowledges, the country's global cultural influence endures through such dimensions as the pervasiveness of its entertainment industry, its status as the leading destination for international students, the dominance of its technology companies, and its Olympic success.

On the fourth criterion of 'interaction preferences', the UK's current national security strategy declares the UK to be positioned 'at the heart of the rules-based international order' as the only nation to be a permanent member of the UN Security Council, as well as a member of NATO, the EU, the Commonwealth, the G7 and G20, the Organization for Security and Cooperation in Europe (OSCE), the Organisation for Economic Co-operation and Development, the World Trade Organization, the International Monetary Fund and the World Bank (HM Government, 2015: 14). It also refers to the 'special relationship' with the US, based on shared values and close bilateral security cooperation, and its amplification through the 'Five Eyes' **intelligence**-sharing partnership with the US, Canada, Australia and New Zealand. The UK's departure from the EU represents a significant strategic adjustment from a declared commitment to multilateralism as well as a broad stance on Europe that had endured since the 1970s. However, the UK's resistance to the deepening of EU integration through the Euro, the Schengen area and – under Conservative-led administrations since 2010 – the strengthening of foreign and defence cooperation (see Whitman, 2015), and a lukewarm commitment to UN and OSCE missions (Smith, 2010), gives some support to Smith's contention that, 'There is little official sense that the UK's international status depends to any significant degree on its being seen as a leading contributor in the multilateral assurance field' (p. 99).

America's commitment to multilateralism is longstanding, as a key post-Second World War sponsor of **collective security** via the UN, NATO and the OSCE, and the strengthening of the international economic system through the global financial institutions (Sperling, 2010c), as well as a leading architect of the League of Nations even though the US ultimately failed to take up membership. However, as Sperling observes, American preferences for multilateral, bilateral or unilateral engagement in response to international challenges have varied from administration to administration and from issue to issue, with NATO seen to represent a multilateral exception rather than the rule in US security policy, and the US often willing to act alone or in 'ad hoc coalitions of the willing', as in the case of the US-led wars in Afghanistan and Iraq (2010c: 175). Bush's actions after 9/11 presented the most extreme examples of US unilateralism since the end of the Cold War (Sperling, 2010c) while, in contrast, Obama's 2015 version of the national security strategy placed significant emphasis on multilateralism (White House, 2015). In turn, Trump's 2017 strategy expresses a critical view of multilateralism, noting the 'competition for influence [that] exists in these institutions' and prioritizing 'better outcomes in multilateral forums' that advance US interests (White House, 2017: 40).

National security architectures from World War to Cold War

Borrowing from the 'high' and 'low' politics dichotomy employed by realist international relations scholars, which was introduced in Chapter 2, the late Canadian criminologist Jean-Paul Brodeur (1983, 2010) employed the concepts of high and low policing to differentiate the roles and functions of state intelligence and policing agencies. Describing how, in the nineteenth century, Napoleon's police minister Joseph Fouché made a distinction between policing tasks to protect the empire and preserving the rule of Emperor Napolean I, and all the other tasks of police including public safety, Brodeur observed that these could be associated with a scale of prestige depending on how close to the seat of power they occurred. The type of security organization that has historically been the most strongly associated with so-called high policing is the **intelligence agency**, defined by Gill as 'an organisation conducting mainly secret activities – targeting, collection, analysis and dissemination – intended to enhance security and/or power by forewarning of threats in time to take preventative action' (2009: 173). Brodeur (2010) identifies four key features of high policing. First, it is preventative: it cannot afford to be mainly reactive, like the police, because a successful terrorist act or political coup has far-reaching consequences, and places a priority on pre-empting or disrupting such activity. Secondly, it is based on surveillance, paired with quick and decisive action to forestall any threatening event uncovered. Because of the need to maintain the secrecy of high policing operatives and tactics, national security intelligence is typically stored away awaiting further action that is often never taken, in contrast with criminal evidence, which is used in court to bring prosecutions. Thirdly, it requires the conflation of powers, since intelligence services rely on very different powers to the police: covert executive orders coming from the top of governments in order to supersede the law and protect their intelligence assets. Powers that are normally distinct – legislative, judicial and executive – are exercised by the executive to facilitate Brodeur's fourth feature, that of extra-legality, whereby the national interest is seen to take priority over all other considerations including human rights. This requires the tension between the national interest and the rule of law to be addressed by either or all of the following measures: cloaking the activities in impenetrable secrecy, making them legal through rules of exception, and making security agencies accountable to an oversight body. Normally all three are used to varying degrees.

The UK's modern intelligence system first originated in response to the growing military threat of Germany prior to the start of the First World War, with espionage made illegal in the UK under the Official Secrets Acts of 1911 and 1920. The primary national security concern internal to the UK in the 20th century came much later, and was associated with the Northern Ireland conflict of 1968 to 1998, known as the 'Troubles', over the constitutional status of Northern Ireland. The precursors to the Secret Intelligence Service (MI6), tasked with the collection of foreign intelligence overseas; the Security Service (MI5), which protects the UK against threats to national security; and the Government Communication Headquarters (GCHQ), responsible for signals intelligence, were originally founded in 1909 and adopted their current names between 1920 and 1946. The UK's armed services – the Army, the Royal Navy and the Royal Air Force – also each maintained significant intelligence capability, and their resources were combined to form the Defence Intelligence Staff (today known simply as Defence Intelligence) when the Ministry of Defence was formed in 1964. The Joint Intelligence Committee, the 'centrepiece of British intelligence' (Goodman, 2014: 137), was established in 1936, made up of the heads of the three intelligence agencies and senior representatives of policy-making departments, with the remit to set intelligence priorities, provide oversight and coordination across the three agencies, and bring them together with policy departments. Police 'special branches' (today often known instead as **counter-terrorism** branches) were dedicated to matters of national security and intelligence, and operated as an executive arm of MI5, undertaking investigations, arrests and questioning of suspects.

In the US prior to the Second World War, the collection and dissemination of foreign intelligence was undertaken by the Department of State and the armed services (see Warner, 2002), while the Bureau of Investigation, established in 1908, was responsible for domestic intelligence and comparable to the UK's MI5. Renamed the Federal Bureau of Investigation (FBI) in 1935, its remit extended to counter-espionage following America's entry into the First World War in 1917, prompted by attacks on American ships, with the Espionage Act 1917 making espionage a federal crime and broadening the Bureau's mandate. From 1924 it began to professionalize and expand under the directorship of J. Edgar Hoover, developing into the country's foremost law enforcement agency, and its counter-espionage capability developed in the early 1940s through successes in identifying and convicting members of a substantial German espionage ring (Batvinis, 2010).

The surprise attack by Japan on the US naval base at Pearl Harbor in Honolulu, Hawaii in December 1941 led the US to join the Second World War, elevating the country to world power status with the need for a commensurate global intelligence capability (Marrin, 2014). Through the remainder of the war and the ensuing decades, a significant investment in 'the most advanced collection technologies available', a powerful FBI responsible for internal security, a substantial foreign intelligence capability, and a robust framework of laws, regulations and oversight mechanisms established the massive and sophisticated intelligence architecture that facilitated US military success over the decades to come (Warner, 2010). The precursor to the Central Intelligence Agency (CIA) was established by President Roosevelt in 1941, and the CIA was formed following the passage of the National Security Act 1947, operating alongside a new National Security Council to advise and assist the President on matters of national security and foreign policy. Shortly afterwards, the Office of National Estimates and the Office of Reports and Estimates were created as departments of the CIA, becoming the National Intelligence Council (NIC) in 1979.

Navigating the new world disorder

After the fall of the Soviet Union in December 1991, marking its disintegration into 15 separate countries, significant reorganization and downsizing of defence and intelligence agencies around the globe was inevitable. Russia's continuing nuclear capability remained a concern to the West yet, as the world entered an age of increasingly open borders, governments around the world had to adapt their capabilities to target a wider range of challenges such as regional instability, nuclear and biological warfare proliferation, terrorism, drug trafficking and other forms of serious organized crime. The proliferation of threats would blur operational boundaries between military, intelligence, border and policing agencies, and require national and international agencies to work much more closely together as the distinction between domestic and foreign policy also became increasingly blurred.

Brodeur (2003) associates the blurring of responsibilities with the growing 'hybridity', 'complexity' and 'transnationality' of contemporary threats. His use of the term 'hybridity' differs from the notion of 'hybrid warfare' exemplified by Russian cyber attacks and disinformation: Brodeur employs the term to refer to the blurring of traditional lines between common criminality and threats to national security requiring different agencies to work together. Examples include terrorism-related offences as captured in Makarenko's (2004) concept of the 'crime–terror nexus', such as the funding of illegal political activities through the proceeds of crime, violent vigilantism by terrorist groups, trafficking in firearms and dangerous substances such as radioactive materials, and the 'narco-terrorism' of drug cartels in Latin America and the Taliban in Afghanistan; as well as organized illegal immigration because of its effect on population control, labour policies and the economy. 'Complexity' reflects the fact that some crimes are becoming so complex that responses often require multidisciplinary expertise. As Brodeur points out, 'organized crime may be crude in its activities, but the laundering of its profits is generally a highly sophisticated operation' (2003: 806). Liberalization of the global economy made all kinds of financial crime possible, and these are among the hardest to detect and police. The development of the internet also offered numerous opportunities for laundering money, defrauding individuals or extorting money from companies: types of crimes that are largely beyond the human and technical resources of police forces. Finally, 'transnationality' is a common characteristic of most of such crimes, which often require inter-agency collaboration across borders.

In the UK the primary focus of MI5 shifted from counter-espionage to counter-terrorism after the Cold War as the threat from foreign intelligence agencies diminished, and the Provisional IRA significantly increased the frequency of their attacks on the British mainland. These had occurred on no more than four days per year between 1977 and 1989, but numbered 19 in 1990 and 47 in 1992 (Andrew, 2009). The Troubles finally came to an end in 1998 with the signing of the Good Friday Agreement, although violence by dissident republicans has continued. The immediate post-Cold War period was also a period of significant organizational reform in the UK's intelligence agencies. MI5 had gained a statutory mandate for the first time in 1989, due to a European Commission on Human Rights ruling that surveillance of political activists from the National Council for Civil Liberties (now just 'Liberty') had breached the European Convention on Human Rights, and its functions and parameters were set out in the Security Service Acts of 1989 and 1996. MI6's existence was officially acknowledged in 1992, and the Intelligence Services Act 1994 provided statutory mandates for MI6 and GCHQ, as well as establishing the Intelligence and Security Committee of Parliament (ISC), a cross-party committee responsible for oversight of the intelligence agencies. Three external Commissioners were added to the regulatory architecture under the provisions of the Regulation of Investigatory Powers Act 2000 (their roles and powers later being combined in the provisions of the Investigatory Powers Act 2016 to form the Investigatory Powers Commissioner's Office).

In the US, the end of the Cold War saw the beginnings of a process of review and reform of the country's intelligence community. In November 1991, shortly before the end of the Cold War, US President George H.W. Bush had issued a directive to heads of all of the country's central government agencies, calling for 'a top to bottom examination of the mission, role and priorities of the Intelligence Community' which would address the country's requirements to 2005. It emphasized the increasing significance of security issues beyond the Soviet Union, including terrorism, the drugs trade, nuclear proliferation, economic espionage and technology transfer, resource scarcities and global health problems, and drew attention to the 'extraordinary uncertainties' now being faced (White House, 1991). Bush's memorandum marked the beginnings of a new way of looking at global security, considering the threats on the horizon up to 2005, and the ways in which the US government needed to adapt. Little changed initially, but the US government was taken by surprise in February 1993 when Islamist terrorists detonated explosives at the base of the World Trade Center, killing six people; again in October that year, when the soldiers of a Somali warlord killed 18 US Special Forces soldiers in Mogadishu; and in February 1994 when investigators from the CIA and FBI discovered that a CIA officer, Aldrich Ames, had spied for the Soviet Union and Russia for over a decade, disclosing details of US agents in Moscow and hundreds of CIA operations (see Johnson, 2004). There was also concern about a protracted campaign by a Democratic Party senator, Daniel Patrick Moynihan (1991), for the CIA to be disbanded, on the grounds that it had consistently exaggerated Soviet economic growth and become too large and difficult to control.

In 1994, under the administration of Bill Clinton, who had taken up the US presidency at the start of 1993, the US Congress established a Commission to carry out an independent review of the American intelligence community. The report of the Aspin–Brown Commission, as it was informally known, noted that the US had established a technical intelligence infrastructure more advanced than any in the world through the Cold War period, yet its maintenance and modernization costs were high, and this investment needed to be appropriately targeted. It advocated a strengthening of the position of the Director of Central Intelligence (DCI), the head of the CIA, to enhance the centralized management of the US intelligence community; intelligence agencies working more closely with the policy community they served; better coordination between agencies to enhance cooperation and improve efficiency; and improving the quality of intelligence by enhancing intelligence analysts' skills, making greater use of experts outside the intelligence community, and harnessing open sources more effectively (Commission on the Roles and Capabilities of the United States Intelligence Community, 1996). Although the Commission did not result in the degree of change that some reformers advocated, and which might have averted the subsequent 9/11 attacks, Johnson (2004) argues that it moved debates about intelligence reform forward in a way that proved fruitful later on, helped intelligence managers address operational weaknesses, and enhanced public understanding of intelligence organizations, budgets and activities. Sperling (2010c: 188) observes that the 1990s also saw the securitization of issues hitherto regarded as domestic law enforcement concerns, with cyber attack, drug trafficking into the US, porous borders and uncontrolled migration, and epidemics featuring in the 1999 national security strategy (White House, 1999).

International terrorism and the widening national security lens

When the major terrorist attacks on New York and Washington shook the US and wider world on 11 September 2001, the immediate response of the US government was to launch a retaliatory 'war on terror'. The US-led international effort to remove the Taliban regime from Afghanistan and destroy al-Qaeda's terrorist network there began with US and UK air strikes on 7 October 2001, and was followed by a NATO-led mission agreed by the UN Security Council in December 2001. This was followed by the controversial US-led intervention in Iraq in 2003, also involving the UK, Australia, Spain and Poland.

The UK has also confronted a significant domestic terrorism problem in the new millennium, including well over 100 terrorism-related deaths (National Consortium for the Study of Terrorism and Responses to Terrorism, 2019), mostly linked to Islamic extremism, but also encompassing an ongoing dissident Irish republican campaign and a more recent and growing far-right terrorism threat. The deadliest attacks were the suicide bombings of 7 July 2005 that targeted commuters travelling on London's public transport system during the morning rush hour, killing 52 people, and the suicide bombing of an Ariana Grande concert at Manchester Arena on 22 May 2017, which killed 22.

Resilience, as previously defined and discussed in Chapters 1 and 3, has become an increasingly significant dimension of national security in the UK, US and elsewhere in the new millennium, with the terms 'resilience' and 'resilient' featuring 64 times in the current national security strategy (HM Government, 2015). This last section of the chapter looks primarily at the way in which resilience thinking has informed policy and practice in both nations, looking at developments in the UK and US in turn.

Resilience in UK national security

In the UK, concern about terrorist attacks against key sites brought emergency preparedness and the concept of resilience to the fore in government policy. A Civil Contingencies Secretariat (CCS) had been established within the Cabinet Office earlier in 2001, following the Y2K bug scare, fuel protests in 2000 and a foot and mouth epidemic in 2001, for the purpose of improving the UK's emergency management policies and structures (Cornish, 2005, 2007). After 9/11, the Civil Contingencies Act (CCA) 2004 established a single framework for civil protection and resilience in conjunction with new counter-terrorism legislation (the Terrorism Act 2000 which preceded 9/11 and the subsequent Anti-Terrorism Crime and Security Act 2001), and defined the obligations of organizations involved in emergency preparedness and response at the local level, including cooperation through multi-agency partnerships called local resilience forums.

The UK approach is often described as a 'lead department' model, as it places responsibility for the anticipation, prevention, planning, response and recovery for any type of civil emergency with the most relevant government department, supported by Cabinet Office, regional and local structures (see Cornish, 2007; Gregory, 2007; Coaffee and Fussey, 2017), hence the COVID-19 pandemic saw the Department of Health fulfilling the lead department role. The UK was one of the first countries to introduce a national risk assessment in order to identify and analyse risks of national significance and inform decision-making (Vlek, 2013), the public version of the document providing a summary of the natural hazards, diseases, major accidents, societal risks (such as industrial action or public disorder), risks in foreign countries to British citizens travelling or living abroad, and malicious attacks on the horizon (see Cabinet Office, 2017). The latter encompasses major cyber attacks; attacks on crowded places, transport systems or infrastructure; and chemical, biological, radiological and nuclear attacks.

A number of government publications, some of which have now gone through multiple editions, set out the strategic direction for the development of UK national security and resilience. These include the *National Security Strategy and Strategic Defence and Security Review* (NSS/SDSR) (HM Government, 2015), the *National Risk Register* (Cabinet Office, 2017), the *National Security Capability Review* of the NSS/SDSR (HM Government, 2018b); and sector or issue-specific strategies including the *Energy Security Strategy* (Department of Energy and Climate Change, 2012), the *National Space Security Policy* (HM Government, 2014a), the *UK National Strategy for Maritime Security* (HM Government, 2014b), the *National Cyber Security Strategy* (HM Government, 2016), the *UK Biological Security Strategy* (HM Government, 2018c) and the national *Counter Terrorism Strategy* (CONTEST) (Home Office, 2018a). CONTEST is split into four work streams called 'Prevent' (preventing radicalization), 'Pursue' (investigating, detecting and prosecuting terrorism suspects), 'Protect' (strengthening protection against an attack, particularly with respect to borders, transport, other **critical national infrastructure** sectors and crowded places), and 'Prepare' (preparedness to respond to and recover from emergencies), and informed the development of the *European Union Counter-Terrorism Strategy* based around the four dimensions of 'Prevent', 'Protect', 'Pursue' and 'Respond' (Council of the European Union, 2005).

Forming a 'central plank of the Government's approach to national security' (House of Commons Defence Committee, 2009: 4), the protective and preparedness measures under CONTEST have become drivers for improving the resilience of critical systems to disaster whatever the cause, not only terrorism (Cornish, 2005). They place an emphasis on the physical security and surveillance of crowded places and 'critical national infrastructure', including energy, utilities, telecommunications, transport, food, health and finance, and defined as:

> those facilities, systems, sites, property, information, people, networks and processes that are needed to keep the UK running and provide the essential services upon which we rely ... which, if disrupted, could have a significant impact on our national security or the functioning of the state. (Home Office, 2018a: 59)

For example, a widespread electricity failure, sometimes described as a 'black sky event', is identified in the *National Risk Register* as having a medium likelihood of occurring in the next five years and a severe impact. Such an event could result from either a natural hazard or a malicious attack, and would have cascading effects to other infrastructures, necessitating what is known as a 'black start' recovery process to restore power from a total or partial shutdown (Cabinet Office, 2017; Electric Infrastructure Security Council, 2018).

Other key aspects of state-directed national resilience identified in the *National Security Strategy* include resilience from **biosecurity** hazards such as a pandemic or a chemical, biological, nuclear or radiological attack; **energy security** (ensuring UK consumers have access to uninterrupted, affordable and sustainable energy sources); and **space security** (resilience from disruption to space services and capabilities, as well as the ability of the UK government, industry and academia to access safely and exploit opportunities in outer space).

A significant dimension of the government's strategy is engagement with regional and local authorities, the business sector and the community, with the aim of embedding resilience in everyday activities and professional practice. Engagement with the business sector includes the publication of advice to organizations on protective security, exemplified in the work of the Centre for the Protection of National Infrastructure, located in the Security Service; and training of security and other public-facing staff in crowded places as part of the Action Counters Terrorism (ACT) initiative of the National Counter Terrorism Security Office police unit. Measures to mobilize the public include National Rail's 'See it. Say it. Sorted' campaign; ACT's campaign to encourage the reporting of suspicious activity; the extension of ACT online training to interested members of the public; and duties placed on local resilience forums under the CCA to educate, warn and inform the public, 'based on the premise that a well-informed public is better able to respond to an emergency and able to help to minimise the impact of an emergency' (Cabinet Office, 2013: 24–25).

More recently, in a review of the NSS/SDSR (HM Government, 2015) and recognizing that 'the world has become more uncertain and volatile since 2015' (p. 3), the UK government announced a new 'whole-of-government approach to national security' (p. 9) called the 'Fusion Doctrine' (HM Government, 2018b: 9). Its purpose is to strengthen the collective response to threats to the nation, the term 'Fusion' being notably similar to that of the Russian 'hybrid' warfare now presenting a distinct challenge to the nation's cyber security and democratic processes (discussed in Chapter 7). The Doctrine places an emphasis on stronger partnerships across government and with the private and third sectors, and fusing together elements of hard and soft power through security, economic, diplomatic and cultural levers. Resilience is a recurring theme of the document, particularly with respect to the UK's 'national resilience' to disasters, including flood resilience, critical national infrastructure (CNI) resilience in general, and resilience to power disruptions in particular, but also in relation to areas as wide-ranging as community resilience from extremist or terrorist radicalization and organized crime; the resilience of IT networks and businesses from cyber attack; the resilience of the global economy and global financial system from economic and financial risks; climate change resilience; and resilience in developing countries. In early 2020, the UK government announced the start of an 'Integrated Review' of its foreign policy, defence, security and international development, to update the NSS/SDSR as well as bringing in foreign policy and development dimensions, with a view to adopting a government-wide approach to its strategy in line with the Fusion Doctrine.

Resilience in US national security

America's internal response to 9/11, in common with the UK, included the immediate passing of new anti-terrorism legislation: the United and Strengthening America by Providing Appropriate Tools Required to Intercept and Obstruct Terrorism (USA PATRIOT) Act 2001 provided the government and its security agencies with a variety of new powers. The concept of resilience did not initially gain the same prominence in post-9/11 government discourse in the US as was the case in the UK, but the underlying principles are very evident in US policy. President George W. Bush also established by Executive Order an Office for Homeland Security (OHS) with a mandate 'to coordinate the executive branch's efforts to detect, prepare for, prevent, protect against, respond to, and recover from terrorist attacks within the United States' (Bush, 2001), and a Homeland Security Council responsible for coordinating domestic security activities among executive departments and agencies.

In 2002, Bush appointed a National Commission on Terrorist Attacks upon the United States (also known as the 9-11 Commission) to provide an independent report into the circumstances surrounding the attacks, the immediate response, and the national preparedness for such an attack. In the Commission's 2004 report, among the noted limitations in capability were a lack of understanding of the gravity of the terrorist threat, insufficient reform of the US security architecture since the end of the Cold War in accordance with the changing nature of the threats to national security, inadequacies in the management and exchange of information within and between key agencies, and permeable borders and aviation security. The US government began to act on these limitations well before the Commission reported, with the majority of initiatives having a domestic focus. It implemented a recommendation by the Commission to appoint a Director of National Intelligence with oversight of the whole of the US intelligence community, having concluded that the failure to share intelligence across agencies was a contributing factor to the failure to protect the country from the attacks. However, the most significant change to America's security architecture to address national protection and preparedness was the establishment in 2002 of a Department of Homeland Security (DHS), through the integration of 22 different federal departments and agencies. Its mission, set out in the Homeland Security Act 2002, was to,

> (a) prevent terrorist attacks within the United States; (b) reduce the vulnerability of the United States to terrorism; (c) minimize the damage, and assist in the recovery, from terrorist attacks that do occur within the United States; (d) carry out all functions of entities transferred to the Department, including by acting as a focal point regarding natural and manmade crises and emergency planning ...

The DHS is now the primary US agency responsible for border protection, securing of transportation and other parts of America's CNI, oversight of emergency services, and working with the private sector to improve preparedness (Department of Homeland Security, 2020). The significance of the latter point is emphasized in the report, with the private sector controlling 85% of the national critical infrastructure, meaning that first responders to an attack on any but a military target will be civilians (National Commission on Terrorist Attacks upon the United States, 2004). The DHS model contrasts markedly with the UK's decentralized approach, overseeing and coordinating national protection and preparedness across America's vast geography, multiple levels of government, numerous agencies and other stakeholders.

Resilience started to become a recurring term in US **homeland security** policy after the devastation of Hurricane Katrina in 2005, as noted by Kahan, Allen and George (2009) and Kahan (2015), who trace its emergence in the official lexicon. It was initially employed in the context of critical infrastructure resilience, most notably in the second edition of the *National Strategy for Homeland Security* (Homeland Security Council, 2007), and then referred to extensively in the 2008 US Presidential campaign by Obama, under whose presidency a Directorate of Resilience was established within the National Security Council (Kahan, 2015). It subsequently appeared in all subsequent editions of the US national security strategy (White House, 2010, 2015, 2017), with the words 'resilience' and 'resilient' being mentioned 23 times in the 2017 document. Although featuring particularly in the first of four pillars, to 'Protect the American People, the Homeland, and the American Way of Life', which focuses on securing US borders and territory, pursuing threats to their source, securing the nation against cyber attack and promoting 'American resilience' to catastrophic events, it is also extended to a wider range of contexts including the resilience of the US economy and energy market, military capability, supply chains, space architecture, and foreign states from domination by rival powers.

Summary

This chapter has examined the national security cultures, threats and architectures of the UK and the US, showing the commonalities of outlook and approach of these two English-speaking nations, and detailing the development of their national security capabilities since the early 20th century. It discussed the ways in which globalization has led to states' internal political issues, traditionally matters of 'low politics', becoming increasingly externalized, as in the case of matters of health and rights; and external political issues becoming increasingly internalized, as events in other states like disasters or massacres have become increasingly politically significant at home (Hough, 2018). As a result, boundaries have been blurred between threats, in terms of what constitute foreign and domestic matters, and the responsibilities of different government security agencies as well as the public and private sectors. The chapter also noted how the accountability of such agencies has become an increasingly prominent issue in today's more open and transparent world. It is argued that among the most significant changes to UK and US national security arrangements in the new millennium has been the much greater emphasis on national resilience, centred around the establishment of the UK civil contingencies system and the DHS in the US and, most recently in the UK, talk of 'whole-of-government' strategies. Such approaches place a significant emphasis on delivery through networks and partnerships, demonstrating that **security governance** is as significant a theme at the national level as it is on the global stage. As observed in the first chapter, the major challenge for governments in the decades ahead will be in the extent they can adapt sufficiently to the continued widening and increasing complexity of the threat landscape.

Study questions

- Identify the distinctive features of your country's 'national security culture', and provide examples of the ways in which these have influenced its domestic and foreign security policies.
- In what ways has the acceleration of globalization influenced governments' national security priorities?
- How well equipped is the defence and security architecture of your country for the effective mitigation of contemporary and future national security challenges?
- What does 'resilience' mean in a national security context?

Further reading

National Security Cultures (Kirchner and Sperling, 2010) provides a useful starting point for the study of national security policy, and the interpretation of different nations' priorities and behaviours on the international stage. An illuminating account of the changing nature of national security and the role of secret intelligence in supporting it, drawing on the author's personal experience in government, is offered by *Securing the State* (Omand, 2010). Further useful texts on the wider landscape of intelligence work are *The Oxford Handbook of National Security Intelligence* (Johnson, 2010), *The Routledge Companion to Intelligence Studies* (Dover, Goodman and Hillebrand, 2015) and *Intelligence in an Insecure World* (Gill and Phythian, 2018). *Everyday Security Threats:*

Perceptions, Experiences, and Consequences (Stevens and Vaughan-Williams, 2017) draws on empirical research on UK public perceptions and experiences of security threats in a rich analysis of 'security threat politics'. On the rise of resilience thinking in domestic and international policy and its practical application, *Resilience: The Governance of Complexity* (Chandler, 2014) offers a comprehensive analysis. For overviews of a selection of topical national security issues, informative chapters can be found in the *Palgrave Handbook of Security, Risk and Intelligence* (2017) by Dolata on energy security and by McLeish on emerging biosecurity frameworks, and in *International Security Studies: Theory and Practice* (2020) by Shields on space security.

5

Securing communities

CHAPTER OUTLINE

Chapter overview

This chapter provides:

- An overview of the concept of the police and the origins of formal policing in the UK.
- An exploration of the ways in which UK police services have developed since the middle of the last century in response to a changing world.
- A discussion of the broadening range of actors engaged in security governance at the local level, and particularly the significant role played by the private security sector.
- A review of wider trends in the way in which security is managed within urban spaces and how this is likely to develop in the future, with resilience principles informing a more holistic approach to the ordering of cities.

Key terms

- Community policing
- Intelligence-led policing
- Neighbourhood policing
- New public management
- Police
- Private security
- Resilience
- Safeguarding
- Smart city
- Surveillance

Introduction

The focus of this chapter is the delivery of security at the local level, with a primary focus on the UK and the evolving role of the **police** in a fast-changing society. In Western democratic countries, the police are the primary coordinators of local security provision, and the chapter's predominant concern is the development and delivery of state policing in the UK, from its 19th-century origins and through the latter half of the 20th century and into the 21st. Over a much longer period, local security has been a matter of individual responsibility, communal self-help and private provision, however, and it is only in a comparatively short phase of history that police forces have come to prominence, while recent decades have seen a resurgence of other actors and especially **private security** (Zedner, 2006).

The chapter begins with a discussion of the development of the police globally and in the UK, before examining the adaptations by the British police over recent decades to a changing nation and a changing world. It is shown how, as police forces have confronted rising crime rates and increasing budgetary pressures, they have had to establish more efficient ways of working and collaborate more closely with other security agencies and public services. The last section of the chapter explores the expanding role of the private sector and other actors in **security governance** at the local level since the end of the last century, and discusses the application and future development of **resilience** thinking to urban development.

The development of the police

One of the most universally applicable explanations of the term 'police' is that of eminent policing scholars Brodeur, Walsh, Kelling, Banton and Whetstone (2020) in the *Encyclopædia Britannica*. Using the simple definition of a 'body of officers representing the civil authority of government', the authors emphasize how, internationally, no uniform, universal system of policing has ever emerged, noting several factors that help to explain the diversity of policing systems, agencies and activities worldwide. History, particularly **colonization**, has shaped the international development of policing systems, early French and British policing models having had great influence in the world. Demographic trends have influenced the nature of provision, since police forces initially emerged in urban areas, with rural areas in continental Europe having been policed according to separate centralized and often military systems as a means of protecting national borders. Political cultures, characterized for example by the degree of a society's democratic advancement, present differing conceptions and systems of police accountability. The types of crime – and methods of committing them – that are most commonly experienced or recognized in a society will determine the way in which policing resources are directed, and the nature of the policing activities carried out. Markedly different qualities and standards of policing therefore apply in different areas of the world. In countries where there are high levels of crime and where corruption and even state-sponsored violence may be common, state security forces may be ineffective at best and, at worst, a threat to the human rights of citizens so that communities are better served by establishing their own security arrangements.

Formal police forces were first established in Europe in the early days of state formation, when monarchs' security concerns were mainly about maintaining their own sovereignty, municipalities were usually left to govern themselves, and military power was exerted over areas recently claimed, or far from the centre of power (e.g. Spain, France). The first formal police arrangements in France took the form of a state military police force, initially called the *Marechaussée* and then re-established after the French Revolution as the *Gendarmerie Nationale*.

This model was transported to other continental European countries as well as its imperial outposts in the Napoleonic conquests, and another such example still in existence today is the Italian *Carabinieri*. In France, the state military model operated mainly in rural areas, with a civilian model employed in the cities.

As capital cities developed, control over them advanced accordingly, in the vein of the municipal police force launched in Paris in 1667 during the reign of King Louis XIV, when Jean-Baptiste Colbert, Minister of Finances, established the office of Lieutenant General of Police of Paris. The main model associated with the UK, Sir Robert Peel's 'New Police', which was established in London in 1829, was a variant of France's urban, civilian model according to Emsley (1999). He observes that, reciprocally, elements of the New Police were incorporated by Napoleon III in the 1850s when he reorganized the police of Paris. This model was also transferred to American cities.

Mawby (1999) suggests that the British may have deliberately created a distinctive, militaristic type of policing for its empire, with more in common with the French *Gendarmerie*. Such a model was considered better suited to controlling colonial populations and was first employed in Ireland, where the police could not rely on public consent, in the form of the Royal Irish Constabulary. The fact that the British government experienced similar problems with maintaining order and eliminating dissent throughout its empire contributed to a uniformity of colonial police systems. This was strengthened through centralized administration and control through the Colonial Police Service based in London, central training for officers, the appointment of an Inspector General of Colonial Police in 1948 and the practice of transferring officers between different countries. Asian states that escaped European colonization were, nonetheless, later influenced by European ideas of policing (Emsley, 2009).

The evolution of urban policing was naturally linked to the development of cities (see Emsley, 2009; Bowling, Reiner and Sheptycki, 2019). Sir Robert Peel introduced the Metropolitan Police in London to address the crime and disorder problems associated with industrialization, particularly the rapid expansion of urban populations as people left their extended families and close communities behind and migrated to the city. Prior to the establishment of police forces, informal social controls were supplemented by disparate localized policing systems, but urban crime soon proved to be beyond their capacity. Peel's 'New Police' model took account of the massive public opposition that he faced in bringing in such a radical new approach to London's security. Londoners were deeply concerned at the prospect of what they saw as a gross threat to their civil liberties and the control of their leisure, based on what they had heard about the French policing model, which was already well established. There was also popular concern about what policing was going to cost citizens through taxation.

The unique character and image of contemporary British policing with the distinctive 'custodian' helmets, and as one of a very small number of national policing models in which officers are not routinely armed, owes much to its historic roots. It revolves around nine principles attributed to Peel and formalized in the Metropolitan Police Act 1829, which provided a philosophy for consensual policing, and which are still published on the Home Office website today. These included the principle: 'To maintain at all times a relationship with the public that gives reality to the historic tradition that the police are the public and that the public are the police' (Home Office, 2012a), in order to promote trust between police officers and the communities they served. To avoid any kind of association with military-style policing, Peel initially attired his officers in distinctive blue long-tailed coats and top hats and armed them only with wooden batons. They adopted an approach that was low profile, highly disciplined, legalistic and preventative in nature, delivered by means of foot patrol and a constant and 'unremitting watch' (Radzinowicz, 1968: 164). Their approach also included wider 'service' functions such as inspecting weights and measures and knocking people up early in the morning for work, which contributed to the securing of legitimacy with the public (Bowling et al., 2019). The 'Instructions to the New Police', published in *The Times* newspaper on 25 September 1829, five days before the new officers hit the streets, set out the functions of a constable:

> The primary object of an efficient police is the prevention of crime: the next that of detection and punishment of offenders if crime is committed. To these ends all the efforts of police must be directed. The protection of life and property, the preservation of public tranquility, and the absence of crime, will alone prove whether those efforts have been successful and whether the objects for which the police were appointed have been attained. (Sir Richard Mayne, Commissioner of the Metropolitan Police)

The intended system of pervasive, pre-emptive **surveillance** proved difficult to realize because of the legal barriers that limited the watch of the New Police to public places, ensuring that their role evolved very quickly into one of 'post-crime responders' coming to the aid of victims of crime, and 'the "front end" of an emerging criminal justice system' (Froestad et al., 2015: 180–181). As Emsley (2014: 3) details, they also absorbed an increasing variety of duties as the 19th century progressed, becoming increasingly responsible for 'the smooth running of a variety of different aspects of society':

> … they regulated traffic, ensured that pavements were unimpeded, kept a watchful eye for unsafe buildings and burning chimneys, administered first aid at accidents and drove ambulances, administered aspects of the Poor Law, looked for missing persons, licensed street sellers and cabs, and supervised the prevention of disease among farm animals.

Today, police activities can include 'everything from unexpected childbirths, drunks, emergency psychiatric cases, family disputes, missing persons and traffic violations to occasional incidents of crime' (Newburn, 2017: 641). Nearly two centuries on from their creation in Britain, the breadth of demands on the police is an aspect of the role that has not altered.

Police adaptations to a changing world

The nature of policing has inevitably had to evolve in accordance with transformations in the wider world, and social, economic and political drivers of reform. This section discusses key aspects of those adaptations from the latter half of the 20th century onwards.

Social adaptations

The post-Second World War period was another important phase in the development of the UK's police, which needed to adapt to the changing composition of society. As the national economy began to recover after the war, citizens of the Commonwealth were encouraged to migrate to the UK to fill jobs, and the ethnic composition of the country began to become more diverse. British social attitudes were slow to adjust to the country's new social diversity, however. New migrants faced widespread hostility and racism, and the overwhelmingly white police shared the attitudes and prejudices of the society from which they were drawn (Whitfield, 2004). The profound lack of police legitimacy among the urban, black community eventually came to a head and to national attention in the Brixton riots in April 1981. Tensions in the community erupted over the aggressive and indiscriminate use by police of their stop and search powers under the Vagrancy Act 1824, known as the 'sus law' (from 'suspected person'), in a plain clothes operation to combat street crime called Operation Swamp 81.

Following an official inquiry led by Lord Scarman into the causes of the disorder, the Scarman Report (1981) concluded that the police had become too remote from the community they served, local citizens should be able to provide input into police planning, and police tactics should be more sensitive to the increasing diversity of major UK cities. Scarman advocated the implementation of '**community policing**', a model originally advanced by John Alderson, Chief Constable of Devon and Cornwall Constabulary, based on establishing collaborative partnerships with the community to develop solutions to crime and disorder problems, as well as measures to increase police accountability. Community policing gained currency through the early 1980s in the UK, US and elsewhere as police chiefs sought to regain public trust, with an underpinning philosophy 'based on the importance of winning and sustaining public confidence in the police as a condition for effective policing' (Weatheritt, 1983: 129) and employing tactics such as foot patrol, community crime prevention and community consultation. The Scarman Report also informed the development of the Police and Criminal Evidence Act 1984, which codified the powers of police officers to search, arrest and detain suspects, including a requirement that a decision to stop and search should be based on 'reasonable suspicion' of an offence.

Lord Scarman considered in the course of his inquiry whether the police were 'institutionally racist', and concluded that they were not, but alluded to practices by 'public bodies' that were 'unwittingly discriminatory against black people' (para 2.22, p. 28). This wider interpretation of institutional racism was adopted nearly two decades later in the Macpherson Report (Home Office, 1999), following an inquiry into the racially motivated murder of young, black Londoner Stephen Lawrence, and the shambolic investigation into his death. The Report concluded that the investigation had been 'marred by a combination of professional incompetence, institutional racism and a failure of leadership' (para 46.1), criticizing the Metropolitan Police as a whole as well as naming specific officers.

The police will always be a reflection of the society they serve and hence, as Bowling et al. (2019) point out, there are plenty of international and historic examples of police forces being employed to maintain systems of exclusion and oppression, such as South Africa under apartheid, the US prior to the civil rights era, and many authoritarian regimes that still exist today, as discussed in the next chapter. Equally, in societies that condone violence against women, police protection and justice for victims of domestic or sexual violence are frequently absent (see UN Office on Drugs and Crime, 2010). Disadvantage and discrimination by age, gender, social class, disability, sexual orientation and gender identity remain widespread in societal structures throughout the world, and prevailing social attitudes in a given society will inevitably be present in the culture of its police. In 2020, the death of George Floyd, a black man in the US, at the hands of police sparked global protests against racism in policing, including 260 UK towns and cities (Mohdin and Swann, 2020). The most recent evidence of ethnic disproportionality in UK policing at the time of writing suggested that people from ethnic minorities were 54% more likely to be fined than white people for violations of COVID-19 lockdown rules (Gidda, 2020). Bowling et al. (2019) pose the question as to whether equal employment would create more equal justice, highlighting historical barriers to police employment of women, ethnic minorities and lesbian, gay, bisexual and transgender (LGBT) people, noting that police staffing that is representative of the local community may be better placed to enhance police legitimacy in a diverse society. Much greater recruitment efforts to establish a genuinely diverse police force are surely essential for Peel's principle 'that the police are the public and that the public are the police' (Home Office, 2012a) to be realized.

Economic adaptations

From the 1970s, escalating crime rates and the politicization of law and order in most of the Western world meant that governments needed to appear to be effective providers of security, while the spiralling costs of criminal justice also required them to constrain both public spending and public expectations (Garland, 1996, 2001). In the public sectors of the major industrialized countries, a 'neoliberal' revival of 19th-century ideas about free market economics, commonly associated with the governments of Margaret Thatcher in the UK and Ronald Reagan in the US, translated into the pursuit from the 1980s of **new public management** (NPM) strategies for greater efficiencies in public sector expenditure. NPM refers to the introduction of private sector management methods and incentive structures such as internal markets into public service provision. In UK police forces, this involved promoting flatter organizational structures, strategic planning, performance management, performance-based contract employment, and decentralized budgeting with an emphasis on local accountability and customer satisfaction. Multi-agency or partnership policing and the outsourcing of non-essential policing tasks also became distinctive features of NPM in the drive for greater economy and efficiency (Fleming, 2009), and there was significant governmental investment in research to improve the organizational and operational effectiveness of the police, fostering the expansion of an evidence-based, policy research tradition.

The parallel challenge of managing public expectations led to the promotion by the UK government of measures to prevent crime, coupled with increasing proactive engagement of other agencies as well as citizens in this task, a process described by O'Malley (1992, 2009) and Garland (1996, 2001) as 'responsibilization'. The new initiatives and campaigns of the 1980s turned the focus towards vulnerable situations, the conduct of potential victims, and specifically 'those routines of everyday life which create criminal opportunities as an unintended byproduct' (Garland, 1996: 451), beginning with the development of crime prevention advice to citizens and the promotion of Neighbourhood Watch schemes. Following the establishment of a Home Office Crime Prevention Unit in 1983, they were informed by the theoretical frameworks of rational choice theory, routine activity theory, crime as opportunity and situational crime prevention theory (see Mayhew, Clarke, Sturman and Hough, 1976; Cornish and Clarke, 1986; Clarke and Felson, 1993; Clarke, 1997; Felson and Boba, 2010). These view crime as an outcome of everyday circumstances that can be controlled and managed through such measures as crime prevention through environmental design (CPTED) (Jeffery, 1971) (defined in Chapter 8), and other forms of situational crime prevention intended to minimize opportunities for crime in specific settings. Strategies to engage other bodies included the funding of local multi-agency crime prevention initiatives under a Safer Cities Programme and, following the election of a new Labour government in 1997, the creation of statutory crime and disorder reduction partnerships between police forces, local authorities and other bodies under the Crime and Disorder Act 1998.

In the new millennium, further legislation and initiatives promoted diversification and partnership working in frontline policing. Frontline private security personnel were given the enhanced legitimacy afforded by a statutory licensing regime, delivered by a new Security Industry Authority under the provisions of the Private Security Industry Act 2001. The Police Reform Act 2002 established arrangements for two-tier policing, allowing police forces to employ civilian staff with limited powers in certain policing roles, most visibly patrol duties through the introduction of police community support officers (PCSOs), and also giving them the authority to bestow powers on non-police patrol personnel employed by local authorities (e.g. neighbourhood wardens in town centres, housing estates and parks) or private employers (e.g. private security personnel in shopping complexes) through community safety accreditation schemes. In 2005, the government launched a five-year Neighbourhood Policing Programme to give renewed priority to community policing. **Neighbourhood policing** teams, known as 'safer neighbourhood teams' in the Metropolitan Police, were intended to make the police more visible and accessible to the community, comprising teams of police officers and PCSOs dedicated to the policing of specific geographic areas 'of a size and character that best serves the needs of local communities' (Centrex, 2006: 18).

The election of a Conservative–Liberal Democrat coalition government in 2010 led to a change of priorities, including the implementation of severe budgetary reductions as discussed further below. One of its first police policy reforms was the introduction of a radically different governance model under the Police Reform and Social Responsibility Act (PRSRA) 2011, putting elected police and crime commissioners (PCCs) in charge of local policing on the basis that they would make forces more accountable to communities. The Home Secretary and chief constables remained part of the governance structure but, from 2012, PCCs replaced the police authorities that had previously overseen the operations of police forces, supported by police and crime panels whose role was limited to an advisory one. At the same time, in recognition of the fact that, in a system of elected representation, national priorities could otherwise be sidelined in favour of the issues that matter most to the local electorate, *The Strategic Policing Requirement* (Home Office, 2012b) provided a guiding framework for PCCs and chief constables on the policing of threats deemed to be of national importance, which included obligations for national and regional cooperation. A further dimension of the reforms under the new government was the establishment in 2012 of a professional body for policing in England and Wales, the College of Policing, responsible for undertaking research, evidence-based standards development and the professional development of police officers.

Strategic adaptations

The challenges of serious crime that transcended force and regional boundaries, much of it transnational in nature, and the availability of increasingly sophisticated technologies for surveillance and information exchange, were among the drivers of further reforms and innovations in strategic UK policing: the centralization of part of the response to serious crime, and the development of **intelligence-led policing** (ILP). A National Criminal Intelligence Service (NCIS) was established in 1992, and six Regional Crime Squads were amalgamated in 1998 to form the National Crime Squad (NCS). A more substantial and powerful organization, the Serious Organized Crime Agency (SOCA), was formed in 2006 through the amalgamation of the NCIS and NCS, along with investigative and intelligence sections of HM Revenue and Customs and the Immigration Service. SOCA officers were authorized to use the legal powers of police, customs and immigration services, making the organization a powerful investigative, intelligence and enforcement agency with unprecedented powers. Its creation extended the scope and authority not only of UK policing, but also the international network of authorities coordinated through Interpol and Europol with a focus on transnational crime, harnessing such information and intelligence-sharing instruments as Europol's Schengen Information System, European Criminal Records Information System and Passenger Name Record data. In 2013, the National Crime Agency absorbed SOCA as well as specialist body the Child Exploitation and Online Protection Centre.

ILP is an approach that favours information gathering and sharing, and collaborative strategic solutions, and forms a central dimension of the national response to serious crime. James (2011) traces its beginnings back to unit beat policing and the introduction of the role of the collator, who maintained and analysed information collected by patrol officers. It differs from community policing, which places street-level officers at the forefront of problem identification and resolution, as a more top-down approach. As Ratcliffe (2009: 177) outlines, 'criminal intelligence flows up to decision makers at the executive level, who set priorities for enforcement and prevention and pass these down to lower levels of the organization as operational taskings'. Intelligence is gained not only from community sources, but the use of informants, surveillance of suspects, offender interviews, and analysis of crime information and calls for service data. ILP thus involves the police acting more like intelligence agencies, and relying on the covert methods more closely associated with such bodies. James (2011) identifies Sir David Phillips, who was Chief Constable of Kent Police, as one of the pioneers in the development of proactive policing strategies in the UK, having introduced the Kent Policing Model, a 'holistic system of intelligence led policing' (Maguire, 2008: 455), in the 1990s as a new way of addressing local crime problems. The success of the model led to its implementation nationally as the National Intelligence Model (NIM). The NIM was developed within the National Criminal Intelligence Service (NCIS) in 1999 and adopted by the Association of Chief Police Officers (predecessors of the National Police Chiefs' Council) in 2000, and is today fully embedded in policing throughout the UK from the local level through to the transnational.

Adapting to changing demands

In 2010, following the 2007/8 global financial crisis and in a drive to reduce the national budget deficit, the Coalition government undertook a spending review and embarked on an austerity programme. The cuts to police funding in England and Wales were unprecedented and amounted to 20% through to 2015. Most forces responded by reducing their spending, usually through cuts to staffing, rather than seeking efficiency savings (Her Majesty's Inspectorate of Constabulary, 2015). An inquiry by the House of Commons Home Affairs Committee on *Policing for the Future* examined changing demands on policing and police capability to meet those demands, concluding that forces are 'badly overstretched' and 'struggling to cope' due to 'changing and rising crimes ... falling staff numbers, outdated technology, capabilities and structures, and fragmented leadership and direction', highlighting online fraud, child sexual abuse and the **safeguarding** of vulnerable people as areas of particular and growing demand (2018b: 6).

Data from the Office for National Statistics (ONS) (2020) show that 'traditional' or 'volume' crime (the most frequent types of crime, such as burglary, shoplifting, vehicle crime, robbery, criminal damage, drug offences and assaults), has generally fallen since the mid-1990s, as shown in Figure 5.1. In the year ending March 2020, approximately 5.7 million crimes were recorded, excluding fraud and computer misuse. There have, however, been increases in some less frequent but higher-harm types of violence, including those involving knives. In 2016, the ONS began measuring crimes of fraud and 'computer misuse', which refers to offences under the Computer Misuse Act 1990, including hacking, unauthorized access to computer systems and purposefully spreading malicious and damaging software (malware), such as viruses. Such **cybercrime**s are widely understood to be significantly under-reported so, given the challenges of measuring actual instances of fraud and computer misuse, ONS data on these offences are based on estimates from the *Crime Survey for England and Wales*, a large-scale victimization survey, rather than crimes recorded by authorities. They are depicted by the second, short line on the right hand side of Figure 5.1, and presented separately so as to maintain the comparability of the crime figures from year to year. The inclusion of such offences in the national crime figures has caused a massive increase, bringing the total up to March 2020 to 10.2 million (ONS, 2020).

The trends illustrated in Figure 5.1 give a clear demonstration of the fact that much contemporary victimization takes place not on the streets but online. As Loveday (2017) observes, they suggest that the average resident in England and Wales is 20 times more likely to experience fraud than robbery, and 10 times more likely to be a victim of fraud than theft from the person. They also represent a significant change in patterns of victimization, since those most likely to be victims of fraud and cybercrime are rural residents, the middle-aged and individuals in managerial and professional positions, as opposed to the young

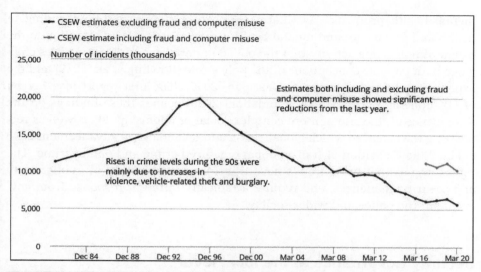

Figure 5.1 Crime in England and Wales from the year ending December 1981 to the year ending March 2020.

Source: Office for National Statistics (2020) Crime in England and Wales: Year Ending March 2020. London: ONS.

people, city-dwellers and manual workers or unemployed who experience 'traditional' crimes most heavily. The growing incidence of fraud and cybercrime led to the creation in 2008 of a national fraud reporting service, Action Fraud, which is now located within the City of London Police. This ended the ability of victims to report the most common types of frauds directly to the police, requiring them instead to record details online or contact a call centre. Very few cases meet the criteria (such as extent of losses) to be judged appropriate for investigation, and most victims are unlikely to hear anything further about their case. Given the considerable gap in service for such victims, Loveday argues that, 'The fast-changing nature of criminal activity suggests that significant re-engineering of the police service may be needed if it is to respond effectively to the growth in online crime' (p. 104).

A College of Policing (2015) analysis on existing demands on the police service addresses further increased pressures in the areas of sexual offences and the safeguarding of vulnerable people, associated with increasing calls for service, more proactive work in the safeguarding of the public, and the decline in police staffing since 2010. The report identifies that non-crime incidents, mostly relating to vulnerability, public protection and safeguarding, account for an increasing proportion of police work, amounting to 84% of all calls for service. Both crime and non-crime incidents of this nature are identified as being particularly resource-intensive as they can be complex and require multi-agency responses, such as in the case of incidents involving people with mental health problems. As Charman observes, cuts to public spending in health and social care and mental health services have drawn attention to the extent of non-crime activity that the police undertake, and these realities challenge both popular conceptions of the police role (Bowling et al., 2019) and the expectations of police recruits (Charman, 2017). The first report of a review of UK policing by the Police Foundation (2020) echoes these findings on the significance of 'the rise of more complex social problems' (p. 3), as well as recognizing the extent to which globalization and technological advancement have enabled the escalation of transnational organized crime and online crime. The report argues that these trends have transformed the nature of public safety and security challenges, and require a radically different response from government, the police and wider society.

Security governance at the local level

While the police play a distinct social role in that they represent the civil authority of government, numerous other bodies and interest groups are involved in policing at the local level. Asserting that a 'restructuring' of policing was taking place in Western societies in the late 20th century, associated with a growing private security sector and an increasing variety of other actors, Bayley and Shearing (1996: 585) went so far as to argue that a turning point had been reached, declaring, 'Modern democratic countries ... have reached a watershed in the evolution of their systems of crime control and law enforcement. Future generations will look upon this era as a time when one system of policing ended and another took its place'. Two decades into the new millennium, the Police Foundation identifies the challenges now facing the police as being so profound that there is a need to manage public expectations and 'think afresh' about 'the role of the police as part of a wider system', with the need for a number of major dilemmas to be resolved, including the appropriate division of roles between the police and other agencies (2020: 6).

The expanding role of non-police service providers in policing, and the variety of different public, private and voluntary bodies now engaged in the activity, has been captured by criminologists in a host of terms. In addition to 'security governance' (Johnston and Shearing, 2003), scholars have referred to the 'security quilt' (Ericson, 1994), 'pluralized policing' (Bayley and Shearing, 1996), 'networked, nodal governance' (Kempa, Carrier, Wood and Shearing, 1999), 'plural policing' (Loader, 2000; Crawford, Lister, Blackburn and Burnett, 2004; Jones and Newburn, 2006), the 'extended police family' (Home Office, 2001), the 'police assemblage' (Brodeur, 2010), and the 'policing web' (Brodeur, 2010). While some have challenged the 'watershed' thesis of Bayley and Shearing (see Jones and Newburn, 2002; Zedner, 2006; White and Gill, 2013), recent decades have seen

Table 5.1 Actors involved in local policing and security in the UK

Public sector	Private sector	Charitable and voluntary sectors

• Home Office police forces (police officers and PCSOs)
• British Transport Police
• Civil Nuclear Constabulary
• Ministry of Defence Police
• Royal Military Police
• Royal Navy Police
• Royal Air Force Police
• Local authority neighbourhood wardens
	• Frontline private security personnel (employed by commercial security companies or in-house by organizations), including:
	  ○ Security officers
	  ○ Door supervisors
	  ○ Close protection officers
		• Street Watch neighbourhood patrols
		• Street Pastors, School Pastors and Rail Pastors from local churches
		• Community Safety Trust volunteers protecting Jewish venues

a growing body of scholars give due weight to the roles played by actors other than the police (see also Wakefield, 2009; Wakefield and Button, 2014; Rogers, 2017; Button, 2019). To take just one dimension of policing, the guarding and patrol functions that are the most visible, the variety of actors in the UK spans the public, private and third sectors, and examples are listed in Table 5.1.

By far the largest of these groups, in terms of the number of personnel employed, is not the police but private security. According to research undertaken by the *Guardian* newspaper, 232,000 private security officers were employed in the UK in 2015, compared with 151,000 civilian police officers (Provost, 2017). This study compiled estimates of the number of private security personnel operating in 82 countries, over 40 of which, including the US, China, Canada, Australia and the UK, were reported to employ more private security personnel than police officers, at an estimated total of 18,744,031 personnel globally. The security officer numbers are limited to 'private guards', and it is assumed that the *Guardian*'s focus is those who are employed by commercial manned guarding companies, since it is more difficult to account for officers employed by organizations in-house. Jones and Newburn (1998) observe that the services undertaken by the private security industry cover much of what the police do, plus further functions that they do not, and the next chapter outlines the other major service areas of the commercial security industry.

The substantial growth of private security in the post-Second World War period, detailed by Johnston (1992) in a UK context, has been underpinned by a variety of social, political and economic factors. Increased prosperity, with more private property and consumer goods to protect, coincided with the rise in crime in many countries, especially from the 1970s to the 1990s. Improvements in security technology (especially alarm, access control and CCTV systems) have led to better, and cheaper, security products with rising appeal to corporate and individual consumers in an increasingly security-conscious world. The proliferation of large, privately controlled, publicly accessible spaces such as shopping centres, leisure parks, business parks and private residential complexes, described by Shearing and Stenning (1981, 1983) as forms of 'mass private property', has driven requirements for dedicated private security teams that can be employed cost-effectively to provide tailored services for such sites. Public spending restrictions led governments to extend their outsourcing of non-core tasks to the private sector, and indeed there has been a general growth in the sub-contracting of security functions within both the public and private sectors. The expansion of private security and other non-police actors in scope and profile within Western democratic countries has also occurred in tandem with the decline of 'secondary social control', attributed by Jones and Newburn (1998) to roles in which social control is not the main purpose, but may be undertaken in the course of wider duties, as in the case of teachers, park-keepers, caretakers, train guards and bus conductors.

A number of studies detail how the owners of mass private property complexes employ security personnel, in conjunction with architectural features and security technologies such as CCTV, to create carefully managed, appealing settings to maximize custom and profit-making (Shearing and Stenning, 1985; Wakefield, 2003; Button, 2006). Local authorities and business communities in retail and business districts of towns and cities have often followed suit, working together to implement local improvements such as additional street cleaning, landscaping, and safety and security measures as a means of competing for custom with mass private property retail developments and rival urban centres. One model is the business improvement district (BID), which first emerged in Canadian and US towns and cities in the 1970s, and spread to New Zealand, South Africa and parts of Europe including the UK (Cook, 2009; Cook and Ward, 2012). Another is town centre management (TCM), which developed in England in the late 1980s, and is mirrored by TCM-like schemes in Australia and several European countries, including France, Italy, Sweden and Spain (Cook, 2009).

The negative side of such developments in locations of public life, irrespective of ownership, is that they can enable the exclusion of individuals from important communal spaces (Wakefield, 2003). Davis (1990) presents a dystopian account of 'Fortress LA' that depicts the division of the city of Los Angeles into fortified enclaves and residual '"places of terror" where the police battle the criminalized poor' (p. 224), while accounts from São Paulo (Caldeira, 1996) and Johannesberg (Bremner, 2004) provide further illustrations of urban spatial segregation. In the UK, the introduction of public spaces protection orders (PSPOs) in 2014 gave local authorities controversial new powers to criminalize specified behaviours in defined areas, building on provisions for dealing with undefined 'anti-social behaviour' that were first introduced in the Crime and Disorder Act 1998. Despite Home Office guidance that PSPOs should not be used to target homeless people, Greenfield and Marsh (2019) found that they were being used by at least 60 councils to prevent rough sleeping and begging.

Such examples show how the market for secure spaces has intensified inequalities between rich and poor, with differential access to such services being especially noticeable in higher crime cities. The security challenges for communities in countries like South Africa, Shearing's home nation, informed his ideas and led him and his colleagues to emphasize the benefits that diversified models of policing can bring (Johnston and Shearing, 2003; Wood and Shearing, 2007). They argue that the 'networking' of non-state nodes with each other as well as those of the state should allow for new forms of accountability that help maximize the strengths and minimize the limitations of private nodes. The authors advocate the empowerment of poor communities in South Africa through capacity-building interventions, including the provision of 'block grants' from public funds to meet their security needs. In later work, Shearing promotes a more active role for the police as part of a 'resilience policing' approach, which would mobilize officers as facilitators in the capacity-building of communities to deal with everyday stresses or survive and manage material shocks should they occur, operating in conjunction with networks of other actors as part of a collaborative approach (Mutongwizo et al., 2019).

Rogers (2016) examines the development of new security and disaster strategies and measures in the new millennium that build further on the disciplinary controls of the urban environment enabled through measures like CPTED, community safety strategies, mass private property, BIDs and PSPOs. Closely related to the heightened terrorism threat, examples include the 'ring of steel' surveillance and security cordon implemented around the City of London to prevent terrorism; automated number plate recognition systems employed in the ring of steel and more widely to monitor and manage traffic; and protective barriers around prestigious buildings and major public venues, often woven into the architectural fabric in the attempt to render them 'invisible'. An independent review into London's preparedness to respond to a major terrorism incident provides numerous further examples of such measures (Harris, 2016). All represent the further application of resilience thinking, a theme of the previous two chapters, to inform a holistic and systematic approach to the ordering of cities, and enhance visitors', workers' and residents' objective and subjective security. So-called '**smart cities**' are the next step in urban evolution, based on intelligent networks of physical devices connected through 'internet of things' technologies (explained in Chapter 7) that are used to improve government services, enhance communication with citizens, and increase operational efficiency and sustainability, including through the automation of security processes (see Willis and Aurigi, 2020).

While offering the potential for enormous quality-of-life enhancements for city users, such measures will substantially deepen mass surveillance, with the potential to significantly erode personal privacy if sufficient commitments to privacy protection and limits to data-sharing are not in-built. China is demonstrating grand ambitions for smart cities and, although Chinese citizens are more accepting of state monitoring (Kostka, 2019), experiments like its social credit schemes have been described as 'Orwellian'. Employed by local governments in a number of Chinese towns and cities, they score citizens for their 'trustworthiness' through points added for good deeds such as voluntary work, and deducted for bad behaviour like late payment of bills, and reward or penalize them based on their scores, for example in the form of travel discounts or restrictions on travel (*Economist*, 2019; Wakefield, 2019). Such schemes present considerable potential for abuse of power, errors associated with incorrect data, or data loss. Smart city technologies also carry the risk that they will worsen inequality and the marginalization of low income and vulnerable groups, exemplified in research showing how facial recognition technologies can build in racial biases (Grother, Ngan and Hanaoka, 2019), again emphasizing the importance of placing the needs of stakeholder groups at the centre of systems design and planning.

Summary

With a primary focus on the evolution of the police and policing more generally in security at the local level, this chapter illustrated how the capacities of UK police forces are now being stretched to an unsustainable degree. This was attributed to high crime rates, the competing challenges of local and global crime, budgetary cuts, and increasing calls on their time associated with non-crime safeguarding incidents that can be linked to cuts to other public services. The chapter detailed how social, economic and strategic challenges over recent decades have stimulated a number of reforms and innovations, including intelligence-led policing, community policing and neighbourhood policing, as well as the centralization of provision to deal with the most serious crime. However, the growing limitations on the police to fulfil all of the security demands of citizens, communities and organizations, and the increased cost-effectiveness of private measures to those who can afford them, were also shown to have ensured a place for other actors, including private sector and community-driven solutions. In the new millennium, the scale of the service gap is such that the Police Foundation (2020) is calling for a radical rethink about the police's future role and relationships with other agencies. A further shift towards a more pluralized framework would not be as radical as it may seem, however, if compared with historical arrangements in the UK prior to the establishment of the New Police in 1829, the experiences of those in less developed societies around the world where the limitations of state policing are much greater and self-help is more commonplace, and the similar diversification of provision across other dimensions of security governance. The growing application of resilience thinking to urban design and management raises further debates and issues about the future of security at the local level, including new questions about the benefits and costs of living in increasingly 'smart' cities.

Study questions

- In what ways have the origins of organized policing in the UK shaped the nature of contemporary policing in the UK and around the world?
- Given the ways in which the profile of crime in the UK is evolving, to what extent are today's police forces fit for purpose?
- What is 'safeguarding', and why has it become such a significant dimension of the contemporary police role in the UK?
- What are the advantages and disadvantages for communities of the growing market for security?

Further reading

On the history of the police in the UK, *The English Police: A Political and Social History* (Emsley, 2014) is recommended, while Emsley's entry on 'History' in the *Sage Dictionary of Policing* (edited by Wakefield and Fleming, 2009) presents useful short, comparative histories of policing in Africa, Australia, China, France, Germany, Latin America, Russia, the UK and the US. *Police Socialisation, Identity and Culture: Becoming Blue* (Charman, 2017) provides an invaluable illustration of the realities of the contemporary police role for front-line officers in the UK compared with common perceptions, particularly the significance and extent of public protection and safeguarding functions. For a holistic analysis of UK policing, Reiner's *The Politics of Police* is a classic text and essential reading, now in its 5th edition with new co-authors (Bowling, Reiner and Sheptycki, 2019), and with a useful final chapter on the multilateral policing of the present age. For more detail on the politics and contemporary role of the private sector, *The Politics of Private Security* (White, 2010) and *Private Policing* (Button, 2019) are recommended. The article 'Resilience policing: an emerging response to shifting harm landscapes' (Mutongwizo et al., 2019) for fresh thinking on policing in a complex era, while *Resilience and the City: Change, (Dis)Order and Disaster* (Rogers, 2016) is essential reading on the way in which resilience principles are increasingly informing urban design and management. For a thorough discussion of the notion of smart cities, the principles and technologies that underpin them and the implications of a future world in which technology is embedded in the very fabric of society, *The Routledge Companion to Smart Cities* (Willis and Aurigi, 2020) is recommended.

6

Security and the individual

Chapter overview

This chapter provides:

- An application of the human security concept and its component dimensions to social problems internationally as well as in the UK.
- An examination of social deprivation and inequalities with respect to access to income (economic security), food (food security) and health care (health security).
- A review of the major global environmental security challenges and their projected impact.
- An appraisal of significant forms of deliberate threats to individuals, communities and societies (personal, community and political security) and those on whom they bear most heavily.

Key terms

- Community security
- Economic security
- Environmental security
- Food security
- Health security
- Human rights
- Human security
- Personal security
- Political security
- Sustainable development

Introduction

The concept of **human security** is distinctive in making people rather than states its reference point, and recognizing the broad range of causes of human insecurity and deprivation. Launched by the United Nations Development Programme (UNDP) (1994) early in the post-Cold War era as the basis of a framework giving more priority to development within the UN, it recognized that the most fundamental human insecurities extend well beyond those caused by war, conflict and violent crime, and can more often be attributed to other challenging social conditions such as poverty, disease and displacement of populations. It also acknowledged that states do not necessarily deliver protection to their citizens and can be the perpetrators of **human rights** abuses and even genocide. As noted in Chapter 3, the concept has been criticized for the fact that it has primarily been applied to poorer countries as a dimension of international aid programmes, and typically excluded from domestic policy agendas (Martin, 2014). However, many of its proponents argue that the concept is universally applicable and as relevant to the social problems affecting countries of the Global North as those in the most challenged regions of the Global South (see Tadjbakhsh, 2013). The UN's Sustainable Development Goals (SDGs), which are underpinned by a 'human security approach' (UN News, 2017), marked a departure from previous development doctrine in explicitly defining sustainable development as being universal in scope (UN General Assembly, 2015).

Social inequality is a challenge throughout the world, and causes all seven dimensions of the UNDP (1994) human security framework – economic, food, health, environmental, personal, community and political security – to bear most heavily on nations' poorer residents. The aim of this chapter is to examine each of the dimensions in turn, making reference to some of the challenges that apply to humans across the globe, as well as domestically within the UK. It seeks to convey that the universal relevance of the human security concept is indisputable, and well-evidenced within the sections of the chapter.

Economic security

The first of the seven dimensions of human security identified by the UNDP is **economic security**, based on individuals' access to an assured basic income. The UK Ministry of Defence (MoD) (2018) predicts that levels of human security will improve globally in the coming decades as more people escape absolute poverty, but that inequality will grow, with the rich getting considerably richer and, particularly in developed countries, the middle class and the poor experiencing slower economic growth. The US National Intelligence Council (NIC) (2017) similarly argues that slow growth, coupled with the automation of jobs and strained welfare budgets, will threaten poverty reduction in the West. The first of the SDGs, which are listed in Table 6.1, is to end poverty, with targets including the eradication by 2030 of 'extreme poverty', which is equated to living on less than $1.25 per day; supporting the implementation of 'nationally appropriate social protection mechanisms' where they are absent; and strengthening the resilience of the poor and those in vulnerable situations to economic, social and environmental shocks and disasters (UN General Assembly, 2015: 19). The last global report of Amnesty International at the time of writing, *The State of the World's Human Rights* (2018), discusses the global impact of governmental austerity measures that followed the global financial crisis of 2008, reported to have been applied in countries from every region and, invariably, hitting poorest people the hardest. It presents them as a human rights issue, as cuts to services across the public sector affect people's access to housing, social security, education, health services, and other economic and social rights.

In the UK, according to the Social Metrics Commission (2019: 5–6), there are 14.3 million people in poverty, including 8.3 million working-age adults, 4.6 million children and 1.3 million pension-age adults. Ethnic minority families experience the higher rates of poverty: 46% of people in families with a black head of household and 37% of people in families with an Asian head of household are in poverty, compared to 19% of people in families with a white head of household. There is also a strong link between poverty and disability: 48% of those in poverty live in a family that includes someone who is disabled. Organisation for Economic Co-operation and Development (OECD) data employed in analyses by the Equality Trust (2020) indicates that income inequality is especially high in the UK compared with other developed countries: in 2018, households in the poorest 20% of the population had an average disposable income of £12,798, whilst the average for the richest 20% was £69,126. The Joseph Rowntree Foundation (JRF) (2018) reports that 1,550,000

Table 6.1 The UN Sustainable Development Goals

1. End poverty in all its forms everywhere
2. End hunger, achieve food security and improved nutrition and promote sustainable agriculture
3. Ensure healthy lives and promote well-being for all at all ages
4. Ensure inclusive and equitable quality education and promote lifelong learning opportunities for all
5. Achieve gender equality and empower all women and girls
6. Ensure availability and sustainable management of water and sanitation for all
7. Ensure access to affordable, reliable, sustainable and modern energy for all
8. Promote sustained, inclusive and sustainable economic growth, full and productive employment and decent work for all
9. Build resilient infrastructure, promote inclusive and sustainable industrialization and foster innovation
10. Reduce inequality within and among countries
11. Make cities and human settlements inclusive, safe, resilient and sustainable
12. Ensure sustainable consumption and production patterns
13. Take urgent action to combat climate change and its impacts
14. Conserve and sustainably use the oceans, seas and marine resources for sustainable development
15. Protect, restore and promote sustainable use of terrestrial ecosystems, sustainably manage forests, combat desertification, and halt and reverse land degradation and halt biodiversity loss
16. Promote peaceful and inclusive societies for sustainable development, provide access to justice for all and build effective, accountable and inclusive institutions at all levels
17. Strengthen the means of implementation and revitalize the global partnership for sustainable development

Source: United Nations General Assembly (2015) Transforming our world: the 2030 Agenda for Sustainable Development. A/RES/70/1.

people, including 365,000 children, experienced 'destitution' over the course of 2017, a definition that is applied when people have lacked two or more of six essentials over the past month because they cannot afford them, including shelter, food and heating. Their research findings suggested that the main routes into destitution were benefit delays, gaps and sanctions; debt recovery; financial and other pressures associated with poor health and disability; the high costs of housing, fuel and other essentials; extremely low levels of benefits, especially for younger people, or no eligibility for benefits, for some migrants. The COVID-19 pandemic has placed further pressure on many, raising serious questions about the ability of states' political and economic systems to deal with a crisis of this nature. A report by the OECD (2020) projects that, as a service-based economy, the UK has been hit especially heavily by the crisis compared to other developed countries.

Food security

Food security relates to individuals' physical and economic access to food at all times. More than 820 million people globally or one person in nine do not have enough to eat, according to the 2019 edition of the annual report *The State of Food Security and Nutrition in the World* by the Food and Agriculture Organization of the UN (FAO) and other organizations. Over 2 billion people are estimated to lack regular access to sufficient safe and nutritious food, and one in seven newborns, or approximately 20.5 million babies, suffered from low birth weight in 2015 (FAO, International Fund for Agricultural Development, UN Children's Fund, World Food Programme and World Health Organization, 2019). The second of the UN's SDGs is to end hunger, achieve food security and improved nutrition, and promote sustainable agriculture (UN General Assembly, 2015), yet the report indicates that continuing poor economic performance in many countries following the 2008 global financial crisis is undermining the international effort to meet the target (FAO et al., 2019).

A further FAO report, *The Future of Food and Agriculture: Alternative Pathways to 2050* (2019), lists the major challenges that have limited the sustainability of food and agricultural systems as including: 'high-input, resource-intensive farming systems that have caused massive deforestation, water scarcity, soil depletion, the loss of biodiversity, antimicrobial resistance of pests and diseases and high levels of GHG [greenhouse gas] emissions', while concerns for the future include 'increasing inequalities, exacerbated climate change effects, uncontrolled migration, increasing conflicts, extreme poverty and undernourishment'. The FAO's observations reflect the interconnectedness of global challenges and the fact that it is difficult to separate out the seven dimensions of human security. It is argued that **sustainable development** with respect to food and agriculture requires a focus on 'the universal challenge – and collective responsibility – of addressing the needs of all countries', with substantial investment necessary throughout all socio-economic and environmental systems to overhaul obsolete capital stock, research and develop new solutions, and implement innovative technologies adapted to different contexts and actors (p. 156).

In the UK, the most visible indicator of food insecurity has been the proliferation of food banks across the country since 2010, when the government embarked on a substantial deficit reduction or 'austerity' programme, making massive cuts to public expenditure. One of the largest providers of food banks is The Trussell Trust, which supports over 1200 food banks and reports that they gave out 1.9 million three-day emergency food parcels in 2019–20 (2020a, 2020b), an increase from about 61,500 in 2010/11 (Loopstra and Lalor, 2017). In qualitative research for the Child Poverty Action Group and the Trussell Trust (Perry, Williams, Sefton, Haddad, 2014), between half and two-thirds of 40 interviewees reported that their food bank use was linked to the operation of the benefits system, and problems that included waiting for benefit payments, sanctions, reduction in disability benefits or waiting for tax credit payments, mirroring the findings of the JRF (2018) report referred to above.

Health security

Health security relates not only to access to health care, but also good nutrition, clean water, a safe environment, as well as safe and affordable contraception and support during pregnancy, again illustrating the interconnections between the seven dimensions of human security. It is captured in the third of the SDGs, to 'ensure healthy lives and promote well-being for all at all ages' (UN General Assembly, 2015). Data from *The Lancet*'s (2018) Global Burden of Disease Study 2017 indicates that in 2017, 73.4% (41 million) of the 55.9 million global deaths were caused by non-communicable diseases such as heart disease, cancer, stroke, diabetes and mental illness. This represents a significant increase on the 60% in 2000 reported by the World Bank (2016), partially due to reductions in deaths from other causes as treatment for infectious diseases improved (MoD, 2018). Lifestyle factors are also a significant factor in this increase, particularly obesity, which could be the world's most pressing health issue by 2050 according to MoD (2018) projections. The NIC (2017) forecasts that non-communicable diseases will far outpace infectious diseases over the coming decades, due to demographic and cultural factors, including ageing, poor nutrition, poor sanitation, urbanization, and widening inequality.

The deadliest communicable diseases were lower respiratory infections, causing 3.8 million deaths in 2017 and accounting for 6.7% of global deaths

(*Lancet*, 2018). Prior to the COVID-19 crisis, the MoD (2018) had given warning of the increasing risk of a global pandemic, due to such factors as high population densities, travel and poverty, with more people projected to be living in cities, and travelling expected to be more frequent and further in distance by 2050. Its report also highlights the growing antimicrobial resistance that will exacerbate the threat from infectious diseases, and the extent of mental health disorders, such as schizophrenia, dementia and depression, estimated to have affected over 700 million people in 2014 and expected to remain a significant issue. It is argued that some forms of mental illness, such as anxiety disorders, may increase in the coming decade due to such factors as the potential for harassment and bullying associated with greater use of social media, and dwindling real-life interactions as more of people's social lives are lived online, increasing loneliness.

With respect to the UK, the Care Quality Commission (CQC, 2020), the independent regulator of health and social care, presents a challenging picture of growing demand across health and social care, due to an ageing population and the increasing complexity of people's needs. The number of patients waiting to start treatment is reported to have risen by 40% from 2014 to 2019, to 4.4 million people, and waiting times for treatment in hospitals and for emergency treatment are increasing. The CQC cites an estimate by the charity Age UK (2018) that 1.4 million older people do not have access to the care and support they need, the number of older people living with an unmet care need having risen by almost 20% in 2 years to nearly one in seven older people. Indicators of declining quality of care in mental health, learning disability and autism services are identified as areas of particular concern, related to issues of poor care from unqualified staff, difficulties in accessing services until reaching crisis point, detention in unsuitable services far from home, and difficulties in accessing care at all. With such gaps in services, it is no surprise that UK police forces are now dealing with a significant increase in non-crime, safeguarding incidents, as reported in the previous chapter.

Environmental security

'**Environmental security**' means a healthy and safe physical environment with, for example, clean water, clean air and productive land. The 2019 edition of the UN Environment Programme's annual global environmental assessment *Global Environment Outlook* details the challenges for the international community as including air pollution, estimated to cause between 6 and 7 million premature deaths per year; biodiversity loss, driving a mass extinction of species including pollinators that compromise the Earth's ecological integrity; marine plastic litter; land degradation; overexploitation and pollution of natural resources, including fresh water and oceans; and inappropriate use of pesticides, heavy metals, plastics and other substances that are contaminating food supplies. It is observed that the impacts of environmental degradation often bear most heavily on the poorest and most vulnerable in society, including indigenous and local communities, particularly in developing countries. Nearly all of the 17 SDGs include targets relating to the environment, but seven directly address environmental sustainability objectives, covering (6) clean water and sanitation, (7) affordable and clean energy, (11) sustainable cities and communities, (12) responsible consumption and production, (13) climate action, (14) marine resources and (5) terrestrial resources (UN General Assembly, 2015).

Hough (2014: 32) identifies three key political dilemmas associated with security threats relating to the environment. First, they are less direct and more complex than more 'traditional' threats, in that they are largely still perceived as 'longer-term creeping emergencies rather than imminent disasters and attacks', lacking a specific enemy. Secondly, measures to address them tend to be costly and require significant compromising of economic interests. Thirdly, often they can only be addressed by globally coordinated political action. International cooperation on climate change has included the establishment of a number of international agreements and frameworks to promote action, including the Sendai Framework for Disaster Risk Reduction 2015–30 (UN, 2015b), the Paris Agreement on climate change of 2015, and the New Urban Agenda (UN General Assembly, 2017), as mentioned in Chapter 3. A substantial and growing environmental movement, comprising a broad church of private citizens, professionals, politicians, scientists and NGOs has influenced the agenda of international politics. Among its latest manifestations are the international youth movement against climate change FridaysForFuture, instigated in 2018 by teenager Greta Thunberg, and the Extinction Rebellion global movement started in the UK in 2018, which uses civil disobedience to call for more urgent action to protect the environment.

According to the MoD (2018), the environmental challenges likely to affect European countries such as the UK include a marked increase in high temperature extremes, droughts and heavy precipitation events; and sea level rises and extreme rainfall increasing coastal and river flood risk. In the winter of 2015 to 2016, the UK experienced the most extreme flooding on record in Cumbria, Lancashire and parts of southern Scotland, causing the flooding of around 5200 homes, the loss of power to tens of thousands due to the flooding of an electricity sub-station, and an estimated insurance bill of more than £1.3bn (BBC News, 2016). The most recent climate change risk assessment (HM Government, 2017) notes a rise in average UK temperatures by around 1°C over the past century, a trend towards warmer winters and hotter summers, rising sea levels around the UK coastline of around 3mm a year, and emerging evidence of changing rainfall patterns. Measures to improve the UK's environmental performance include the Climate Change Act 2008, which set a target to reduce carbon emissions by 80% by 2050, requires the government to publish a climate change risk assessment every 5 years, and established a statutory Committee on Climate Change responsible for advising the UK government on emissions targets, monitoring progress, and conducting and disseminating evidence and analysis. The UK government also made a commitment to the international community to reduce its emissions under the Paris Agreement, as part of a joint pledge by members of the European Union (EU) to achieve by 2030 at least a 40% reduction in emissions below 1990 levels. Its goals for improving the environment are set out in *A Green Future: Our 25 Year Plan to Improve the Environment* (Department for Environment, Food and Rural Affairs, 2018). The *Sustainable Security Index* for 2020 (Oxford Research Group, 2020) ranks the UK second in the world for environmental governance, but argues that it could improve its commitment to reducing carbon emissions, use of renewable energy and investment in research.

Personal security

Personal security is concerned with individuals' security from physical harm arising from conflict, crime, industrial and traffic accidents, and threats to the self, such as suicide and drug use. Relevant SDGs and targets relate to reducing substance abuse and deaths and injuries from road traffic accidents (goal 3), eliminating violence and harmful practices affecting women and girls (5), eradicating forced labour and providing safe and secure working environments (8), improving the safety of public spaces and public transport (11), and reducing all forms of violence (16) (UN General Assembly, 2015). According to indicators informing the country peacefulness rankings of the Global Peace Index 2020 (Institute for Economics and Peace, 2020), the average level of global peacefulness has deteriorated by 2.5% since the Index was created in 2008, and the gap between the least and most peaceful countries is growing. The total number of conflicts fought globally and the overall intensity of internal conflict were found to have increased, although the total number of conflicts and the number of deaths from both internal and external conflict fell due to the defeat of ISIL in Syria and Iraq, and the easing of the civil war in Syria. The Uppsala Conflict Data Program estimates that there were 76,000 fatalities globally due to organized violence in 2018, which is the lowest level since 2012, the primary reduction being in state-based armed conflict, while the number of armed conflicts is at its highest level since the early 1990s (Pettersson, Högbladh and Öberg, 2019).

Such fatalities make up just a fraction of deaths worldwide from interpersonal violence, however, which accounted for 405,000 deaths in 2017, according to *The Lancet* (2018). Physical injuries as a whole accounted for 8% of deaths worldwide (4.48 million) in 2017, with road injuries accounting for the highest proportion of injury deaths (27.7%, or 1.24 million), and other major causes of death including self-harm (794,000), falls (696,000), substance use disorders (352,000) and drowning (295,000). Human trafficking and modern slavery are an especially significant and disturbing dimension of the global threats to personal security, with 40.3 million people estimated to have been victims of modern slavery in 2016, including sexual slavery and forced marriage (International Labour Organization and Walk Free Foundation, 2017).

In the UK, there has been a fall in 'traditional' or 'volume' crime since the mid-1990s, as noted in Chapter 5, but an increase from 2019 to 2020 in specific violent offences, including homicide, robbery and offences involving knives or sharp instruments (Office for National Statistics [ONS], 2020). The 10% increase in homicides is mainly due to one incident in which the bodies of 39 Vietnamese people were found in a lorry in Grays, Essex in October 2019 (BBC News, 2020). A spate of knife-related killings among young people in recent years has prompted a growing focus on strategies to prevent knife violence. Grimshaw and Ford (2018) extend the analysis to possession offences, noting a steady increase of 27% since the year ending March 2013, following a fall of nearly half from 2009, although they clarify that changes in police practices have a significant impact on the level of possession offences. They identify a number of possible explanations for the rise in knife violence, including an increase since 2014 in the vulnerable population, in terms of children in care, children excluded from school, and homeless adults; an association between income inequality and all types of violent crime demonstrated in the combined results of a number of research studies; a connection between mental health and violence; and the growing prevalence of drugs misuse and the 'county lines' model of distributing and selling drugs, with the accompanying problems of violent 'turf wars' between gangs, and vulnerable people being forced to work for them. Indeed, this form of criminal exploitation is reported by police to have overtaken sexual or labour exploitation as the most common reason to class someone as a modern slave (Dodd, 2020).

Community security

The concept of **community security** reflects how people gain security through their membership of groups – families, communities, organizations and ethnic groups, for example – while also recognising that particular groups can be vulnerable to identity-based marginalization and oppression, including ethnic minorities, indigenous groups, women, children, the disabled and members of the LGBT community. The main sources of community-based threat according to the UN Office for the Coordination of Humanitarian Affairs are 'inter-ethnic, religious and other identity based tensions' (2009: 7). While the initial UNDP (1994) definition of community security was primarily focused on sources of insecurity for members of ethnic minority groups, a later document expands the focus to women and children, recognising their specific vulnerabilities. It identifies seven main forms of threat to personal and group security: 'threats from the state' (physical torture), threats from other states in the case of war, threats from other groups of people (ethnic tension), threats from individuals or gangs, threats directed against women (rape, domestic violence), threats directed at children (child abuse), and threats to self (suicide, drug use) (UNDP, 2009: 13–14). Most of the SDGs relating to personal security also apply to community security, along with other goals and targets that refer to the specific vulnerabilities of the poor or marginalized groups – 'all children, youth, persons with disabilities (of whom more than 80 per cent live in poverty), people living with HIV/AIDS, older persons, indigenous peoples, refugees and internally displaced persons and migrants' – as part of a pledge that 'no one will be left behind' (UN General Assembly, 2015: 7, 1).

Social division is a significant theme of the NIC (2017) and the MoD (2018) forecasts for the coming decades, as well as the Amnesty International (2018) report *The State of the World's Human Rights*, which observed 'the bitter fruits of a rising politics of demonization' across the globe. The MoD (2018) observes a rise in inequality and people's sense of injustice, religious intolerance, nationalism and intolerance of immigrants, providing the conditions for violent ideologies to flourish, particularly in regions of continuing instability such as the Middle East and South Asia, and with some actors such as Russia employing disinformation and propaganda to exploit grievances, erode trust in governments and provoke conflict. Its report also draws attention to the growing division in many developed and developing countries between those with liberal attitudes and those with more traditional values, with those who are willing and able to travel in search of better education or employment tending to become richer and more liberal, and those less willing or unable to do so often being less educated, poorer and more culturally conservative. Such a phenomenon, also discussed by Goodhart (2017) in relation to the UK in the aftermath of the Brexit referendum, presents enormous challenges to governments. More positively, the *Global Peace Index 2019* indicates that, while community acceptance of immigration has declined by 3% globally since 2014, acceptance of minority groups such as racial and ethnic minorities and LGBT people has improved globally since 2008 (Institute for Economics and Peace, 2019) (the 2020 report does not refer to these indicators).

In the UK and many other jurisdictions, criminal acts that are judged to be motivated by identity-based discrimination are categorized as hate crime, defined by the UK government as 'any criminal offence which is perceived, by the victim or any other person, to be motivated by hostility or prejudice towards someone based on a personal characteristic' (Home Office, 2018b: 8). Five areas of hate crime are centrally monitored: race or ethnicity, religion or beliefs, sexual orientation, disability, and gender identity, while incidents related to gender and age are recorded by the police but fall outside the hate crime statistics. Hate crime scholars and campaigners emphasize that such crimes are often intersectional in nature, in that individuals may belong to more than one marginalized group and face overlapping forms of prejudice, though current arrangements do not allow this to be recorded (All Party Parliamentary Group on Hate Crime, 2019).

In 2017/18, as detailed by Allen and Zayed (2018), there were 94,098 hate crime offences recorded by the police in England and Wales where one or more of the centrally monitored strands were deemed to be a motivating factor, representing a 17% increase on the previous year's figures, and accounting for around 2% of all police recorded crime. Their report partially attributes the rise in police recorded hate crimes to an improvement in the recording of these crimes, with growing public awareness of the problem, although there were short-term increases following the EU referendum in June 2016 and the terrorist attacks of 2017. While gender is not treated as a hate crime category, domestic and sexual violence bear most heavily on women and children, 13% of all crimes recorded by the police in England and Wales being marked as being domestic abuse-related, and sexual assaults making up 2.2% of crimes (ONS, 2020). The COVID lockdown caused domestic abuse to soar, with more than double the number of homicides occurring in the first 3 weeks than during the same period the previous year (Grierson, 2020). A much debated issue in the UK as well as international scholarship and policy is the extent to which research findings on fear of crime indicate that certain groups, particularly women and the elderly, are disproportionately fearful, since official figures have consistently suggested that they experience lower rates of 'traditional' (as opposed to online) crime victimization. These assumptions have, however, been challenged by arguments and research highlighting the wide range of hidden and under-reported threats to women ranging from street harassment to domestic violence through to rape (Stanko, 1988), and evidence that male respondents to fear of crime surveys are more inclined to provide socially desirable rather than fully candid responses and downplay their fears (Sutton and Farrall, 2005).

Political security

Political security means living in a society that honours one's basic human rights, as laid out in the Universal Declaration of Human Rights (UDHR), 30 rights and freedoms proclaimed by the UN General Assembly in 1948. These encompass civil and political rights, such as the right to life, liberty, freedom from torture, asylum, free speech and privacy; and economic, social and cultural rights, such as the right to social security, health and education. The UDHR has no enforcement mechanism, but it has informed international and national legislation, including the European Convention on Human Rights, and the UK's Human Rights Act 1998. The SDGs and targets most relevant to the promotion of political security are those of goal 16, to promote just, peaceful and inclusive societies (UN General Assembly, 2015), placing an emphasis on human rights and effective governance based on the rule of law, and recognizing that abuses are most prevalent in states where there is conflict or no rule of law. The MoD (2018) predicts that, over the coming decades, 'democracy will increasingly come under pressure from authoritarian leaders', and the world will become less liberal (2018: 122). According to the Economist Intelligence Unit (2020) Democracy Index 2019, only 76 out of the 167 countries covered in the index can be considered to be democracies, and 22 to be 'full democracies'. Just over a third of the global population are classified as living under authoritarian rule, with a large share represented by China, and only 5.7% to be living in full democracies.

McLaughlin (2019) groups crimes perpetrated by states into four categories: acts of political criminality (including corruption, intimidation, manipulating the electoral process and censorship); criminality associated with the military and police forces (including acts of genocide, torture, disappearance and assassination); criminality associated with economic activities (including monopolization practices, violations of health and safety regulations and illegal collaboration with multinational corporations); and criminality at the social and cultural levels (including material immiseration of sections of the community, institutional racism and cultural vandalism). The Amnesty International (2018) report *The State of the World's Human Rights* offers many examples of each type. Recent years have seen China drafting and enacting sweeping national security-related laws and regulations, giving authorities greater powers to silence dissent, censor information and harass and prosecute human rights activists, while Hong Kong residents have staged major protests against a series of measures that diminish their democratic rights. Among many cases across the globe of military criminality and ethnic cleansing is the plight of the Muslim Rohingya ethnic minority in the north of Rakhine State in Myanmar, described by one UN representative as 'the most persecuted minority in the world' (Office of the UN High Commissioner for Human Rights, 2017). Unsafe working environments are globally prevalent: every year, 2.78 million people die as the result of exposure to safety and health hazards at work, while 374 million workers suffer non-fatal occupational accidents (International Labour Organization, 2020). While many industrialized countries such as the UK have comprehensive regulatory regimes for health and safety at work, it is much harder to guarantee safe working conditions in businesses making up global supply chains, one of the worst tragedies being the collapse of the Dhaka garment factory in Bangladesh in 2013, killing 1135 people (Reuters, 2016).

Amnesty International (2018) addresses a number of areas of concern over human rights in the UK, as does an article by Coles (2019). Both draw attention to areas of gender discrimination, including restrictions in Northern Ireland on women's access to abortion, gender inequalities in pay, and unequal representation of women in Parliament, while Coles highlights criticism by the UN over the impact of social security cuts on disabled people, and of legal aid cuts on vulnerable people such as the disabled and women who have suffered domestic violence. Other areas of inequality highlighted by Amnesty International include the inability of same-sex couples in Northern Ireland to marry, and the over-representation of ethnic minorities in the UK prison population. Both publications are critical of aspects of police practice, including high levels of police stop and search under Schedule 7 of the Terrorism Act 2000, which requires no suspicion of wrongdoing; the use of tasers, which the UN has condemned as weapons of torture, and which had caused 16 deaths by mid-2016; and police infiltration of activist groups. Ongoing legal action by Amnesty International and other bodies over the legality of UK mass surveillance regimes and intelligence-sharing practices is also highlighted. With respect to foreign policy, Coles points to UK support to America's rendition programme, while Amnesty International raises concerns about the UK's continuing supply of arms to Saudi Arabia, despite ongoing serious violations of international humanitarian law by the Saudi Arabia-led coalition in Yemen. Finally, the Amnesty International report refers to the Grenfell Tower tragedy in June 2017, when at least 71 people died in a fire in a council-controlled residential tower block in Kensington, London, raising questions over public authorities' and private actors' compliance with their human rights obligations including protection of the right to life and guaranteeing an adequate standard of living, including the right to adequate housing.

Summary

This chapter applied the concept of human security and its seven dimensions (UNDP, 1994) to major social problems experienced globally and nationally within the UK. Although it has predominantly been applied by the international community to developing countries, the UN Sustainable Development Goals, which are grounded in a human security approach, marked a distinct change from previous development doctrine in defining sustainable development as being universal in scope (UN General Assembly, 2015). In accordance with the UN's universalist approach, human security principles have been shown in this chapter to have equal relevance to the developed world, where social inequalities expose many to the threats and insecurities that governments of the Global North more commonly ascribe to other regions. There are demonstrable inequalities both globally and in the UK in access to income, food and healthcare (economic, food and health security), the human impact of environmental degradation (environmental security), and experiences of deliberate threat (personal, community and political security). Global and national inequalities thus have a bearing on humans' vulnerability to insecurity, their access to its remedies, as well as their experiences as the targets of authorities' security measures. Human security's seven dimensions are not discrete issues but rather are inter-related, and those experiencing material deprivation are more likely also to be exposed to more direct and deliberate threats. Human security is clearly a powerful concept that brings together a range of issues that are rarely addressed in tandem in countries of the Global North. However, there is so far little sign of it gaining much currency beyond the international development sphere.

Study questions

- In your country, what should be the main policy priorities in order to improve health security?
- To what extent is the international community making progress in its efforts to prevent severe global warming in the decades ahead?
- What is the relationship between material deprivation and individual experiences of deliberate threats such as interpersonal violence?
- In what ways can communities be oppressive to their own people?

Further reading

Human Security: Theory and Action (Andersen-Rodgers and Crawford, 2018), provides a comprehensive overview of the concept and its contemporary applications, complementing Tadjbakhsh and Chenoy (2007), as recommended in Chapter 3. For criminological 'harm' perspectives that have parallels with human security thinking, *Beyond Criminology: Taking Harm Seriously* (edited by Hillyard et al., 2004) provides an insightful critique of mainstream criminology and justification for a more inclusive 'social harm' conception of crime. Green criminology is based on similar assumptions with a particular focus on environmental harms, and is well represented in the *Routledge International Handbook of Green Criminology* (Brisman and South, 2020), which complements Hough's (2014) comprehensive text on *Environmental Security*, while his chapters on food (2020a) and health (2020b) security in *International Security Studies: Theory and Practice* (Hough et al., 2020) offer valuable recent overviews of these topics. *County Lines: Exploitation and Drug Dealing among Urban Street Gangs* (Harding, 2020) presents a comprehensive analysis of a contemporary UK phenomenon and the associated issues of gangs, drugs, youth violence and exploitation. For an in-depth examination of hate crime as a global challenge, *Blood, Threats and Fears: The Hidden Worlds of Hate Crime Victims* (Hardy and Chakraborti, 2020) is recommended. The challenges for governments around the world in reconciling issues of security with a respect for fundamental human rights are comprehensively explored in *Security and Human Rights* (edited by Goold and Lazarus, 2019).

7

Securing the internet

Chapter overview

This chapter provides:

- An account of the development of the internet and the World Wide Web, and the projected evolution of the Web over the coming decades.
- An introduction to the concept of the fourth industrial revolution, which offers a framework within which to consider the collective opportunities and challenges for society that are associated with technological advancement.
- An assessment of the distinct security challenges associated with cyberspace, as they relate to individuals, states and corporations.
- A discussion of the concepts of internet governance and cyber security governance, and the practices and challenges associated with both.

Key terms

- Artificial intelligence
- Big data analytics
- Cyber security
- Cyber security governance
- Cybercrime
- Cyberspace
- Dark web
- Fourth industrial revolution
- Internet governance
- Internet of things

Introduction

Technological advancement has significantly driven, and been driven by, **globalization**. Many social theorists see today's world as being defined by technology, describing our era as the 'information age' (Castells, 1996) or the 'digital age', bringing about a 'network society' (van Dijk, 1991; Castells, 1996), 'information society' (e.g. Webster, 2014) or 'surveillance society' (e.g. Lyon, 2001). These perspectives observe the pace of technological advancement from the late 20th century onwards and the central position of technology in the economy and society, viewing contemporary social structures as being primarily organized around electronically processed information networks. Nye describes the rapid growth of **cyberspace** as 'an important new context in world politics' (2010: 1) that is changing the nature of power and increasing its diffusion, mirroring wider trends in contemporary global politics. Smaller actors, such as non-state actors and small states, face much more of a level playing field than on land or at sea and have significantly more capacity to exert hard and soft power, benefitting from the low price of entry to the cyber realm, virtual anonymity, and asymmetries in vulnerability compared with governments and large corporations that have much more to lose. Individuals able to access the internet also have access to the power that information provides. For Nye, these are examples of 'cyber power', which can be defined as 'the ability to use cyberspace to create advantages and influence events in other operational environments and across the instruments of power' (Kuehl, 2009: 38).

This chapter is primarily concerned with the security of cyberspace, beginning with an overview of its development and projected future evolution. The focus then turns to internet security threats, discussing how '**cybercrimes**' can be defined and categorized, and examining the challenges they present to individuals, states and corporations. The final section addresses the governance of the internet and **cyber security governance**, which Mueller (2017) presents as two competing ways of thinking about internet regulation that are underpinned by conflicting agendas on the control and purpose of the internet and the Web.

The landscape of cyberspace

The internet is a computer network or a 'network of networks' (Castells, 1996). A network links computers together, enabling communication and information exchange between them. Networks of information and communications technology (ICT) have been around for many decades – in financial markets, the military, corporations and government departments, for example – but the internet provided the means to connect the many networks in existence. The term 'cyberspace', initially coined by science fiction writer William Gibson in the novel *Neuromancer* (1984), describes the virtual space that exists within the scope of the internet. From here, as Yar and Steinmetz (2019) note, the prefix 'cyber' caught on in the 1980s and 1990s and was attached to various nouns denoting a relationship with computers and the internet. This section explores the landscape of cyberspace, focusing on the development of the internet and World Wide Web and the projected evolution of the Web, as well as introducing the concept of the **fourth industrial revolution** (4IR), which refers to the technologically advanced age that we are now entering.

The global penetration of the internet

Since the commercialization of the internet in the mid-1990s, its growth has been exponential. Between 1990 and 2000, the number of countries connected to the internet increased from 20 to 208 (Internet Telecommunications Union, 2003), and the number of internet hosts (computers connected to the internet) from 200,000 to 104 million (Dholakia, Dholakia and Kshetri, 2004). In 2019, 53.6% of the global population, or 4.1 billion people, were estimated to be using the internet (Internet Telecommunications Union, 2019). According to Internet World Stats (2020), as shown in Table 7.1, North America has the highest internet penetration, with 90.3% of the population having access, Europe next at 87.2% and, at the other end of the spectrum, Africa remains markedly behind the rest of the world, with just 42.2% internet penetration. Within countries, unequal access follows existing lines of exclusion, so factors like employment, income, education, ethnicity, gender and disability have an association with internet use. For example, the proportion of women using the internet globally is 48%, compared to 58% of men, the gap being most marked – and growing – in developing countries (Internet Telecommunications Union, 2019).

When the UN General Assembly adopted the 2030 Agenda for Sustainable Development, containing 17 Sustainable Development Goals and 169 associated targets, it declared that 'the spread of information and communications technology and global interconnectedness has great potential to accelerate human progress, to bridge the digital divide and to develop knowledge

Table 7.1 World internet usage and population statistics, June 2019

World regions	Population (2019 est.)	Population % of world	Internet users 30 June 2019	Penetration rate (% population)	Growth 2000–2019	Internet use % of world
Africa	1,340,598,447	17.2%	566,138,772	42.2%	12,441%	11.7%
Asia	4,294,516,659	55.1%	2,525,033,874	58.8%	2,109%	52.2%
Europe	834,995,197	10.7%	727,848,547	87.2%	592%	15.1%
Latin America / Caribbean	654,287,232	8.4%	467,817,332	71.5%	2,489%	9.7%
Middle East	260,991,690	3.3%	184,856,813	70.8%	5,527%	3.8%
North America	368,869,647	4.7%	332,908,868	90.3%	208%	6.9%
Oceania / Australia	42,690,838	0.5%	28,917,600	67.7%	279%	0.6%
World Total	7,796,949,710	100.0%	4,833,521,806	62.0%	1,239%	100.0%

Source: World Internet Users and 2020 Population Stats. https://internetworldstats.com/stats.htm.

societies' (2015: para 5). While there is no goal specifically dedicated to ICT, it features in numerous targets, and seven out of 232 of the indicators employed to measure progress towards the goals and targets. These include a target of 70% global internet penetration by 2023, and 75% by 2025 (International Telecommunications Union, 2018).

The development of the internet and the World Wide Web

The origins of the internet can be traced back to the development of a network called ARPANET in the 1960s. This project of the US military was intended to establish a means for secure communication and coordination of military activities during the Cold War period, and was up and running by 1969, initially linking together a handful of university research communities with government agencies. In 1990, the ARPANET was released to civilian control through the National Science Foundation, a US government agency to support research, enabling worldwide participation in the development of new networking technologies and the merger of many networks. One of the largest internet nodes was the CERN physics lab in Switzerland, where Tim Berners-Lee put forward a proposal to join hypertext with the internet and create the World Wide Web, for which he designed and built the first web browser. The first commercial browsers, 'Netscape' and 'Internet Explorer', were released in 1994 and 1995, allowing internet access from personal PCs. Numerous commercial internet service providers (ISPs) entered the market in the mid-1990s offering internet connections to anyone with a computer and a telephone line. In 1998, the Internet Corporation for Assigned Names and Numbers (ICANN) was established under contract to the US Department of Justice to coordinate the domain name system (DNS) and assign Internet Protocol (IP) addresses, and ensure the internet's stable and secure operation, with control transitioning to the global, multi-stakeholder community in 2016. While the terms 'internet' and 'World Wide Web' are often used interchangeably, the former refers to the physical network of networks, whereas the World Wide Web is the information space where web pages can be found by means of their URLs (unique resource locators) and accessed over the internet.

The Web is now regarded as having developed and continuing to evolve through a series of distinct phases (see Kambil, 2008; Patel, 2013; Choudhury, 2014). Retrospectively termed 'Web 1.0', the 'read-only Web' or the 'information Web', the first phase of the Web up to around 2005 consisted mainly of static HTML web pages with little interactivity except for basic online shopping carts. As the World Wide Web progressed to a more interactive experience, whereby users were able to collaborate and share information online, it came to be known as 'Web 2.0', the 'read-write Web' or the 'social Web', lasting until around 2016. The new forms of interactive and user-generated content that marked this phase of web development included discussion forums, social media (e.g. MySpace, Facebook and Twitter), instant messaging, voice and video communication (e.g. Skype), collaborative tools (e.g. Wikipedia), blogs, video and picture sharing (e.g. YouTube and Instagram), aggregation services, such as RSS feeds, and crowdsourcing (e.g. Just-Giving, Indigogo). The rise of smart phones and tablets enabled a new level of connectedness to such Web 2.0 tools, the term 'smart' referring to applications and devices that are programmed to be able to harness large amounts of data and use analytics, **artificial intelligence** (AI) and machine learning (an approach to achieving AI whereby a machine is able to learn from data) to deliver tailored solutions.

As devices, data, connections, processes and people have become increasingly integrated, a third generation of the Web covering the period to around 2020 has come to be described as 'Web 3.0', the 'read-write-execute Web' or the 'semantic Web'. It is a more individually oriented, intelligent web, in which information applications and systems are able to be linked in order to deliver such features as personalized advertisements and smart applications. This era of web development has brought about a greater dependence on smart phones and tablets, as well as new **'internet of things'** (IoT) technologies. Referring to the idea of 'things' connecting directly with each other via the internet and machine-to-machine communication, these include activity trackers, 'virtual assistants' like Amazon Alexa, and smart household devices such as speakers, baby monitors, refrigerators and heating thermostats, though any device with an on–off switch can now technically be connected to the internet. IoT technologies also assist industries in optimizing production, and will enable the development of the **'smart cities'** of the future as mentioned in Chapter 5. The semantic Web capitalizes on new technologies such as **big data analytics**, which refers to the analytical capabilities for mining the massive amount of data produced by internet users; cloud computing, enabling mass data storage and accessibility; the increasing array of mobile devices; sensor networks enabling technologies to be remotely activated; and social media, a source of big data. Such concepts and technologies provide the foundations for the more profound changes that will characterize future generations of the Web.

'Web 4.0' is also described as the 'mobile Web', as it will be ubiquitous and always in action; the 'intelligent Web'; or the 'symbiotic Web' to reflect interactions between humans and machines in symbiosis. The idea is of a 'read-write-execution-concurrency' Web that provides smart interactions with users and will demonstrate increasing levels of intelligence, able to communicate with humans like personal assistants. Web 5.0, a 'sensory Web' or 'emotive Web' that is more aware of human feelings and able to respond dynamically to them, is anticipated from around 2030. Its technologies will be able to assess various physiological and neurological states of the user with, predicts Kambil, 'the potential to change the WWW from a noisy environment to a richer place of thoughtful and affable interactions', while 'it could also become a manipulative and disruptive space for individuals' (2008: 57). As he concludes, only time will tell how these capabilities will come to be used.

The dark web

Another notable dimension of the development of the Web is that of the '**dark web**', encompassing content from the World Wide Web that exists on encrypted networks (also known as 'dark nets' or 'darknets') like Tor (The Onion Routing project) and I2P (Invisible Internet Project) and cannot be found through traditional browsers and search engines. The dark web forms part of the 'deep web', which describes all parts of the web not indexed by search engines. The Tor dark net enables anonymous internet communication, and the Tor browser and Tor-accessible sites are identified by the domain '.onion', while I2P specializes in the anonymous hosting of websites. The US Naval Research Laboratory originally financed and developed Tor during the 1990s to enable encrypted communications in the military and intelligence communities, releasing the code to the public in 2004, after which it was financially supported by the Electronic Frontier Foundation, a digital rights organization. It now has millions of users worldwide.

In an era of increasing social concern about online privacy and data protection, the dark net offers users obvious benefits, but has become controversial due to associations with numerous forms of organized crime, child sex abuse images and identity theft. After 2009, the release of the Bitcoin cryptocurrency provided a new framework for encrypted online payments, and gave significant impetus to the development of digital black markets. The first major dark net market was Silk Road, launched in 2011 and shut down by the FBI in 2013, while its successor Silk Road 2.0 was shut down by the FBI and Europol in 2014. A study by Owen and Savage (2015) of content on the Tor dark net over a period of 6 months found that the majority of sites were criminally oriented, with drug marketplaces being especially common, and that sites hosting child abuse imagery were the most frequently requested. Moore and Rid (2015) classified the contents of 2723 live dark web sites over 5 weeks and found that 57% hosted illicit material, while a study by McGuire (2018) concluded that 60% of dark web listings are potentially harmful.

Advocates of the dark net contend that it is excessively maligned, and provides necessary internet privacy in an era when standard internet platforms all feed users' personal data to corporations and governments, leaving internet users open to monitoring, exploitation and, potentially, repression. It provides a space for sensitive communications, such as among activists in repressive regimes, and between journalists and whistleblowers. The Tor Project team (2020) argue that it served as an instrumental tool during the Arab Spring uprisings in the Middle East and North Africa in the early 2010s, and that the need for tools safeguarding against mass surveillance was substantiated by the Snowden disclosures in 2013 of mass internet and phone surveillance by the US National Security Agency (NSA) and its international partners (see Macaskill and Dance, 2013).

Digital transformation and the fourth industrial revolution

The concept of 4IR, sometimes alternatively referred to as 'Industry 4.0' (see Rojko, 2017), provides a useful framework for thinking about the collective impact and implications of an increasingly technologically integrated world. Coined by Klaus Schwab, Founder of the World Economic Forum, it refers to the advanced stage of industrial development that we are now entering, which is driven by the fusion of technologies across the physical, digital and biological worlds, and significantly impacting the ways in which humans live, work and relate to each other. The first industrial revolution of around 1760 to 1840 had been characterized by the mechanization of production through water and steam power, while the second occurred in the late 19th century and created mass production fuelled by electricity, gas and oil. The third industrial revolution, also known as the 'digital revolution', beginning in the 1960s, was brought about through the development of electronics, mainframe computing, personal computing and the internet.

According to Schwab (2017), 4IR is bringing about an unprecedented speed and scale of innovation and change, disrupting most industries across the world. It is seen to have started early in the new millennium, facilitated by the internet, using the power of digitization and information technology to enable all dimensions of production to be connected in real time. 4IR is characterized by the growing interrelationship between physical innovations (such as autonomous vehicles, 3D printing, advanced robotics, and new materials, including advanced nanomaterials such as graphene); digital innovations (such as the technologies enabling IoT, blockchain technology, and the on-demand economy epitomised by Uber, Airbnb and Deliveroo); and biological innovations (such as genome editing – the modification of DNA in living organisms – which raise profound ethical issues but have significant implications for spheres such as medicine, agriculture and biofuels).

Schwab (2018b) argues that 4IR requires widespread changes in approach, for example, governments must invest in more agile approaches to governance that empower communities and deeply engage business and civil society; businesses need to be aware of the opportunities that 4IR presents and develop ways of working that are sensitive to their impact on employees, customers and communities; and individuals must get involved in conversations about the implications of 4IR and experience the technologies associated with it. Presenting threats as well as opportunities, key areas for attention that he identifies include ensuring ethical considerations are built into technological development processes, and preparing people adequately for the changing nature of work and particularly the impact of accelerating automation. Indeed, the World Economic Forum (2018) already notes that the employee skills profile viewed by employers as being required to perform most jobs is evolving rapidly and requires ongoing re- and upskilling. The most sought-after job skills by 2022, according to their survey, are analytical thinking and innovation; active learning and learning strategies; creativity, originality and initiative; technology design and programming; critical thinking and analysis; and complex problem-solving.

Schwab's thesis is written in an optimistic, galvanizing tone but, as the speed of technological advancement is already challenging governments, their capacity to adapt adequately as it accelerates further is open to question. As the Ministry of Defence (MoD) (2018) acknowledges, managing this process may be especially difficult in political systems with short election cycles; less democratic countries without such vulnerabilities may be more adaptive to these new challenges and opportunities. To mitigate the adverse impacts of 4IR, it is certain that bold political decisions will be needed.

Internet security threats

As Nye observes, 'the internet was designed for ease of use rather than security' (2010: 5), as users are diverse and sometimes anonymous, physical distance is inconsequential, and the costs of committing a cyber offence can be negligible. The widening range of benefits brought about by the development of the internet have been accompanied by an 'explosion of crime and criminality' (Yar and Steinmetz, 2019: 3). McGuire (2018) estimates that, although cybercrime constitutes a relatively new criminal economy, it is already generating at least $1.5 trillion in revenue every year. As time goes on, and an increasing number of people spend more of their time conducting a widening range of activities in cyberspace, information is becoming more central both to humanity and to conflict (MoD, 2018), and advancing technologies will present opportunities for exploitation by rogue states, terrorists and criminals on an even greater scale through such means as the malicious use of AI. This section examines different types of internet security threat, firstly considering how the commonly-used term 'cybercrime' is best defined, and then examining threats to individuals, states and corporations in turn.

Defining 'cybercrime'

Human dependence on the internet presents new and evolving risks. The concept of 'cybercrime' has become commonplace in the new millennium, its various definitions including references to 'computer mediated activities which are either illegal or considered illicit by certain parties and which can be conducted through global electronic networks' (Thomas and Loader, 2000: 3) and criminal acts that have been 'transformed by networked technologies' (Wall, 2009: 74). Yar and Steinmetz offer a straightforward interpretation covering 'computer-mediated activities that are illegal' (2019: 12), which can then be broken down into categories, a task that has been approached in different ways. Wall (2001) distinguishes between four types of cybercrime that have become prevalent in recent decades according to established legal categories: 'cyber-trespass' (e.g. hacking, defacement, viruses), 'cyber-deceptions and thefts' (e.g. fraud and product 'piracy': copyright infringement of digital content), 'cyber-pornography' (breaching obscenity/decency laws), and 'cyber-violence', which may incite physical harm or cause psychological harm (e.g. hate speech and stalking). This is the preferred approach of Yar and Steinmetz (2019), as it maps most effectively to existing frameworks for classifying crimes, and allows cybercrime to be broken down according to the target of the offence to denote crimes against property (addressing Wall's first two categories), crimes against morality and crimes against persons. To these Yar and Steinmetz add 'crimes against the state' to encompass activities that threaten the integrity of the state and its infrastructure (e.g. disclosure of official secrets, espionage and terrorism).

Various alternative classifications are based on the relationship of the offence with technology (e.g. Furnell, 2002; Lilley, 2002; Smith et al., 2004; Gordon and Ford, 2006; Wall, 2007; McGuire and Dowling, 2013). The most straightforward is that employed by McGuire and Dowling, distinguishing between 'cyber-dependent' and 'cyber-enabled' crimes; a categorization that is now widely used across government and law enforcement in the UK, and employed in the *National Cyber Security Strategy 2016–2021* (HM Government, 2016). The former are crimes that can only be committed through the use of ICT devices, and are primarily directed against computers or network resources (such as the spread of malware, hacking, or denial of service attacks). The latter category refers to traditional crimes that have increased in scale or reach through the use of ICT devices (such as cyber-enabled fraud, data theft, trafficking in drugs and other illicit goods, various forms of harassment, and sexual offences against children). A significant contemporary dimension of cyber-enabled crime is the spreading of misinformation. The media has always carried a certain amount of so-called 'fake news', some of which may be seen simply as careless reporting or gossip. However, in today's technology-driven media landscape, the problem is magnified many times over, and presents a major threat to individuals, states and corporations.

Threats to individuals

The development of the internet has transformed the pattern of crime against individuals. Fraud and computer misuse offences make up a large proportion of such cybercrime, as discussed in Chapter 5, and may become more refined and effective in the future as offenders employ AI and machine learning to increase the scale of their attacks and the sophistication of their scams. Alongside such well-established threats as 'phishing' and 'spoofing', misinformation presents a growing threat to individuals as a further tool for social engineering: the manipulation of individuals into breaking security procedures. This type of threat sees both fake and real news being weaponized, with trending stories and sensational headlines being used to draw people's attention. Lures range from the very basic to the highly tailored, based on individuals' social media activity. They can lead to the sharing of malware via email attachments, banner advertisements directing users who click on them to malicious sites, or 'watering hole' sites, infected with malware, dressed up as news sites (Scott, 2017).

Online platforms have also made prevalent the most serious illegal content and activity, including online harassment and cyber-bullying, the sharing of sexual images of children, and organized hate and terrorism. The former can take a variety of forms, as detailed by Strickland and Dent (2017), including 'trolling' (the sending of menacing or upsetting messages), identity theft, doxxing (sharing someone's personal information) and cyber stalking, which affect both adults and children. They observe that, for children, online bullying can be more pervasive than face-to-face bullying, as it can follow children wherever they go and have a highly detrimental effect on their mental health. Strickland and Dent also highlight the problem of online abuse of politicians, identified as particularly affecting females and especially women from ethnic minorities, which is not only harmful to the individuals affected but also to democratic processes, with the potential to put off citizens – and especially under-represented groups – from getting involved in politics (see also Committee on Standards in Public Life, 2017; Babuta and Krasodomski-Jones, 2018). Acts of online harassment and bullying typically fall under the same legislation as similar offline offences covering stalking, harassment, sending malicious communications and improper use of a public electronic communications network, while the offence of 'revenge pornography' was recently incorporated in the Criminal Justice and Courts Act 2015.

The circulation of sexual images of minors online is an aspect of cybercrime that provokes particular concern, and is vast in its scale. The National Center for Missing and Exploited Children (NCMEC) (2020), a US-based NGO, received 16.9 million reports of child sexual abuse imagery in 2019. In the first quarter of 2020, Facebook (2020) reported removing 8.6 million pieces of content that breached policies on child nudity and sexual exploitation. The Internet Watch Foundation (IWF) (2020), a British NGO, estimates that around

46% of the child sexual abuse material it finds online contains children aged 10 or under, and 64% of this imagery falls into the most serious categories of abuse. Pornhub, the world's largest pornography website, is heavily criticized for not doing enough to prevent the hosting of child sexual abuse content as well as non-consensual content of adults, and for aiding human trafficking (see Gordine, 2020). Organized hate and terrorism are also prevalent online, Facebook (2020) having reported the removal of 4.7 million pieces of content violating policies on organized hate, and 7.5 million pieces of content violating policies on terrorist activity in the first quarter of 2020. The extent of the threat to the UK of various categories of illegal and unacceptable online content and activity was explored in a government consultation and report in 2019 (HM Government, 2019).

Threats to states

The rapid growth of cyberspace is having a significant bearing on international politics and global governance. Nye (2010: 1) observes how smaller actors have more capacity to exercise hard and soft power in cyberspace, 'a new and a volatile manmade environment' than is the case in more traditional domains of politics. The diffusion of what he terms 'cyber power', enabled by the low cost of entry to the internet, opportunity for anonymity, and asymmetries in vulnerability that bear most heavily on its largest actors, mean that governments are limited in their ability to counter attacks or defeat the enemy, and internet security relies heavily on preventative measures. The total costs and harms of cybercrime to states are hard to quantify, but the economic and social costs are considerable (Home Office, 2018c). The challenge for governments is not to prevent individual attacks, but to protect the whole of a society that has become digitized, and which is evolving faster than governments can keep up with. As the internet has expanded beyond computers, tablets and mobile phones to encompass pervasive IoT technologies and the smart systems that these enable, a whole range of new technologies are vulnerable to interference, such as satellites, power grids, industrial plants, air traffic control systems, traffic signals and autonomous vehicles. There is also the threat of attack through the deployment of autonomous weapons (see Brundage et al., 2018). In the coming years, AI is likely to accelerate the security 'arms race' between those protecting systems and their attackers.

The vulnerabilities to a nation lie in the fact that much of the hardware and software on which the internet and cyberspace are built has prioritized efficiency, cost and convenience but not always security, leaving gaps that malicious actors can readily exploit, exemplified by the WannaCry ransomware attack on the UK's National Health Service in 2017 (see Smart, 2018). These include an expanding range of devices, poor cyber hygiene and compliance, insufficient training and skills, legacy and unpatched systems, and the ready availability online of hacking resources. The range of threat actors looking to take advantage of such vulnerabilities encompasses cyber criminals, terrorists, 'hactivists' (digital activists), 'script kiddies' – less skilled individuals who conduct cyber attacks using scripts or programmes developed by others – and states. States have come to be seen as one of the most dangerous threat actors, prominent examples of offensive state operations including the US NSA spying revealed by the Snowden disclosures; attacks on Sony and the Bangladesh Central Bank as well as the WannaCry outbreak, attributed to North Korea; observations of Chinese intelligence services hacking NGOs; and Russia's attack on the Democratic National Committee during the 2016 US Presidential elections (van Eeten, 2017).

Propaganda and disinformation now present significant contemporary threats to states that promote an open and democratic internet. Having played a significant role in the First and Second World Wars, they are now recognised as a significant element of contemporary 'hybrid' warfare (defined in Chapter 2), as demonstrated in Russia's actions in Ukraine (see Lanoszka, 2016; Fox and Rossow, 2017) and against the West and elsewhere (see Fridman, 2018) to undermine confidence in national governments and manipulate democratic processes. Lucas and Pomerantsev (2016) observe how the nature of online media, and especially social media, allows propagandists to play to audiences who are already mistrustful of their own systems and are seeking information that confirms their biases, identifying and exploiting 'echo chambers' where facts and fact-checkers have little effect. Major concerns have been raised about the use of big data analytics for profiling citizens, including for political purposes. Reports on the strategy used by US data mining company Cambridge Analytica as part of the campaigns of Ted Cruz and Donald Trump for the US presidency, and the Brexit referendum campaign in the UK, have revealed how political messages can be tailored to individual social media users through data analytics of online activity (see Rosenberg, Confessore and Cadwalladr, 2018). Digital advertising is becoming an increasingly significant feature of political campaigning yet, at the time of writing, still falls outside the scope of electoral regulation in the UK (see Electoral Commission, 2018). It is not only the spread of fake text content that can be used to manipulate public opinion: machine learning and AI can be used to produce synthetic images that are virtually indistinguishable from photographs, known as 'deepfakes' (combining 'deep learning' – a subset of machine learning whereby a machine is enabled to learn and make decisions – and 'fake').

Equally serious for national – and global – security are forms of misinformation and disinformation that promote distrust in science and misperceptions of scientific knowledge. This can be observed in relation to the denial of climate change (van der Linden, Leiserowitz, Rosenthal and Maibach, 2017), undermining the large-scale changes in human behaviour and political decision-making that are needed to mitigate its effects; and erroneous information about vaccines (Broniatowski et al., 2018) and COVID-19 (Brennen, Simon, Howard and Nielsen, 2020), making it more difficult to contain communicable disease. The World Health Organization (2020) has declared a COVID-19 'infodemic' of misinformation to be accompanying the pandemic. Such threats to the integrity of information undermine administrations' capacity to deal with major crises of different forms, which require evidence-based understandings of the problems at hand, trust between partners involved in responding to the crisis, and effective public information campaigns to communicate risk information and advice to the public. If such elements are lacking, a crisis response will be seriously impaired.

Threats to businesses

According to the *State of Cyber Security 2020* report by ISACA and RSA (2020), 53% of the world's businesses expect to be hacked in the year ahead, and attacks are increasing. Since their data collection preceded the COVID-19 pandemic, which led many organizations to favour remote working that shifted business services and resources outside the traditional perimeter, it is expected that future data will reflect a shift in visible attacks. Survey respondents identified social engineering, advanced persistent threats, ransomware and exploitation of unpatched systems as being the most common methods; and cybercriminals as the top threat actors, followed by hackers, malicious insiders, non-malicious insiders, states and hacktivists. In response to the growing threat of states to the business sector as well as to other states (Mueller, 2017), Microsoft has called for a Digital Geneva Convention to establish standards in international law that protect civilian use of the internet, committing governments to avoiding cyber attacks on the private sector or critical infrastructure, or the use of hacking to steal intellectual property (Smith, 2017).

The threat of cyber attack to businesses and charities in the UK is assessed annually by the government in its Cyber Security Breaches Survey (Department for Media, Culture and Sport, 2020). The 2020 survey found that almost half of the UK businesses (46%) and over a quarter of the charities (26%) participating in the research had experienced **cyber security** breaches or attacks in the last 12 months, while three-quarters of the large businesses, and well over half of the high-income charities (57%) were affected. Typically, organizations incurred no specific financial cost from cyber security breaches, since most breaches or attacks did not lead to a loss of assets or data. When losses did occur, the average cost of breaches was modest, at £1560 for charities and £3230 for businesses (£5220 for medium and large firms). However, the total cost of cybercrime to businesses is significant, based not only on the cost of attacks but, more significantly, the costs of the necessary cyber security measures, making it a major threat to states' national and economic security. Button, Shepherd and Blackbourn (2017) estimated that fraud costs the UK private sector £140 billion and charities £2.3 billion annually, with the total annual cost of fraud to the UK assessed to be £190 billion, while Gee and Button (2019) estimate the annual global cost of fraud as being £3.89 trillion.

Misinformation also presents significant reputational risks to the corporate world, since the brand is often an organization's biggest asset, and may be employed by competitors or cyber criminals seeking to gain stock market advantages. In 2013, a hacker posted a bogus tweet by the Associated Press about an explosion at the White House, which led to over £90 billion being temporarily wiped off the US stock market (Foster, 2013). Market manipulation hoaxes may also target specific companies, giving cyber criminals opportunities to profit from short-term share price rises and falls, to which companies are typically alerted after the fact when share prices are already moving (see Mancusi-Ungaro, 2016). A report by the Ponemon Institute (2016) concludes that the threats to companies of online incidents and cyber attacks that fall outside the traditional corporate security perimeter are high, yet the capabilities to mitigate these are low.

Cyber security governance

Cyberspace is a global system, and its governance is difficult because it is without boundaries, accessible to all and fast-changing (Jasper, 2014). Mueller (2017) asserts that the governance of cyberspace can be looked at in two ways: an **internet governance** perspective, concerned with control over internet resources, systems and services through multi-stakeholder institutions, which is primarily civilian in outlook; and a cyber security governance perspective, which views the internet through a national security lens and has military and governmental roots. For those adopting the former, cyber security is just one dimension of governance, contributing to wider goals for commerce, communication, privacy and freedom.

One of the major challenges for individual, state and corporate users of the internet lies in establishing the right balance for each between competing utility, security and privacy goals. Thomas and Loader (2000) argue that the following objectives need to be prioritized in weighing up such considerations: secure electronic commerce, protection of intellectual property rights, data protection for citizens, and safeguarding rights of freedom of expression. Yet market, political and community pressures as well as legal constraints all make this difficult. If threats are high or exaggerated, moral panic may ensue, which is often when individual privacy is most at risk, yet authoritarian governments and unscrupulous commercial vendors of security measures have vested interests in sensationalizing cybercrimes. Technological advancement presents further challenges: AI, for example, can be used for both progressive and malicious purposes. It will offer authoritarians better tools for monitoring dissent, controlling populations, and targeting certain people, and democracy will suffer (Wilner, 2018).

Internet governance encompasses a variety of multi-stakeholder institutions, forums and processes. These include ICANN as described above, which is now a private organization with 178 member states and territories represented on its Governmental Advisory Committee, and 38 Observer Organizations; the International Telecommunications Union, the specialized United Nations (UN) body for information and communications technologies (ICTs), which allocates global radio frequency bands and satellite orbital positions and develops technical standards; and the Internet Governance Forum (IGF), which convenes annual meetings of diverse stakeholders for debates on internet governance policy under the aegis of the UN. Jayawardene, Larik and Jackson (2015) note that, while it is commonly recognized that the rule of law in cyberspace needs strengthening, international legal commitments are rare, since its governance has major implications for states' prosperity, security and political stability. The only international instrument addressing cyber security is the Budapest Convention on Cybercrime of 2001, which serves as an international standard for national legislation against cybercrime and a framework for international cooperation between states.

One of the reasons for states' reluctance to establish international treaties is their differing national priorities: Jayawardene et al. contrast Western nations' particular concern with guarding against copyright infringement and industrial espionage while protecting freedom of expression online, with that of Russia and China, which emphasize their sovereignty in cyberspace, seeking to monitor and control the flow of information within their borders. In 2019, to the disappointment of the US, the UN General Assembly passed a Russia-backed cybercrime resolution titled 'Countering the use of information and communications technologies for criminal purposes', which empowers an expert group to draft terms of reference for a multilateral treaty. Countries' support for internet openness may well have decreased in accordance with an increasing sense of the risks, such as disinformation, spying and global ransomware attacks, coupled with a shift towards more authoritarian regimes (Sherman and Raymond, 2019).

Governmental regulation of the internet thus varies markedly from country to country. The measures available encompass a combination of rules, charges, fines and threat of prosecution. Some governments, such as those of China, Russia and Singapore, impose controls on citizens' internet use via governmental monitoring organizations or state ISPs. Indeed, in 2019 Russia passed a new 'sovereign internet' law that has been described as a 'digital iron curtain', creating a national network that can operate independently from the rest of the world, and can be shut off from external traffic exchange (Ilyushina, Hodge and Gold, 2019). In the West, notes van Eeten, 'the actual policies of states to protect the internet – or perhaps one should say "their internet" are still remarkably hands off' (2017: 430), with national cyber security strategies relying heavily on voluntary action by the private actors operating its networks, systems and services. In democratic countries, the major challenge in the governance of the internet is to mitigate growing vulnerabilities while seeking to balance the needs of different internet stakeholders as effectively and ethically as possible.

Cybersecurity governance is overwhelmingly forward-looking, seeking to minimize the likelihood and impact of harms. The **police** forces that are often relied upon to respond to 'traditional' crimes are poorly equipped to manage cybercrime, due to its often cross-jurisdictional nature, and the fact that such crimes are often too prevalent and too minor to warrant the financial resources needed to investigate them, as discussed in Chapter 5. Kuerbis and Badiei (2017) provide a framework for conceptualizing cyber security governance based on three categories of governance – markets, hierarchies and networks – borrowed from Williamson (1996), an institutional economist. Market-based cybersecurity governance is driven by information and the price mechanism, enforced by law and contract, and including the purchase of security equipment, software and consulting services; and by the legal liabilities held by organizations that publish internet content, such as internet service providers and social media companies. Hierarchical governance structures are those whereby actions are compelled by authorities, and include formal inter-governmental arrangements, national laws and organizational cyber security policies. Networked governance structures are those based on voluntary collaboration. Cyber security regulations and standards may fall into any of these categories. A baseline standard employed across many sectors voluntarily is ISO 27001, a globally recognized framework for information security management good practice (International Standards Organization and the International Electrotechnical Commission, 2013). The Framework for Improving Critical Infrastructure Cybersecurity (National Institute of Standards and Technology, 2014), usually abbreviated to the 'NIST Cybersecurity Framework', was created and ratified by the US Congress in 2014. Aimed at US private-sector owners and operators of critical infrastructure, it is widely used in organizations across the globe. In the European Union, the Security of Network and Information Systems (NIS) Directive requires operators of critical infrastructure services to adopt certain security measures and mandatory breach notifications, and the General Data Protection Regulation focuses on the protection of personal data, both of which were adopted in 2016.

The UK's current national cyber security strategy is based around three objectives, labelled 'Defend', 'Deter' and 'Develop' (HM Government, 2016: 9).

'Defend' is focused on the prevention of threats to UK networks, data and systems and effective responses to incidents, by bolstering the capabilities of citizens, businesses and the public sector. 'Deter' encompasses offensive actions to 'detect, understand, investigate and disrupt hostile action taken against us, pursuing and prosecuting offenders'. 'Develop' is concerned with bolstering cyber security skills in the population and fostering innovation through research and development, to equip the UK to address future threats and challenges. The strategy also encompasses a commitment to 'international action' through collaboration with international partners to enhance the global governance of cybercrime. The government has published an *Initial National Cyber Security Skills Strategy* (HM Government, 2018a) to support the building of the national workforce capability to address future challenges, having created a Cyber Security Body of Knowledge (CYBOK) (www.cybok.org) to define the parameters and scope of cyber security and inform education and training for the sector, and commenced work on the creation of a Cyber Security Council to serve as a professional body. A National Cyber Security Centre (NCSC) was established as part of GCHQ in 2016 as the UK's technical authority for cyber threats, providing information, guidance and support on cyber security to the public and private sectors and the general public, and working collaboratively with other government agencies, international partners, industry and academia.

The national police response to cybercrime in the UK is led by the National Crime Agency's Cyber Crime Unit, working in conjunction with police forces, regional organized crime units and other agencies, including transnational policing organizations such as Europol, Interpol and the Virtual Global Taskforce network against online child sexual abuse. Other stakeholders involved in policing cyberspace include NGOs such as reporting centres the IWF, which also searches for and removes online child abuse content, and NCMEC, which also works directly with affected families, law enforcement and community organizations to help deter child exploitation and recover missing children. Other user groups and individual users police the internet voluntarily, targeting the sharing of child sex abuse images in particular (see Hadjimatheou, 2019).

Summary

The focus of this chapter was the securing of cyberspace, the virtual space that exists within the scope of the internet. The opening discussion on the landscape of cyberspace examined the extent of global internet penetration, demonstrating that significant inequalities between regions remain, and the ways in which the development of the internet and the World Wide Web have profoundly changed and are changing the world. The concept of 4IR was introduced as a framework in which to consider the cumulative societal effects of rapid technological advancement and the possibilities and challenges presented, with significant implications for governance, commerce and the workforce. The chapter also discussed the distinct threats presented by the internet, often categorized as 'cyber-dependent' and 'cyber-enabled' threats, and their impact on individuals, states and corporations; as well as the governance of the internet and of cyber security, which may be regarded as different models for internet regulation (Mueller, 2017). As a dimension of the **global commons**, cyberspace is, as is the case with the oceans (the focus of Chapter 9), very difficult to regulate, requiring the cooperation of multiple stakeholders, often with competing interests. It has been shown to raise fundamental questions about the roles and responsibilities of states, which are reflected in the conflicting internet governance agendas of Western states (in which the internet originated) that value a free and open internet; and Russia, China and other states that seek greater security and sovereign control. Even in the UK, an increasing sense of the risks of cyber attack and disinformation, much of which is perpetrated by other states, is seen to be driving an increased focus on cyber security. However, this remains primarily forward-looking, risk management-based and market-driven, due to the challenges of policing a vast, open, multi-jurisdictional environment. The distinctive feature of cyber security governance for citizens in Western democracies is that, while we count on the state to protect us from serious physical threats, in the virtual environment we are expected largely to look after ourselves.

Study questions

- What are the main opportunities and challenges for society associated with 4IR?
- In what ways do internet technologies help and hinder human security?
- What are the parameters and scope of cyber security as a profession?
- Given the scale of contemporary and future internet-based security threats, to what extent is a free and open internet still desirable?

Further reading

Misunderstanding the Internet (Curran, Fenton and Freedman, 2016) is recommended for a critical appraisal of the development and impact of the internet, while the journal article 'World Wide Web: a survey of its development and possible future trends' (Algosaibi, Albahli and Melton, 2015) gives a thorough and informative overview of the stages of development of web technologies and their anticipated future development. For a review of technological advancements to come, *Artificial Intelligence: A Modern Approach* (Russell and Norvig, 2020) is an extensively cited text, now in its fourth edition, that examines the breadth of the field of AI. On the many ways in which technology is penetrating crime and criminal justice, *The Routledge Handbook of Technology, Crime and Justice* (edited by McGuire and Holt, 2017) is an invaluable compendium. *Cybercrime and Society* (Yar and Steinmetz, 2019), now in its third edition, is one of the most definitive and successful textbooks on the many facets of cybercrime, written from a criminological/sociological perspective and with a useful chapter on policing the internet. For a national security perspective on cyber security, Moran's (2020) chapter in *International Security Studies: Theory and Practice* provides a helpful overview, and research reports from the Royal United Services Institute are informative on two topical national security issues: *The Personal Security of Individuals in British Public Life* (Babuta and Krasodomski-Jones, 2018) on an emerging social media-driven problem for democracies, and *Artificial Intelligence and UK National Security: Policy Considerations* (Babuta, Oswald and Janjeva, 2020) on the potential applications of AI in national security and their ethical implications. *Governing New Frontiers in the Information Age: Toward Cyber Peace* (Shackleford, 2020) is recommended for a comprehensive and up-to-date appraisal of internet and cyber security governance, as well as comparisons with governance challenges and arrangements for the other dimensions of the global commons: the oceans and outer space.

8

Securing corporations

CHAPTER OUTLINE

Chapter overview

This chapter provides:

- An outline of the development of corporate security into a substantial business function.
- A review of the types of security risk that are of most concern to businesses.
- An overview of the key characteristics of security risk mitigation in the corporate sector.
- An examination of the main market sectors making up the commercial security industry supplying security products and services to corporate, governmental and individual clients.

Key terms

- Business continuity management
- Commercial security
- Corporate governance
- Corporate security
- Information security
- Personnel security
- Physical security
- Private security
- Risk

Introduction

Companies on the Fortune Global 500 list, an annual ranking of the world's top 500 corporations, generated $33.3 trillion in revenues and $2.1 trillion in profits in 2019, and employ 69.9 million people worldwide (Fortune, 2020). Corporations are significant political actors, with market structures and corporate strategies governing many aspects of life, shaping trade patterns, labour market practices, consumer identities and environmental impacts (Levy and Newell, 2006). **Critical national infrastructure** (CNI) falls predominantly under private ownership, and technological innovation is primarily driven by private corporations. Corporations need to protect themselves from a range of security risks, with **risk** profiles that vary according to their market sectors. In an intensely corporatized world, corporate security departments have evolved to become significant players in security governance.

Corporate security can be defined as 'security provision that seeks to achieve corporate organizational goals' (Walby and Lippert, 2014: 2). Alternative terms include 'organizational' or 'in-house' security; 'end users', when contrasted with security vendors (**commercial security** services); and 'industrial security' which, as Walby and Lippert observe, tends to reflect sector-specific provisions (e.g. aviation, maritime, or oil and gas). It is largely hidden from public view, with relatively little call for it to be held to account (Gill, 2014). This chapter examines the development of the corporate security sector, the major security threats it faces, and the strategies it employs to mitigate them, including the important role of security partnerships and networks. The final section of the chapter then explores the primary market sectors of the commercial security industry that supplies specialist products and services to corporations and other organizational and individual clients.

The evolution of corporate security

North American research ascribes both the corporate buyers and the sellers of security services a dubious past, focusing on their deployment by US companies between the mid-19th century and the early 20th century to maintain labour discipline prior to the establishment of trade unions, as documented by critical sociologist R.P. Weiss (1978, 2014). This was a period of aggressive industrial expansion and declining informal labour controls, during which commercial security agencies, most famously the Pinkerton National Detective Agency, found that employers were willing to pay for information on employee dishonesty, dissent and organized resistance. The increasingly lucrative market associated with an advancing, under-regulated economy extended to the supply of private armies, after the mining and railroad industries in Pennsylvania, operating in remote and rural locations unprotected by state policing, successfully lobbied for policing powers that could be bestowed by local sheriffs under the Coal and Iron Police Act 1867. Pinkerton's chequered history culminated in the Homestead Riots in 1892, when its guards were hired to challenge an employee siege of the Carnegie Steel Plant, which resulted in 12 deaths.

Weiss (2014) draws on US Senate reports from the late 1930s to note records of over 200 detective agencies engaged in industrial espionage and strikebreaking services by this time, with America's automobile industry making especially heavy use of these. The Ford Motor Company, he observes, were distinctive in employing their own personnel for these purposes, and for employing a level of workforce regulation that extended to all areas of their workers' lives by recruiting thousands of spies from within the company and local community. Walby and Lippert (2015) identified a similar approach to the regulation of employees as having been employed slightly earlier, from 1917 to the early 1920s, within the US Department of War's Plant Protection Service, demonstrating that such practices were not exclusive to the private sector. Private industrial policing went into decline in the US following legislation in 1935 that substantially increased labour rights and, according to Weiss, led to labour discipline functions shifting to conservative trade unions employing the same tactics hitherto used by employers: 'espionage, blacklisting, use of strikebreakers during "outlaw" or "wildcat" strikes, fines, intimidation, red baiting, etc.' (1978: 42). In the case of Ford, however, Weiss (2014) observes that such regulation was enabled in part through a 'partnership' with trade union leadership, and extended to the policing of workers' drinking, sexual and purchasing habits.

More typically, corporate security provisions in the 20th century were relatively hidden, being primarily seen as overhead costs and therefore considered to be of relatively low status in organizational hierarchies, and well removed from board level decision-making (Lippert and Walby, 2014). Dalton (2003) describes this as the 'green shack' era, referring to the lowly position from which security personnel operated and the limited resources available. This was the first of four phases of development that he identifies, reflecting the evolution of corporate security from an operational, to a tactical, and finally to a strategic function in organizations with a well-developed security department. Dalton termed the second the **'physical security'** era, which saw a more direct focus on the protection of assets, with many units coming to be labelled 'loss prevention' departments. His third 'corporate security' phase reflected the emergence of this new label and the expansion of security responsibilities beyond physical security, as they began to feature in wider business plans. Dalton's fourth and final phase, the 'total asset protection era', refers to its further expansion and collaboration with other business units to encompass the protection of assets both tangible and intangible (without physical form, such as reputation or intellectual property), and increased involvement in corporate strategic planning and business development (such as undertaking political and security risk analysis and due diligence to support decision-making on entering new and sometimes unstable markets overseas). A related trend that Dalton notes elsewhere in the book is the gradual emergence of 'chief security officer' roles, beginning just before the terrorist attacks of 11 September 2001 (9/11). More recently, this phase has seen an increasing focus on the 'convergence' of different security-related business functions that have historically been managed separately. Most attention has been given to that of physical and **information security** (Aleem, Wakefield and Button, 2013; Wakefield, 2014), but international research by the ASIS Foundation (Beck, Gips and McFarland Pierce, 2019) suggests that the convergence of either physical security or **cyber security** with **business continuity management** (BCM) – the advance planning and preparation undertaken by organizations to enable them to restore their business functions following disruption – is more commonplace, reported in nearly half of the organizations surveyed.

To these, Walby and Lippert (2014) have added a fifth phase, which they term the era of 'corporate security creep'. This has seen corporate security models and practices for governing conduct, places and information increasingly permeating the public sphere, from central government departments to local authorities, universities and parks, all of which are becoming subject to more and more vigilant monitoring and regulation. This is exemplified in the UK government's Security Policy Framework (Cabinet Office, 2018), the Australian government's Protective Security Policy Framework (Australian Government Attorney-General's Department, 2018), the establishment of the Government Security Profession in UK central government, and associations supporting knowledge exchange in public sector practitioner groups like the Association of University Chief Security Officers and the National Association of Healthcare Security. Walby and Lippert see these developments as being linked to a professionalization trend that they call 'the new security credentialism', evidenced in corporate security executives' increasing pursuit of security qualifications and participation in generalist professional associations like ASIS International, with over 34,000 members globally (ASIS International, 2020), and the UK's Security Institute, with over 3500 members (Security Institute, 2020).

Security risks to corporations

A survey by the Economist Intelligence Unit (2018) of 600 senior executives from around the world asked participants to rank the likelihood and impact of 46 global risks. The results indicated the extent of corporate concern about major security risks – specifically, international terrorism and cyber attacks – alongside a broader range of corporate risks. The top 10 were: (1) retrenchment of globalization/increase in protectionism, (2) oil price shock, (3) asset price collapse, (4) emergence of disruptive business model, (5) international terrorism, (6) unexpected regulatory change, (7) global recession, (8) instability in the Middle East, (9) increased competition from emerging market companies and (10) talent shortages. Cyber security risks were relatively low in the list, but spread across several categories: (29) cyberterrorism, (36) exposure of confidential data and (37) disruption to business from viruses, spyware and malware. Further threats associated with businesses' technological dependence were also ranked, so that, in total, six of the 46 risks were IT-related, extending to (32) power outage, (33) talent/skills shortages in IT and (38) systems failure/downtime of essential IT services.

Corporate security executives are a group among which little research has been conducted, although a survey undertaken in 2006 as part of a study by Briggs and Edwards illustrated the breadth of security concerns in the corporate sector at that time. The top five identified by participants who appeared to be drawn primarily from the UK, the US, South Africa and India were, in order of importance, crime, IT security, fraud, natural disasters and terrorism. The researchers noted that such threats are becoming more complex, with many – such as terrorism, organized crime and information security – being asymmetric and networked, and therefore difficult to manage. An updated picture focused on corporate security executives in North America is provided in an annual survey conducted by Securitas, the 2019 edition identifying threats to internet/intranet networks, active shooter attacks, workplace violence, business continuity threats and threats to mobile technology as the top five concerns, indicating the extent to which cyber security threats have increased in priority, and also the distinct challenges in the region associated with high gun ownership and America's pervasive gun culture. As recognized in a research study by Gill, Owen and Lawson (2010), crimes against organizations are substantially under-reported, making it difficult to estimate the scale of the problem. This section examines security risks to corporations in more detail, covering external threats, internal threats, compliance challenges and crises and disasters.

External threats

Companies face wide–ranging threats from external predators, ranging from traditional thefts and acts of violence to more complex challenges such as the theft or malicious destruction of data, fraud, extortion or terrorism. As the Economist Intelligence Unit (2018) survey indicates, international terrorism has become a significant concern for the corporate world. Although terrorism is not a new problem, the UK having operated in the shadow of the IRA campaign for many years and continuing to face a threat from dissident groups, 9/11 and al-Qaeda/Islamic State-inspired terrorism raised the threat level to corporations. Many of the mass casualty, civilian targets of international terrorism have been corporate assets, including the World Trade Center, major hotels, airlines, concert halls and other crowded places. In the study by Briggs and Edwards (2006: 28), 9/11 was found to have served as 'an important turning point in corporate security' since it 'focused minds, worried staff and made boards ask questions about how their security was being managed'. Almost a third of the corporate security executives in their survey reported having made significant alterations in their approach to corporate security after those attacks. The research noted that for many companies the threat of politically motivated violence and damage extends more widely to groups such as the Animal Liberation Front (ALF), anti-**globalization** groups, and local activist movements in specific locations.

The challenge of **cybercrime** for businesses, introduced in the previous chapter, has grown substantially in recent years. The value of companies' information assets has increased exponentially relative to their physical assets, encompassing the personal data of customers and employees, as well as all types of business information. Historically, information security has been the remit of corporate IT departments, which have protected companies from viruses and hackers through technical safeguards and counter-measures embedded in operating systems and networks. However, it has become an increasingly significant element of the corporate security executive's role as organizations have recognized the need to address their risks more holistically, and 'converged' approaches to security have become more commonplace, as noted above.

The related problem of fraud, including identity, insurance and investment fraud (see Action Fraud, 2020 for a list of its many types), comes at significant financial cost to the corporate sector, as the last chapter showed. Intellectual property fraud, also known as product counterfeiting or piracy, is another significant dimension of the problem for corporations, affecting numerous industries and products, from tobacco, alcohol, food and pharmaceuticals to cosmetics, clothing, electronics and illegal streaming. Counterfeit products are estimated by the UK government's Intellectual Property Office and IP Crime Group 2019 (2019) to account for almost 4% of UK imports (£9.3 billion in value) and £4 billion in lost tax revenue, while the Organisation for Economic Co-operation and Development and European Union Intellectual Property Office (2019) assesses fake goods as accounting for 3.3% of world trade, at a value of $509 billion. Other acquisitive crimes against which businesses must protect themselves include theft, burglary and robbery. The retail sector suffers external losses from theft particularly acutely. Planet Retail RNG (2018) estimated the annual cost of 'shrinkage' to the retail industry in the 14 countries they surveyed to be $99.56 billion, while a survey in 24 countries by The Smart Cube and Ernie Deyle (2015) assessed the cost at $123.39 billion in 2014 to 2015, equivalent to 1.23% of retail sales, with shoplifting accounting for 38% of the losses.

Acts of violence by perpetrators who are usually (but not exclusively) external to the organization can occur in any sector, but are more prevalent in certain industries or areas of work. According to a 2011 survey by the European Agency for Safety and Health at Work, the four areas in which the risk of experiencing both threats and violence is highest are health and education, public administration and defence, transport and communication, and hospitality. Corporations operating in areas of political instability also have to take account of a spectrum of physical risks, ranging from petty criminal activity such as pick pocketing and mugging; to health risks, ranging from problems with the water supply to poor local health care; to serious incidents such as kidnap, extortion, violent crime and terrorist attacks (Briggs, 2003). The COVID pandemic has drawn attention to the risks that some employees may even experience in their homes, as national lockdowns have led to an increase in domestic abuse incidents around the world (Graham-Harrison, Giuffrida, Smith and Ford, 2020). The UK's Safe Lives charity reported that more companies have subsequently been working with them to establish domestic abuse awareness training and resources and implementing measures to protect staff (Topping, 2020).

Internal threats

Most organizations will also experience some level of internal or insider crime, the internal theft of data now being an area of particular concern to employers. A study by the Centre for the Protection of National Infrastructure (2013) identified five main types of insider malfeasance: unauthorized disclosure of sensitive information; process corruption (defined as illegitimately altering an internal process or system to achieve a specific, non-authorized objective); facilitation of third party access to an organization's assets; physical sabotage; and electronic or IT sabotage. The most common by far were found to be unauthorized disclosure of sensitive information (47%) and process corruption (42%). The study identified three types of insider behaviour: deliberate insiders, who obtain employment with the deliberate intent of abusing their access; volunteer/self-initiated insiders, who obtain employment without deliberate intent to abuse their access but at some point personally decide to do so; and exploited/recruited insiders who obtain employment without deliberate intent to abuse their access but at some point are exploited or recruited by a third party to do so.

Physical items that are the subject of internal theft, according to Fischer, Halibozek and Green (2018), encompass company finances and any items that may be useful or have a resale value. They highlight theft of merchandise in transit as being a particular problem, as insiders are able to exploit vulnerabilities such as poor access controls at the loading and departure points, lax control over vehicles and poor or overly complicated administrative systems, often in collusion with others. Research into internal theft has typically been particularly concentrated in the retail sector due to its acute nature in this industry. Retail merchandise needs to be received, stored and moved to display areas on the shop floor, as well as being carefully monitored through effective record-keeping, with each of these operations carrying risks. The Smart Cube and Ernie Deyle (2015) attributed 39% of the losses in their study to employee theft, and 7% to vendor/supplier fraud.

Compliance challenges

The new millennium has seen an increased emphasis on **corporate governance** – how large organizations are directed and controlled – leading to a tightening of compliance regulations relating to money laundering, terrorist financing, bribery and corruption. The research by Briggs and Edwards (2006) identified that convergence between corporate security and corporate governance was taking place as companies became increasingly aware of the relationship between security risks and operating practices. This was seen to have contributed to the widening of the corporate security role and its rising status within the corporation, supporting Dalton's (2003) typology.

After 9/11, anti-money laundering controls expanded internationally to target the financing structures of terrorist networks, for example in the provisions of the USA PATRIOT Act 2001, and in the UK via the Proceeds of Crime Act 2002. In 2010, the UK introduced rigorous anti-bribery legislation in the Bribery Act 2010, finally catching up with the US, which had led the way with the Foreign Corrupt Practices Act of 1977, and reflecting the growing intolerance of corporations that condone such practices. Described by Breslin, Ezickson and Kocoras as 'the toughest anti-corruption legislation in the world' (2010: 362), the Bribery Act created a new, strict liability offence of failure by a commercial organization to prevent payment of bribes by employees or others working on its behalf, requiring companies to be able to show that they have adequate procedures in place to prevent bribery by intermediaries (who may be employed in high risk environments) as well as their own employees. It also increased the maximum jail term for bribery from 7 to 10 years. Companies caught engaging in such practices can suffer significant reputational and financial costs, as well as the prosecution of any individual directors or employees implicated.

The UK is also recognized by the Walk Free Foundation (2019) to be the country doing the most to combat modern slavery. Its Modern Slavery Act 2015 includes provisions to prevent labour exploitation and increase the transparency of labour practices in supply chains. The transparency requirements apply to any commercial organization that conducts business in the UK and has a global annual turnover of £36 million or more, requiring it to produce an annual slavery and human trafficking statement setting out the steps it has taken in the past year to identify and eradicate modern slavery from its business and its supply chain. The Government Commercial Function (2019) identifies numerous risk factors to help companies assess their contracts, including sectors that are labour intensive, workforces that rely on predominantly low or unskilled labour, inadequate labour laws or high levels of poverty or unemployment in the country of origin, and reliance on sub-contracting and complex supply chains.

Crises and disasters

A final area of focus for corporate security departments is unforeseen events that can substantially disrupt business activity. Their causes may be natural (e.g. flooding, pandemic, hurricane or earthquake), man-made (e.g. fire, explosion or accident), or intentional (e.g. terrorism or cyber attack), and major disruptions can have national security implications since states' CNI falls predominantly under private ownership. As Smith (2006) observes, crises that lead to accident investigations or public inquiries have generated extensive information available to researchers to analyse, such as the loss of the space shuttles Challenger (1986) and Colombia (2003), the nuclear accidents at Three Mile Island in the US (1979) and Chernobyl in Ukraine (1986), the gas leak at Bhopal in India (1984), the 9/11 terrorist attacks (2001) and Hurricane Katrina over New Orleans in the US (2005). However, he notes that much of the theoretical development in this area has consequently been based on the experiences of the most extreme events, not more routine types of emergency. A survey by the Chartered Management Institute (2013) identified severe weather conditions as having been the leading cause of disruption to UK businesses for four years in a row up to that time with, for example, only 23% of participants reporting no disruption at all due to snow (p. 4). Adverse weather was the most commonly cited reason for activating BCM procedures (69%), followed by loss of IT (38%) and loss of telecommunications (24%) (p. 13).

In risk, crisis and disaster management the words 'incident', 'emergency', 'crisis' and 'disaster' all describe events that can have disruptive or devastating effects, an incident being an unforeseen event that, if not handled appropriately, can escalate into an emergency, crisis or disaster (Borodzicz, 2005). Former UK Prime Minister Tony Blair placed BCM on the national agenda in the late 1990s, when he called for a concerted approach to confront the much anticipated millennium computer bug, which was mitigated successfully with few major failures globally (Thomas, 2019). By that time BCM was already emerging as a distinct area of professional practice, with the UK-based Business Continuity Institute (BCI) having been established in 1994 and declaring a membership of over 9000 members in over a hundred countries (BCI, 2020). The Civil Contingencies Secretariat (CCS) of the UK government's Cabinet Office now actively promotes BCM across the public and private sectors as part of its Resilience Capabilities Programme to enhance the nation's preparedness for emergencies.

Risk mitigation strategies

As Shearing and Stenning observed in an early article on **private security**, it is characterized by a 'preventative approach to the protection of assets and maximization of profits' (1981: 210), an emphasis that distinguishes its approach from the primary focus of criminal justice scholars on 'past-focused governance processes' (Shearing, 2015: 259), and the practices of the police. Their account of a trip to Disney World provides an extreme example of the difference in approach when applied to the management of a public venue, detailing the ways in which social controls at this famed mass entertainment complex are pervasive, subtle and embedded, so that order 'is a designed in feature' and it 'seems to run like clockwork' (Shearing and Stenning, 1985: 300). Subsequent ethnographic studies by Wakefield (2003) and Button (2006) explored in more detail the controls employed in corporate, quasi-public spaces; management measures that are so successful that they have been imported into competing high street trading environments, as noted in Chapter 5.

The securing of public venues under private control is just one small aspect of corporate security management practice, however, the scope of which has been examined in a number of studies (Nalla, 2001; Nalla and Morash, 2002; Brooks, 2013; Coole, Brooks and Minaar, 2017). Brooks' (2013) 'integrated framework of organisational security' presents its core disciplines as comprising risk management, BCM, technology (IT security as well as electronic systems such as closed circuit television [CCTV], access control and intrusion detection), physical security, **personnel security** and industrial security (industry-specific measures, such as the aviation security requirements of International Civil Aviation Organization legislation). Investigations, law, criminology, facility management, fire and life safety, safety and **intelligence** are listed as ancillary disciplines.

Security risks are just one dimension of an increasingly diverse set of corporate risks that must be seen as part of a wider strategic process and therefore integrated with the wider 'enterprise risk management' of an organization, so that they are considered holistically and addressed through cross-functional partnerships (see Wakefield, 2014). In the new millennium, major financial scandals, including those of Enron, Worldcom and Tyco, prompted new corporate governance regulations and best practices that placed more emphasis on risk management. At the same time, 9/11 led to more priority being afforded to business continuity and crisis management both by corporations and governments, leading to the concept of 'organizational **resilience**' gaining currency in tandem with the rise of resilience thinking in the public sector (see Braes and Brooks, 2011). ISO 31000, an international risk management standard, was first published in 2009 and provides a set of common principles and steps for managing risk irrespective of the risk category, type of organization, its size, or the level or function within the organization at which the process is being applied (International Standards Organization [ISO], 2018), enabling closer alignment between departments when collaborating over risks of common concern. Risks to businesses may fall under the categories of strategic, financial, operational or hazard risk, each of which break down into multiple sub-categories and include physical security, information security, personnel security (insider threats), business continuity, and health and safety risk, some or all of which may fall within the portfolio of a chief security officer (Wakefield, 2014). International and national regulations, standards and guidelines support practitioners in the delivery of these functions, the most prominent standards organization being the ISO, with many security standards being generated by ISO Technical Committee 292 Security and Resilience.

Numerous approaches are employed by corporate security teams to deliver aspects of the corporate security strategy. One that has been applied to the protection of assets for centuries and lies at the heart of corporate security practice is 'defence-in-depth', a strategy for the protective security of people, property and information, based on the idea of employing layered defences through a succession of barriers to restrict penetration and allow time for response and recovery (Smith, 2003; Coole, Corkill and Woodward, 2012). Coole et al. see it as being compatible with routine activity and rational choice criminological theories, as well as **systems theory**, which is concerned with 'the behavior of a system in terms of that of its constituent components and the interrelationships between those components' (Koopmans, 2017: 21). Another commonplace strategy is crime prevention through environmental design (CPTED) (Jeffery, 1971), a multi-disciplinary approach to designing the built environment in order to reduce the incidence and fear of crime and enhance quality of life, which has had significant influence in public policy as well as the corporate sector.

Security networks and partnerships

As with other dimensions of security governance, networks and partnerships are an essential aspect of corporate security. The reliance on the private sector to ensure the resilience of the majority of states' CNI requires the coordination of numerous organizations across the public and private sector, as well as different parts of the economy. This is exemplified in 'black start' scenarios and procedures following a total or partial shutdown of the national energy supply, mentioned in Chapter 4. In the UK, local resilience forums established under the provisions of the Civil Contingencies Act 2004 bring representatives of the corporate sector together with public sector partners to prepare for civil emergencies, while the Department for Homeland Security fulfils such a coordination function in the US. As Rosemont (2015: 286–287) observes, 'the significant variety and new types of public–private cooperation that emerged after 9/11 (and especially after 7/7 [the London terrorist bombings of 2005]) represent nothing short of a major revolution in the way that the Government interacts with non-state actors to implement its security objectives'.

Other forums and organizations allow for advice- and information-sharing, UK examples of the former including the security advice supplied to

UK businesses through the Centre for the Protection of National Infrastructure, the National Cyber Security Centre and the Action Counters Terrorism police initiative, as noted in Chapter 4. Information-sharing is facilitated by bodies like the Overseas Security Advisory Council (OSAC), a joint venture between the US Department of State and American private sector interests overseas, and Cross-sector Safety and Security Communications (CSSC) in the UK, a mechanism for disseminating authoritative and timely security information across the private sector. Security partnerships and networks can also be made up primarily or exclusively of private sector organizations, as in the case of the Business Improvement Districts mentioned in Chapter 5, or through industry bodies and professional associations. Sector-specific information- and intelligence-sharing partnerships are likely to have a minimal public profile, but one body that maintains a website is the Telecommunications United Kingdom Fraud Forum, which brings together members of the UK telecommunications sector to share information and expertise relating to fraud and crime.

In past empirical research I observed the nature and quality of interactions between security teams in three large shopping and/or leisure sites in the UK and their local police forces. Five primary types of activity brought the two sectors together to support each other: 'responding to crimes in progress', 'investigating crime', 'intelligence sharing', 'knowledge sharing' and 'partnership working' primarily for crime prevention purposes. Interactions were found to operate most successfully in cases where individual police officers had invested time in developing good relationships (Wakefield, 2003). A study by Gill, Owen and Lawson (2010) provided a useful insight into broader relations between the corporate security sector and the police in the UK, based on interviews with 43 representatives of police and police-related organizations (including 32 at assistant chief constable level or above) and 25 representatives of the corporate and commercial security sectors, and an online survey of police superintendents. The research uncovered a distinct lack of mutual understanding between the police and business community, the former prioritizing the prevention, detection and prosecution of crime, and the latter treating crime as a risk to be managed to the degree and in the manner that makes most economic sense, even if this allowed a certain amount of crime to be tolerated. The study participants emphasized the need for better quality interactions between the two sectors to enhance understanding and trust, and allow for better sharing of resources and expertise.

The commercial security industry

The commercial security industry is a multi-billion dollar industry serving the needs of corporate, governmental, third sector and individual end-users. The scale and relevance of its global contribution is articulated by Abrahamsen and

Williams (2011: 2), who observe that, 'The routine, commonplace activities of commercial private security belie its importance to contemporary social order, and its expansion is crucial to world politics and the shifting politics of protection across the globe.' The global market for private security services was estimated to be worth $220bn in 2020, and projected to grow to $263bn by 2024 (Freedonia Group, 2020), although a study by ASIS International and the Institute of Finance and Management some years earlier (2013) valued the market significantly more highly, at $350 billion in the US alone. It can be divided into a number of sectors, although these are no longer as distinct as they once were: a growing market for integrated security services and systems has led physical security companies to expand into the digital arena, and vice versa, for example. Many larger vendors in particular are increasingly operating as 'one-stop shops' for a complete package of security services, following a business model that has become commonplace throughout the industry.

Manned guarding companies are the most visible element of the industry. They range from the highly localized through to major global operators, the largest of which are the Anglo-Danish company G4S, with approximately 533,000 employees in 85 countries (G4S, 2020), and the Swedish firm Securitas, employing around 370,000 people in 57 countries (Securitas, 2020). As noted in Chapter 5, research by the *Guardian* newspaper suggests that nearly 19 million frontline security personnel are employed globally (Provost, 2017). Uniformed security personnel are contracted to protect a variety of locations, and they fulfil a wide range of functions, as detailed by Wakefield (2003), Nalla and Wakefield (2014) and Button (2019). Other dimensions of this sector are door supervisors or 'bouncers', the protection of cash and valuables in transit, and close protection (bodyguards) (see Button, 2019).

Frontline private security also extends to armed security services, often termed 'private military and security companies' in academic and policy circles, which play an important role in maintaining security in unstable but strategically important regions of the world (see Abrahamsen and Leander, 2016). The downsizing by many states of their military forces after the end of the Cold War provided extensive opportunity for the private sector to play a role in defence, security, peacekeeping and reconstruction, and fostered the expansion of such services. As Avant (2005: 34) observes, 'global trends demonstrated a mismatch between security concerns and national military institutions', with the rapid growth of armed private security services being driven by the forces of supply and demand. A flood of trained military personnel was suddenly available to meet the needs of several categories of client that she identifies: Western states with newly downsized militaries; countries seeking to upgrade their militaries as a condition of entry into Western institutions; rulers of weak, failed or transitional states; and private firms and NGOs operating overseas. For corporations operating in or seeking to expand into emerging markets, armed private security can form part of an essential portfolio of services to maintain the security of business operations and personnel, and satisfy the insurance requirements associated with risky overseas ventures.

Private investigation is another significant dimension of commercial security, described by Gill and Hart (1997) as ranging in the UK from 'home-based' lone investigators, often with a prior background in the police, to 'high street' sole traders or partnerships, larger 'regional' entities that may have multiple offices, and major 'prestige' companies based in London and supplying services to 'blue chip' companies. Button (2019) reports a more recent trend of professional services companies offering investigative services that complement other areas of their business, including audit firms undertaking fraud investigation and legal firms fulfilling investigative functions rather than contracting with an external provider. The many types of private investigative service that he identifies extend across such areas as criminal defence, industrial espionage, due diligence, asset tracing, person tracing, vetting and matrimonial cases.

A wide-ranging security consultancy sector comprises a vast array of generalist and niche consulting firms, again extending from sole traders operating locally to large firms with a global reach, some of which include consultancy among a broad range of security services. The website of the UK-based Association of Security Consultants (2020) lists nearly 30 areas of service covered by its members, including crisis management planning and response, information security, security systems design, technical counter-surveillance measures and counter-terrorism. As Button (2019) notes, information/cyber security consultancy has become a huge and growing area, bringing many new operatives into commercial security. Very little academic literature has been produced about this sector which, by virtue of the market structure and company characteristics, is difficult to define and measure. Czerniawska (1999) observes of the management consultancy sector as a whole, and O'Reilly (2010) of global security consultancies, that little is known about such companies, since most firms are unlisted and not subject to the financial disclosure requirements applying to public companies, and client confidentiality concerns and operational discretion about the services offered further limit the amount of publicly available information.

The industry also supplies security equipment and software for a considerable range of purposes, with information/cyber security once again representing a newer, significant and still-growing dimension. Button (2019) lists a selection of further areas, including locks, safes, intruder alarms, access control systems, CCTV systems, specialist barriers (e.g. fencing, bollards), unmanned aerial vehicles ('drones') and integrated systems. He also notes the increasing prevalence of security technologies replacing or minimizing human intervention, in line with the advances characterizing the fourth industrial revolution as discussed in the previous chapter, such as automatic number plate recognition or the use of drones for patrols or surveillance.

Summary

This chapter has demonstrated the substantial role played by the private sector in the governance of security, with reference both to organizations' corporate security management arrangements, and the substantial commercial security industry that supplies services to corporations and other client sectors. It discussed the historical development of corporate security departments and the commercial security providers which, in the US, had a dubious past, including involvement in strikebreaking activities in the mid-19th and early 20th centuries, prior to the development of trade unions. Since then, corporate security departments were shown to have evolved in accordance with the developing needs of businesses, from a relatively low position in organizations centred on the provision of security guarding, to a much more significant role in the corporate hierarchy protecting both tangible and intangible assets and more actively involved in corporations' strategic decision-making. As the world enters a more uncertain phase, the range of risks facing corporations will continue to widen, and their capacity to navigate and manage these will be key to competitive advantage.

The major challenges to countries' national resilience, including international terrorism, cyber attack, instability overseas and natural disaster, apply equally to the private sector, Chapter 4 having exemplified how governmental measures to protect against terrorism are now increasingly focused on crowded places and CNI that typically fall under private control. Given the extent of societal dependence on corporations, and the scale of the activity undertaken by organizations to secure their assets, they have become key players in the international security governance complex, and this chapter has provided a number of examples of the security partnerships to which the private sector contributes. The global prevalence and scope of the commercial security industry was also shown to be significant, information and cyber security products and services having been a particular area of growth in recent years, in accordance with the evolving profile of threats to the corporate sector as well as to governments and individuals.

Study questions

- What have been the main driving factors in the development of corporate security?
- How does the corporate sector manage security risk, and how do its objectives and approach differ from those of government and law enforcement?
- Why are networks and partnerships important to the delivery of corporate security?
- In what ways is the commercial security market evolving, and what are the key drivers?

Further reading

The most definitive resource on topics covered in this chapter is *The Handbook of Security* (edited by Gill, 2014) and including contributions from many of the authors cited in this chapter, with a completely revised third edition expected in late 2021. *Corporate Security in the 21st Century* (edited by Walby and Lippert, 2014) is a rare text in an under-researched area, which demystifies much of corporate security practice and explains its development and key parameters. Despite its age, the research report by Briggs and Edwards (2006) for the UK's Demos think tank, *The Business of Resilience*, is illuminative on the strategic delivery of corporate security, drawing on interviews with security executives from several countries, and observations that remain pertinent today. For a more in-depth insight into the principles and techniques underpinning corporate security, *The Rules of Security* by Paul Martin (2019) is an insightful and engaging guide from a Cambridge behavioural scientist turned senior government security practitioner. For perspectives on the day-to-day delivery of corporate security, 'From the panopticon to Disney World: the development of discipline' (Shearing and Stenning, 1985) offers a vivid illustration of many of the distinctive features of corporate social control, and the book based on my PhD, *Selling Security: The Private Policing of Public Space* (Wakefield, 2003), similarly employs an ethnographic approach in documenting corporate security arrangements in the management of public venues, in this case based on three case studies. Finally, on the commercial dimensions of private security, the *Routledge Handbook of Private Security Studies* (Abrahamsen and Leander, 2016) is an invaluable compendium alongside earlier reading recommendations in Chapter 5.

9

Securing the seas

CHAPTER OUTLINE

Chapter overview

This chapter provides:

- An overview of the framework for the governance of the oceans laid out in the 1982 United Nations Convention on the Law of the Sea (UNCLOS).
- An appraisal of the major threats associated with marine and maritime settings, including the construction of migration as a security threat.
- A discussion of the contested concept of 'maritime security', including the advocacy of an expansive definition that encompasses wider human and environmental concerns.
- An examination of the diverse actors and strategies involved in maritime security governance and the importance of multi-stakeholder collaboration, exemplified by the successful efforts to mitigate maritime piracy off the coast of Somalia.

Key terms

- Blue economy
- Border security
- Flag state
- Global commons
- Human security
- Maritime security
- Maritime piracy
- Ocean governance
- Universal jurisdiction

Introduction

Oceans and seas make up 71% of the earth's surface and contain 97% of its water (National Oceanic Atmospheric Administration, 2018b). They provide us with oxygen and food, absorb carbon dioxide, recycle nutrients and regulate the global climate and temperature. More than 80% of the oceans remain unmapped and unexplored (National Oceanic Atmospheric Administration, 2018a), while some parts are very well travelled, serving as the highway to global trade. They support numerous industries, and millions of people depend on what is known as the **'blue economy'** for their income.

The marine environment also presents distinct security challenges. It is multi-jurisdictional and legally complex. The vastness of the oceans makes them difficult to police; a vacuum that criminals are often available to fill.

Conditions at sea can be harsh and unpredictable. This chapter examines the key features of the marine environment as a dimension for security, the distinctive security threats presented, the major actors involved in **maritime security** and the strategies employed to mitigate threats.

The marine environment

The marine environment comprises oceans, seas, bays, estuaries and other bodies of salt water. Around two-thirds of the world's oceans belong to the **'global commons'**, areas and resources beyond sovereign jurisdiction, meaning that they fall outside the protection of governments, and are vulnerable to over-exploitation, pollution and ecological degradation, which undermine vital ecosystems. The focus of this section is the governance of the oceans and the blue economy that is dependent on their sustainability.

The governance of the oceans

The way that humans use the sea and its resources is governed by a complex of institutions, agreements, rules and processes to protect the ocean environment, including 576 bilateral and multilateral agreements (UN Educational, Scientific and Cultural Organization, 2020). **Ocean governance** relates to the high seas and the international seabed area, and rules on the conduct of the ocean are established through international agreements. The United Nations Convention on the Law of the Sea (UNCLOS), adopted in 1982, lays down in a single instrument a comprehensive set of rules governing all uses of the oceans and their resources, and provides a framework for further development of areas of the law of the sea. It balances seafarers' rights of freedom of navigation with states' desire to preserve their sovereign coastal rights (Percy, 2018). The Convention came into force in 1994 and, at the time of writing, had been ratified by 168 parties, including China and Russia but excluding the US, although President Reagan's (1983) *Ocean Policy Statement* had announced the intention of the US generally to follow the Convention's rules. UNCLOS established a number of maritime zones, depicted in Figure 9.1, which each afford different levels of rights and control to coastal states, relating to access to resources, such as fisheries, oil and gas, and the ability to exert security controls to manage forms of cross-border crime.

The zones comprise territorial seas, archipelagic waters, the continental shelf, the contiguous zone, the exclusive economic zone (EEZ), the high seas and the deep seabed. Territorial seas are coastal waters extending up to 12

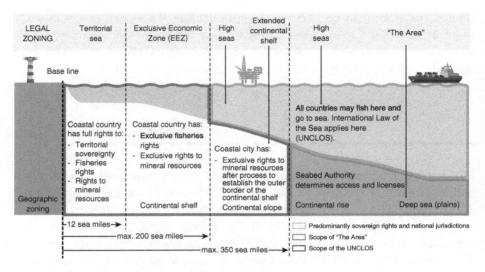

Figure 9.1   Maritime zones and boundaries

nautical miles (22.2 km; 13.8 mi) from the baseline (usually the mean low-water line) of a coastal state. Within these boundaries, coastal states have full sovereignty over the air space above the sea, established in the Convention on International Civil Aviation in 1944, and over the seabed and subsoil. Archipelagic waters are the waters inside and around an archipelago (an island group or chain). The continental shelf of a coastal state is the edge of the continent that lies under the ocean, up to 200 nautical miles from the shoreline or up to the end of the physical shelf, whichever is greater.

The contiguous zone is an area immediately beyond the territorial sea, which may not extend beyond 24 nautical miles from the baseline from which the breadth of the territorial sea is measured. Here, a coastal state has the authority to exercise the control necessary to: '(a) prevent infringement of its customs, fiscal, immigration or sanitary laws and regulations within its territory or territorial sea; (b) punish infringement of the above laws and regulations committed within its territory or territorial sea' (Article 33). The exclusive economic zone is defined in Part V, Article 55 as 'an area beyond and adjacent to the territorial sea, subject to the specific legal regime established in this Part, under which the rights and jurisdiction of the coastal State and the rights and freedoms of other States are governed by the relevant provisions of this Convention'. Such special rights can encompass exploration, exploitation, management and conservation of natural resources and marine research. Kraska (2011) argues that EEZs, comprising 36% of the oceans, 'rich in natural resources, crowded with people, and enmeshed in vessel traffic' (p. 6), are the most important of the zones in international law and politics and where most international disagreements occur. The high seas are open to all States, whether coastal or land-locked (similarly, airspace outside any country's territorial limit is considered to be international). The deep seabed is also deemed to be beyond national jurisdiction and its mineral resources are considered part of the 'common heritage of mankind' (part 11, section 2, Article 136), to be administered for the benefit of mankind as a whole. All mineral exploration and exploitation activities must be sponsored by a state party to UNCLOS and approved by the International Seabed Authority, an autonomous inter-governmental organization (IGO) established under the Convention.

The '**flag state**' (the state under whose laws a vessel is licensed) also serves as a legal jurisdiction on the high seas, applicable both within the confines of the ship, and with respect to criminal acts it may come across at sea, such as piracy or drug trafficking. Ships must sail under the flag of one state only and are subject to its jurisdiction on the high seas. The flag state therefore acts as a regulatory body, in that a ship must meet the standards it lays down in relation to a range of areas such as construction, equipment, seaworthiness, manning, crew training and labour conditions. In reality, however, the use of 'flags of convenience' is prevalent, which refers to the practice of registering a merchant flag under a different state to that of the ship's owners, in order to reduce operating costs by flying under a flag with lower regulatory standards. According to Wing, this 'dysfunctional' system is a product of the prohibition era in the US in the 1920s, as it allowed US vessels to avoid the restrictions on serving alcohol, and it became lucrative for both states and ship owners as a way for businesses to avoid tax, labour and other regulations. She observes, 'Those nations whose open registries have become the most popular also tend to be those who possess the most lax labor, safety, and environmental codes' (2003: 176). Panama, Liberia, the Marshall Islands, Hong Kong and Singapore are named by the shipping news journal *Lloyd's List* (2019) as the largest flag states in 2019 in terms of gross tonnage.

UNCLOS also codifies international law provisions on **universal jurisdiction** in respect of piracy. Universal jurisdiction is a concept that has evolved over centuries and affords to every state jurisdiction over a limited range of offences that are generally recognized as being of universal concern, irrespective of the location of the offence and the nationalities of the offender and victim. According to Article 105 of the Convention,

On the high seas, or in any other place outside the jurisdiction of any State, every State may seize a pirate ship or aircraft, or a ship or aircraft taken by piracy and under the control of pirates, and arrest the persons and seize the property on board. The courts of the State which carried out the seizure may decide upon the penalties to be imposed, and may also determine the action to be taken with regard to the ships, aircraft or property, subject to the rights of third parties acting in good faith. Although its initial focus was piracy, as the scope of international law has broadened, the scope of universal jurisdiction has extended accordingly to include such crimes as genocide, torture and human trafficking (see Macedo, 2004; Archibugi and Pease, 2018).

The body that establishes instruments for implementing UNCLOS provisions is the International Maritime Organization (IMO), a specialized agency of the UN, serving as the global standard-setting authority for the safety, security and environmental performance of international shipping. It was established in the Convention on the International Maritime Organization in 1948 and came into being in 1958. The UK's Ministry of Defence (MoD) (2018) predicts that, while the UNCLOS and IMO are likely to continue to provide the primary governance framework for the seas over the coming decades, it will probably face challenges relating to territorial claims and access to resources as discussed further below. It also anticipates that the IMO will need to modify regulations in response to advances in technology, such as automated shipping and more energy-efficient means of propulsion such as solar power or modern sails.

The blue economy

Also useful to understanding the marine environment and its governance is the concept of the 'blue economy', which reflects the world's dependence on the oceans. It is defined by the World Bank (2020) as the 'sustainable use of ocean resources for economic growth, improved livelihoods and jobs, and ocean ecosystem health', and encompasses established sectors such as fisheries, ports, shipping, shipbuilding and tourism; and emerging industries like deep-sea mining, offshore energy and biotechnology. The term, along with that of 'blue growth', was proposed at the 2012 Rio + 20 UN Conference on Sustainable Development, having been coined by Pauli (2010), and informing the framework for Sustainable Development Goal (SDG) 14, to 'Conserve and sustainably use the oceans, seas and marine resources for sustainable development' (UN General Assembly, 2015). The Organisation for Economic Co-operation and Development (OECD) (2016) estimates that the oceans contributed $1.5 trillion annually to the overall global economy in 2010, and will contribute £3 trillion by 2030, while 31 million people were employed in ocean-based industries in 2010, expected to rise to 40 million by 2030. There is a global economic dependence on secure commercial shipping, offshore oil and gas and port facilities: the IMO (2020a) estimates that over 90% of the world's trade is carried by sea, while the OECD (2019) forecasts that global freight trade will grow by 3.1% annually, leading to a near tripling of maritime trade volumes by 2050. The container shipping industry has revolutionized world trade and access to cheap, consumer goods, and is a thriving industry. Even the world's digital connectivity is dependent on the sea, as over 95% of all intercontinental digital traffic travels through underwater cables rather than satellites (HM Government, 2014b).

The *UK National Strategy for Maritime Security* (HM Government, 2014b) observes the extent of the country's dependence on the global maritime economy. It is an essential aspect of the nation's food security: with 40% of the food consumed by the UK being imported, over 91% of that arrives by sea. The UK's maritime industry is estimated to support one in every 50 jobs and account for over 2% of the economy. It includes a large network of ports and maritime infrastructure, as well as the extensive resources provided by a large coastline, including fisheries and energy. Shipping carries 95% of British trade by volume, with UK ports handling an estimated 393 million tonnes of international cargo and over 4.4 million containers per year, and the value of UK goods imported/exported by sea assessed at over £500 billion/annum. There are said to be around 1500 large commercial ships off the UK coast at any one time, and between 500 and 600 ships using the Dover Strait – the world's busiest shipping lane – every day (Guinness World Records, 2020). Critical energy assets along the UK coastline include much of the civil nuclear power infrastructure, providing around 16% of the UK's electricity, and gas and oil import terminals, while the UK Marine Area is home to around 300 gas and oil rigs, undersea pipelines critical to the delivery of the energy supply, and a growing number of offshore wind farms. As the foreword of the *National Strategy* emphasises, 'Almost every aspect of our national life depends on our connections to the wider world, and most of these connections are provided by the sea' (p. 7).

Maritime security threats

The marine environment presents distinct security challenges. As with **cyber-space**, its vastness and multi-jurisdictional complexity means that it lacks adequate policing, and it is inevitable that such a vacuum will be filled to some extent by criminality. The United Nations General Assembly (2008: para. 39) identified the major areas of maritime security threat as encompassing: direct threats to the territorial integrity of a State, such as an armed attack from a military vessel ... crimes at sea, such as piracy, armed robbery against ships, and terrorist acts ... intentional and unlawful damage to the marine environment, including from illegal dumping and the discharge of pollutants from vessels, and depletion of natural resources, such as from IUU [illegal, unreported and unregulated] fishing. The number of illegal maritime incidents since the mid-1990s is noted by the MoD (2018) to have grown, a trend that it expects to continue over the coming decades, with piracy, smuggling and human trafficking in particular anticipated to remain significant problems. This section considers the challenges of maritime conflict, terrorism, piracy, environmental crime, other forms of maritime crime, as well as migration and its construction as a security issue.

Maritime conflict

The laws of the sea reflect competing interests and priorities. As Percy notes: 'on the one hand, they preserve the right to freedom of navigation, especially on the high seas, while on the other, the creation of EEZs moves to territorialize the oceans' (2018: 610). While states seek to extend their sovereignty over resources in their immediate neighbourhood, all states need to be able to navigate the oceans freely for purposes of trade. States seeking to assert claims over the oceans will inevitably conflict with states seeking freedom of navigation. The territorial dispute in the South China Sea between Brunei, China, Indonesia, Malaysia, the Philippines, Taiwan and Vietnam provides a clear example of such conflict. China is challenging the current demarcation of territorial waters and EEZs, viewing its claim as being vital to its physical and economic security (MoD, 2018). Since islands can allow a state to claim an EEZ, it has built artificial islands in disputed waters on which it continues to construct military and industrial outposts. If its constructions were recognized as islands, it would have access to natural resources on the seabed, and be able to limit freedom of navigation through essential shipping routes. The MoD anticipates that the oceans will become the focus of increasing competition, and possibly conflict, over the coming decades as states compete for resources and influence. Noting that deep sea mining is already technologically feasible, with vast deposits of minerals and precious metals already having been identified, it expects competition to claim the rights to these deposits, and notes new vulnerabilities being created as an increasing number of pipelines and cables are being laid across the seabed. Competition for resources in the Arctic and Antarctic is also expected, particularly as the Arctic sea ice melts and opens up shipping routes.

Maritime terrorism

A widely used definition of 'maritime terrorism' is that of the Council for Security Cooperation in the Asia Pacific Working Group, which refers to 'the undertaking of terrorist acts and activities (1) within the maritime environment, (2) using or against vessels or fixed platforms at sea or in port, or against any one of their passengers or personnel, (3) against coastal facilities or settlements, including tourist resorts, port areas and port towns or cities' (cited in Chalk, 2008). Maritime terrorist attacks have been few in number compared to land-based attacks, however. According to the *RAND Database of Worldwide Terrorism Incidents*, which compiled data from 1968 to 2009, only 10 terrorist attacks between 1977 and 2007 were related to maritime facilities or ships (RAND, 2020). Chalk (2008) relates this to the costs of expanding into the maritime realm and its unpredictability, as well as the fact that maritime targets are out of sight, and less likely to elicit the same publicity as a strike on land-based targets.

Nonetheless, a number of high profile incidents have brought the threat of maritime terrorism to international notice, and demonstrate its potential to have a significant impact on global shipping. In 1985, members of the Palestine Liberation Front hijacked the *MS Achille Lauro* cruise ship, carrying 400 passengers, off the coast of Egypt, killing one passenger. Suicide bombings were employed by al-Qaeda in attacks in 2000 on the US Naval destroyer *USS Cole* while it was harboured and being refuelled in the Yemeni port of Aden, killing 17 US sailors and injuring 39; and in 2002 on the French oil tanker *MV Limburg*, also off Yemen, in which one crew member was killed and over 90,000 barrels of oil were sent pouring into the Gulf of Aden. The most devastating attacks occurred in 2004, when 116 people were killed in the bombing of the passenger ferry *SuperFerry 14* by Philippine Islamist separatists, and in 2008, when terrorists hijacked a boat and landed in Mumbai where they undertook 12 coordinated shooting and bombing attacks over four days, killing 174 people. In 2011, German intelligence uncovered an al-Qaeda plan to highjack a cruise ship and then start killing passengers while demanding the release of prisoners (Robertson, Cruickshank and Lister, 2012).

Chalk (2008) identifies several reasons why the maritime sector may be attractive to terrorist organizations. Many of the vulnerabilities that facilitated the re-emergence of **maritime piracy** as a significant international security threat also apply to terrorism, including minimal coastal surveillance, weak port security, skeleton crews of vessels, the dependence of maritime trade on passage through specific routes where vessels are exposed to attacks, and a profusion of targets. The maritime sports market offers terrorists accessibility to the necessary training and resources for operating at sea. Maritime attacks offer the potential for terrorists to cause significant economic destabilization, given the dependence of the global economy on tightly integrated supply chains that keep costs low by feeding goods to users just before they are needed and in just the right amounts, with little excess capacity in the event of disruption. Finally, passenger ferries and cruise ships offer the opportunity to commit mass casualty attacks that attract significant publicity.

The resurgence of piracy

The historic problem of maritime piracy, which has existed for as long as valuable assets have been transported by sea, and has impacted merchant shipping for centuries, started to become a contemporary concern to the international community in the new millennium. According to the 1958 Geneva Convention on the High Seas (Article 15) and Article 101 of UNCLOS 1982 (Part VII, Article 101):

Piracy consists of any of the following acts:

a. any illegal acts of violence or detention, or any act of depredation, committed for private ends by the crew or the passengers of a private ship or a private aircraft, and directed: (i) on the high seas, against another ship or aircraft, or against persons or property on board such ship or aircraft; (ii) against a ship, aircraft, persons or property in a place outside the jurisdiction of any State;

b. any act of voluntary participation in the operation of a ship or of an aircraft with knowledge of facts making it a pirate ship or aircraft;

c. any act of inciting or of intentionally facilitating an act described in subparagraph (a) or (b).

The key aspects of the definition are that it must be committed on the high seas or in a place outside the jurisdiction of any State; pirates need to use a ship to attack another ship, which excludes mutiny and privateering (private ships in warfare); it needs to be committed for private ends, which excludes the acts of terrorists or environmental activists; and it must be committed from a privately owned vessel, which excludes attacks by naval craft. Given its exclusions, the problem of piracy is often considered in conjunction with that of 'armed robbery against ships', the IMO Assembly (2009, annex, para. 2.2) having clarified:

Armed robbery against ships means any of the following acts:

d. any illegal act of violence or detention or any act of depredation, or threat thereof, other than an act of piracy, committed for private ends and directed against a ship or against persons or property on board such a ship, within a State's internal waters, archipelagic waters and territorial sea;

e. any act of inciting or of intentionally facilitating an act described above.

From 2000 and especially after 2006, piracy off the coast of Somalia and particularly the Gulf of Aden rapidly escalated and became a major threat to commercial shipping, with an estimated 40% of the world's sea trade passing through that region (UN Conference on Trade and Development [UNCTAD], 2014). Central government in Somalia had collapsed in 1991 when the 22-year dictatorship of President Siad Barre was overthrown, leading to the breakdown of law and order. Activities in the 1990s by armed groups that claimed to be protecting Somali waters from illegal fishing absorbed more and more people, with their tactics evolving and levels of violence increasing (Lucas, 2013). Piracy was recognized as an international security concern from 2008, when UN Security Council Resolution 1816 called upon states to increase and coordinate their counter-piracy efforts and send their naval forces into Somali territorial waters for a period of 6 months. It was declared as a threat to the UK in a House of Commons Foreign Affairs Committee (2011) report, which identified the major threat as being to the country's economy, affecting its banking, insurance and shipping industries, and threatening the large volume of goods transported to the UK by sea. The same year it was announced that ships sailing under a British flag would be allowed to carry armed guards (BBC News, 2011).

The problem reached its peak in 2010 (UNCTAD, 2014; Statista, 2019), with the level of piracy off the east coast of Africa beginning to fall as security measures being put in place by shipping companies, governments and IGOs began to take effect. However, it simultaneously began to increase in other regions, particularly off the west coast of Africa and in South China Sea. Oil tankers and offshore energy exploration infrastructure became the main targets in west Africa, a major oil-producing region where forms of oil theft are commonplace, with the aim of capturing and reselling cargo (UNCTAD, 2014). The IMO (2020b) reports that in 2019, 193 piracy and armed robbery at sea incidents were reported worldwide in 2019, marking a drop from 223 incidents in 2018, and the areas most affected were West Africa (67 incidents), the Straits of Malacca and Singapore (45 incidents) and the South China Sea (34 incidents), followed by the South America Pacific region (14 incidents), the South America Caribbean region (12 incidents), and the Indian Ocean (10 incidents). Looking ahead to the coming decades, the MoD (2018) highlights the risk that climate change, including flooding and storm damage, as well as disruption to fisheries, will destabilize some coastal communities in developing countries, potentially leading to an increase in piracy and associated disruption to trade routes.

Environmental crime

The UN General Assembly (2008) identified 'intentional and unlawful damage to the marine environment' as a significant maritime security threat to states, particularly coastal states, including loss of marine habitats, loss of species and reduced fish catch, coral bleaching and decreased biodiversity. Such offences are reported to directly impact the social and economic interests of coastal states; lead to direct conflict or exacerbate other causes of conflict, such as poverty, migration, infectious diseases, poor governance and declining economic productivity; and often have a link to organized crime. Interpol (2018) undertook its first global multi-agency operation against marine pollution crime throughout the month of October 2018, codenamed '30 Days at Sea', during which 276 law enforcement and environmental agencies across 58 countries detected more than 500 offences, including illegal discharges of oil and refuse from vessels, shipbreaking, breaches of ship emissions regulations, and river and sea pollution.

Other forms of maritime crime

The broad category of maritime crime encompasses crimes against maritime and marine assets, as well as the exploitation of the maritime environment to commit crimes. Crimes still to be mentioned include numerous forms of trafficking, including that of human beings, drugs, firearms, money, cigarettes, counterfeit goods or other contraband, as well as theft of or from craft, cyber attack, robbery, illegal fishing and illegal exploitation of the seabed. Many of these are interlinked, as vessels used in illegal fishing can also be used for piracy and smuggling, and smuggling routes can be repurposed to carry different illegal goods (Percy, 2016, 2018). They may also pose a more direct threat to states, as effective ways of smuggling weapons or insurgents, or an indirect threat if the proceeds of crime are channelled towards insurgency or terrorism. Another significant dimension of crime at sea is cruise ship crime which, although thought to be infrequent, raises challenges for victims who often lack the level of access to law enforcement and emergency services, as well as avenues for recourse, that they would receive at home (US Senate Committee on Commerce, Science, and Transportation, 2013; Klein, 2016).

Percy (2018) notes that many of the longstanding rules of the sea were created to control a very different world, making crime on the high seas difficult to police and facilitating many types of maritime crime. Particular challenges for law enforcement are the restrictions on the right to board vessels on which crime is suspected without the owner's permissions when on the high seas, except when slavery, piracy or illegal broadcasting is suspected; and those associated with the system of flags of convenience, with some registries located in states with poor standards of administration, and others located in another jurisdiction entirely, as in the case of the Marshall Islands and Liberian registries which are based in the state of Virginia in the US. In addition, ownership of vessels is often hidden through complicated shell company arrangements, and suspected criminal vessels are often able to escape before an owner can be found. A newer challenge to the maritime sector as it relies increasingly on digital technology is that of cyber attack. In 2018, for example, the 'NotPetya' virus infected computers right across the network of the shipping conglomerate Maersk, causing estimated damage of $300m (Graham, 2018).

Irregular migration

A significant **human security** issue both in and beyond the maritime sphere relates to irregular migration, reflecting the considerable risks that individuals are prepared to take to reach their destinations, and the prevalence of people smugglers willing to capitalize on their desperation. Since the end of the Cold War, migration has been increasingly constructed in politics and the media as a danger to cultural identity, economic stability and national security, and one of the most significant new security issues of the 'new world order' (see Wæver, Buzan, Kelstrup and Lemaitre, 1993; Bigo, 2002).

The increased border fortifications that have resulted in many countries are adding to the precariousness of the journeys. The International Organization for Migration (IOM) (2020) has recorded the deaths of 34,532 people on migration routes worldwide since 2014 through its Missing Migrants Project, and Weber and Pickering (2011: 1) estimate that for every recovered body there are two additional deaths.

In 2015 to 2016, Europe experienced the biggest influx of migrants and refugees since the Second World War. Approximately one million people arrived in Europe in 2015, according to estimates by the UN High Commissioner for Refugees (UNHCR) and the IOM (2015), most having crossed the Mediterranean Sea. Their data suggest that half of those crossing the Mediterranean were Syrians escaping the war in their country, while Afghans accounted for 20% and Iraqis for 7%. The number of people displaced by war and conflict was the highest seen in Europe since the 1990s, following conflicts in the former Yugoslavia. The number crossing the Mediterranean dropped to about 362,000 in 2016, falling sharply after a deal between the European Union (EU) and Turkey, new border fences in the Balkans, and a 2017 bilateral arrangement between Italy and Libya, but tens of thousands of people are still trying to reach Europe. Since the start of 2017, over 2700 people are believed to have died or gone missing while crossing the Mediterranean to reach Europe (UNHCR, 2019).

More recently, the UK has experienced a growing number of migrants attempting to travel by small boat from France across the Dover Strait, the narrowest part of the English Channel and an expedition so treacherous that police have likened it to trying to 'cross the M25 at rush-hour on foot' (BBC News, 2018). Up to 4343 people were thought to have attempted the journey between January and August 2020, thought to be due to the suspension of the UK's refugee resettlement arrangements and the disruption of clandestine travel routes due to the COVID-19 pandemic (Edwards and Edmunds, 2020; see also Timberlake, 2020). The nature and impact of border fortifications as a dimension of maritime security are discussed further below.

Maritime security governance

Maritime security is a field that has developed in accordance with threats to the maritime and marine environments, as these have gained recognition on the international stage. Transnational criminal activity presents a common challenge to states and has become a growing area of collaboration in the maritime domain, as in the case of Interpol's '30 Days at Sea' operation described above. States are increasingly recognizing and responding to the devastating effects of environmental crimes like illegal fishing and marine pollution.

The priority being attached to maritime security in the new millennium is evident in the governmental and inter-governmental strategies that have been developed, such as those of the US (US Government, 2005), the North Atlantic Treaty Organization (NATO) (2011), African Union (2012), UK (HM Government, 2014b), EU (Council of the European Union, 2014), France (Premier Ministre de la République Française, 2015), and India (Indian Navy, 2015), collective statements such as the G7 declaration on maritime security, and as a major theme of the annual Our Ocean international conference, established in 2014 under the leadership of then US Secretary of State John Kerry and first held in Washington, DC (Bueger and Edmunds, 2017).

The complexity of the maritime realm favours multi-agency responses to maritime threats. A vessel being used for people smuggling originates in one state, crosses territorial waters into an EEZ and onto the high seas, and then into the territorial waters of the destination state, with different rules governing how the matter can be addressed in the different zones. This section examines some of the key dimensions of maritime security, considering its definition and scope, as well as looking in more detail at responses to piracy as an example of the inter-governmental and multi-agency nature of maritime security, the fortification of borders in response to transnational crime and the securitization of migration, and maritime security in the UK.

The scope of maritime security

'Maritime security' is a fairly new concept, reported by Bueger and Edmunds (2017) to have initially been coined in the 1990s, and gained growing attention since 2000 due to heightened concerns over maritime terrorism, the rise of modern piracy, the prevalence of maritime crimes such as people smuggling and human trafficking, and increased international recognition of the importance of a sustainable blue economy. The term is difficult to define, because it can be applied to a wide range of actors and activities. Just as the concept of 'security' is contested, 'maritime security' can also mean different things to different people.

The UK government defines it in relation to its contribution to the country's national security, as 'The advancement and protection of the UK's national interests, at home and abroad, through the active management of risks and opportunities in and from the maritime domain, in order to strengthen and extend the UK's prosperity, security and resilience and to help shape a stable world' (HM Government, 2014: 14). For some, it is about the 'stable order of the oceans' (Kraska and Pedrozo, 2013: 1) or 'good order at sea', such as safe sea routes, safe access to resources, and dominium and jurisdiction (Vreÿ, 2013: 1). Germond employs a simple, practical definition that refers to the 'set of policies, regulations, measures and operations to secure the maritime domain'

(2015: 137). More expansive interpretations take account of the dimensions requiring protection and the threats being protected against, Klein's (2011: 1) interpretation referring to 'the protection of a state's land and maritime territory, infrastructure, economy, environment, and society from certain harmful acts occurring at sea', including 'piracy, terrorism, illicit trafficking in drugs and weapons, people smuggling, illegal fishing, and intentional and unlawful environmental damage'.

Bueger (2015) adopts the broadest approach of all, employing a matrix as depicted in Figure 9.2 to encompass four inter-connected domains of maritime security: the marine environment (with a focus on marine safety), economic development (with a focus on the blue economy), national security (with a focus on sea power) and human security (with a focus on **resilience**). Different maritime security issues such as climate change, accidents, pollution, smuggling, piracy, human trafficking, IUU fishing, inter-state disputes, arms proliferation and terrorist acts are then placed at appropriate points on the matrix. He argues that the meaning of maritime security relates to its relationship to the other terms in the matrix, and the relationships of those terms with each other, so that they form a web of relations. For example, dimensions of the blue economy, such as food security and the resilience of coastal populations, are prerequisites of human security, while conventional security threats can arise when there is an absence of human security, requiring the mobilization of sea power.

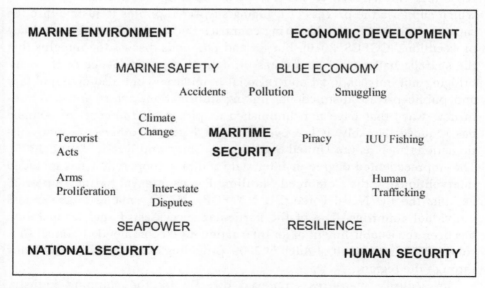

Figure 9.2 Bueger's maritime security matrix

Source: Bueger, C. (2015) 'What is maritime security?' *Marine Policy*, 53: 159-164.

In a subsequent paper, Bueger identifies four distinguishing characteristics of the maritime security agenda. These are the interconnected and sometimes interdependent nature of the challenges; their liminality, in that most are not problems of the marine environment alone, and are usually linked with challenges on land; their transnational nature, often transcending the boundaries of governmental responsibility; and a cross-jurisdictional, or at least jurisdictionally complex, character (Bueger and Edmunds, 2017). His matrix provides a useful framework that takes account of these complexities and the competing agendas associated with them, and recognizes the broad scope of contemporary security governance.

Responses to piracy and armed robbery at sea

Piracy offers a case example of these four characteristics and, as a result, the many stakeholders playing a role in maritime security. The emergence of piracy in the Gulf of Aden and surrounding region led to action by the UN Security Council action and prompted new collaborative interventions by navies and other stakeholders. One example of this is the Contact Group on Piracy off the Coast of Somalia (CGPCS), which was initially set up by the participating nations, and later expanded to include non-state organizations. Established in 2009, its activities include a bi-annual plenary attended by representatives of over 60 states, as well as representatives from navies, IGOs and NGOs, such as the UN Office on Drugs and Crime (UNODC), which supports the process of bringing suspected pirates to justice through capacity building in neighbouring countries that agree to undertake piracy prosecutions (CGPCS, 2019). Bueger and Edmunds discuss the impetus that the shared challenge of piracy has brought to the governance of the seas, bridging not only national and regional boundaries, but also civil–military and public–private distinctions, linking information, actors and activities in new ways that have not diminished as piracy off the coast of Somalia has reduced. Notably, it has even brought together 'otherwise antagonistic nations such as the United States, Iran, China and Russia' (2017: 1305). The unprecedented degree of inter-state military cooperation has included interventions by the Combined Maritime Forces, a naval partnership of 33 nations; the EU Naval Force (EU NAVFOR), NATO, smaller alliances and individual countries. One of the particular successes of such cooperation has been the establishment of an Internationally Recommended Transit Corridor (IRTC) in the Gulf of Aden in 2009, providing escorts to ships travelling through the region.

The security measures employed directly by the shipping industry developed rapidly as the challenge of piracy grew. International legislation requiring merchant ships and ports to be certified to a certain security standard was already in place, in the form of the International Ship and Port Security (ISPS) Code, which had been part of a new chapter inserted into the 1974 Safety of Life at Sea Convention in response to the attacks of 11 September 2001 (9/11), setting out mandatory obligations for contracting states, ship-owning companies and port facility administrations. The industry is further governed by the policy conditions of shipping insurance, as well as other forms of insurance such as kidnap and ransom ('K&R') insurance. Shipping good practice is laid out in a series of industry Best Management Practices publications, to which associations of ship owners such as BIMCO (the Baltic and International Maritime Council) are signatories, including *BMP 5: Best Management Practices to Deter Piracy and Enhance Maritime Security in the Red Sea, Gulf of Aden, Indian Ocean and Arabian Sea* (BIMCO, International Chamber of Shipping, International Group of P&I Clubs, INTERTANKO and Oil Companies International Marine Forum, 2018). The International Maritime Bureau (IMB), part of the International Chamber of Commerce which represents the business internationally (e.g. as a consultative body to the UN), provides an international Piracy Reporting Centre (www.icc-ccs.org/piracy-reporting-centre). Established in 1992 and employing the UNCLOS definition of piracy, it provides a single point of contact for shipmasters to report piracy, armed robbery or stowaway incidents; relays information to local law enforcement and other vessels in the same region, and monitors incident trends, which are depicted in its Live Piracy Map. The range of counter measures that shipmasters may have at their disposal include X-band radar (for early detection of hostile vessels), increased speed (although some vessels such as oil tankers cannot reach high speeds), armed guards on ships, and citadels/strongholds, which are secure spaces equipped with emergency supplies and means for communication with the outside world.

Alongside military, security and criminal justice measures, various international missions have been established to help address the root causes of piracy in Somalia, and continued to gain momentum after the decline in piracy incidents (Bueger and Edmunds, 2017). The UN Development Programme (UNDP) has delivered development projects in Somalia since 1991. The UN Political Office for Somalia (UNPOS), which ran from 1995 to 2013, and its successor, the UN Assistance Mission in Somalia (UNSOM), have assisted with peace and reconciliation in the region. The African Union Military Observer Mission in Somalia (AMISOM) has run since 2007, mandated by the UN Security Council to deploy a peacekeeping operation to support Somalia's long-term stabilization and post-conflict restoration. The UNODC Regional Programme Promoting the Rule of Law and Human Security in East Africa was established in 2009, tasked with responding to evolving security threats and promoting the rule of law and human security in 13 countries, including Somalia.

The fortification of borders

On the matter of international border control, Franko (2020) observes that global mobility is not a privilege that all enjoy equally. The well-off are able to enjoy frictionless movement, corporate international travellers inhabiting 'a world of safety that extends across national boundaries and that links secure enclaves', while tour operators like Club Med have established a successful business model that extends the safety and luxury of the developed world into the 'undeveloped' world (Johnston and Shearing, 2003: 9). Franko cites Klein's (2003) concept of 'fortress continents' to describe the way in which blocs of the richer nations are hardening their external borders while liberalizing internal migration at the same time, in order to increase access to cheap labour, as in the case of the North American Free Trade Agreement between the US, Canada and Mexico from 1994, and the policies of the EU.

The facilitation of free movement within the EU Schengen Area from 1995, and its expansion from 2004 to include countries of Central and Eastern Europe (plus Malta and Cyprus), were introduced in conjunction with the fortification of external border controls: the creation of Frontex, the European agency for cooperation at the external border, to coordinate border control efforts; the extension of visa requirements to a much longer list of countries; and the strengthening of judicial and security cooperation. Migrants and refugees travelling to Europe by sea have also been intercepted and forced back to the ports of departure by the authorities of the Mediterranean countries they were attempting to reach. In the US, since the inauguration of US President Donald Trump, who made illegal immigration and an 'America First' approach to policy-making central planks of his 2016 election campaign, the country has tightened its borders, including those with its immediate neighbours, embarking on the construction of a substantial barrier at the US–Mexican border, and heavily restricting the issuing of visas to travellers from 13 predominantly Muslim countries (Kanno-Youngs, 2020).

The attacks of 9/11 provided the catalyst for the securitization of migration and migrants by many states. In the UK, the Home Office (2002) swiftly released a white paper on migration and border control which outlined a high-tech, integrated and flexible approach to the UK border. Subsequent terrorist attacks at home and overseas in the new millennium gave further impetus to such controls. Vaughan-Williams (2010) identified three key characteristics of the UK's vision for **border security** at the time of writing, under the leadership of then Prime Minister Gordon Brown: the 'offshoring' of the border outside UK territory, the employment of technologically advanced forms of identity management, and a pre-emptive approach based on risk profiling. He observed, 'Today borders are not only territorially defined sites of control but also complex assemblages that are increasingly offshored, decentred, diffused and as mobile as the people, services, and goods they seek to control', facilitated by a host of new technologies (p. 1082). The subsequent government placed more emphasis on migration management, and in 2012 then UK Home Secretary Theresa May told the *Telegraph* that her aim was 'to create here in Britain a really hostile environment for illegal migration' (Kirkup and Winnett, 2012). What became widely labelled as the UK government's 'hostile environment policy' (House of Commons Home Affairs Committee, 2018a; Taylor, 2018) peaked with the Windrush scandal in 2018 when, as Prime Minister, May was forced to apologise to the leaders of 12 Caribbean nations for the wrongful deportation of at least 83 British subjects who were born in Caribbean countries of the British Commonwealth and arrived in the UK before 1973, when new controls under the Immigration Act 1971 came into force (see Williams, 2020).

The term 'militarization' refers to the process of becoming ready for war, conflict and violence, but is now also commonly used to describe the mechanisms increasingly being employed at the borders of countries in the **Global North**, including enhanced physical barriers, increased security budgets and staffing, and technologies such as unmanned aerial vehicles ('drones'), motion and heat sensors, and smart border solutions. Jones and Johnson (2016) see such measures as being linked to the dehumanization of migrant 'others' and increasing numbers of deaths at borders, including 28 shootings by US Border Patrol agents between 2010 and 2014 attributed to agents behaving like paramilitaries. They argue that, while officials point to instances when their actions have saved migrants stranded at sea, or crossing desert with insufficient water, the militarization of borders is making journeys riskier, and the accompanying ethos of border agents leading to increased violence at the border. As the global population continues to grow, the extent of mass migration will only increase, and Global North countries will need to give more attention to the factors driving people from their home countries if they are to be more successful at managing the volume of travellers (Raadschelders, Larrison and Thapar, 2019).

Summary

This chapter has demonstrated how, as a dimension of the global commons, the marine environment is highly complex and challenging, involving multiple jurisdictions, multiple stakeholders, and multiple security actors facing a diverse and evolving range of security challenges. Its scale is such that more than 80% of the oceans remain unmapped and unexplored, and around two-thirds fall outside sovereign jurisdiction. As is the case with cyberspace, the oceans are extremely difficult to police, creating ample opportunity for criminality to thrive. The major threats to maritime security as detailed in this chapter encompass conflict, terrorism, multiple forms of organized crime, piracy, human security challenges, and environmental crimes, with disputes over territories and resources being a key area of future unpredictability. Maritime security has been shown to be equally multifaceted, the problem of piracy providing an illustration of the variety of agendas and actors. One of the success stories of maritime security has been the effectiveness of multi-sector, multi-agency collaboration, which has been particularly successful with respect to piracy off the coast of Somalia. The fortification and militarization of borders has been one of the most negative aspects, as regional instability and strife leads increasing numbers of people to seek better lives elsewhere, drawing attention to the stark inequalities of a world that the most privileged are allowed to traverse with little restriction. It also illustrates the limitations of maritime security solutions to problems that originate on land.

Study questions

- Is the UNCLOS system of maritime governance fit for purpose?
- To what extent should migration be regarded as a security threat?
- What should be the main objective of maritime security?
- What are the main challenges for maritime security stakeholders in combating major crimes at sea?

Further reading

The articles 'What is maritime security?' (Bueger, 2015) and 'Beyond seablindness: a new agenda for maritime security studies' (Bueger and Edmunds, 2017) together present an expansive, holistic perspective on maritime security that embraces human security, environmental and economic considerations as well as more traditional defence, piracy, terrorism and crime concerns, and the range of organized responses to them. The latter features in *Maritime Security and the Law of the Sea: Help or Hindrance?* (edited by Evans and Galani, 2020), which examines a range of topical maritime issues. *Global Responses to Maritime Violence: Cooperation and Collective Action* (edited by Shemella, 2016) provides a useful collection of papers on forms of maritime violence, particularly terrorism, piracy and robbery, as well as the dimensions of international responses to them, such as maritime governance structures, legal frameworks, anti-piracy initiatives in different regions, and port security. *The Routledge Handbook on Crime and International Migration* (Pickering and Ham, 2014) is a valuable compendium on the securitization of immigration and borders, and the blog of the Border Criminologies research network at Oxford University is recommended for up-to-date original research and first-hand accounts of border control (www.law.ox.ac.uk/research-subject-groups/centre-criminology/centreborder-criminologies/blog).

10

Conclusion: Building a resilient future

CHAPTER OUTLINE

Chapter overview

This chapter provides:

- A discussion of the implications presented by some of the book's recurrent themes for scholarship and practice.
- An introduction to complexity theory and related ideas and concepts, and their application across multiple disciplines.
- An overview of approaches being put forward to facilitate the governance of complexity.
- Reflections on the adaptations that the criminology discipline needs to make in order to adapt to a more complex, more security-focused world.

Key terms

- Complexity theory
- Resilience
- Risk
- Security
- Security governance
- Systems theory
- Wicked problem

Introduction

Security is essential to the functioning of any society. It is not only about the protection of a country's citizens, but also its assets, its infrastructure and services, its political stability and its economy and prosperity. To deliver security, it is necessary to understand the nature and causes of insecurity; develop means to predict, prevent and manage the **risk**s and threats; and ensure that appropriate legal and governance structures are in place to balance security goals with civil liberties, **human rights** and ethical considerations. Conceptions of security vary enormously, however, from the objective to the subjective, the narrow to the broad (in terms of the range of concerns deemed to fall under the security umbrella), and the shallow to the deep (from the state-centred to the human-centred). Most applications of the concept focus on deliberate physical threats, yet the UK and US government's strategic **intelligence** forecasts (Ministry of Defence, 2018; National Intelligence Council, 2017) that were used to set the scene for the book emphasize that politicians, policy-makers and practitioners concerned with security cannot ignore wider human security concerns.

This book has explored the political, economic and other influences and transformations that have shaped and continue to shape our world, and the implications of these for security across a range of dimensions. Recognizing the bewildering array of issues that can be associated with the subject of security, its aims were to present a holistic framework in which to consider a diversity of security challenges, actors and strategies, drawing on a variety of disciplinary perspectives. The framework employed has adopted a 'wide' and 'deep' interpretation of security, as defined in Chapter 2, across dimensions ranging from the international to the personal, exploring their distinctive challenges and mitigation strategies as well as highlighting many common threads and interconnections. The task of this concluding chapter is to consider the implications associated with some of the book's recurrent themes for scholarship and practice, and it takes complexity as its main theme, revisiting the overarching challenges presented by a complex world, the analytical frameworks being developed to address them, and the ways in which **security governance** structures must continue to evolve to mitigate complexity. It concludes with some brief reflections on the adaptations that the criminological discipline needs to make to contribute most effectively to the search for solutions.

Theorizing complexity

The breadth of security challenges facing the world today is formidable, and global risks and threats are becoming more complex and difficult to predict. Since the 1990s, there has been increasing interest within the social sciences in importing concepts and approaches from the natural sciences relating to the study of complex systems, often collectively referred to as '**complexity theory**', as a means of understanding and helping to address complex problems. Some prefer the terms 'complexity science' or 'complexity research' on the basis that there is no single identifiable complexity theory (Kavalski, 2007). It can be regarded as a subset of **systems theory** (defined in Chapter 8), and is a similarly interdisciplinary endeavour that grew out of the study of the mathematical properties of 'non-linear dynamical systems'. In such systems, changes in the outputs are not necessarily proportionate to inputs, so that small influences can have large effects. This is captured in the well-known metaphor of the 'butterfly effect' after Lorenz (1972), a meteorologist, suggested that the mere flap of a butterfly's wings could ultimately set off a tornado. A 'complex adaptive system' (CAS) is a type of non-linear dynamical system, and can be defined as a system 'whose component parts interact with sufficient intricacy that they cannot be predicted by standard linear equations'; rather, 'so many variables are at work in the system that its overall behavior can only be understood as an emergent consequence of the holistic sum of all the myriad behaviors embedded within' (Levy, 1993: 34). Examples include immune systems, traffic systems, ecosystems, weather systems and economies.

Complexity has been a recurring theme across academic disciplines even where it is not explicitly mentioned by the authors, as Urry (2005) illustrates with a number of prominent examples by analysts of modernity and globalization. These include Harvey's (1989) idea of 'time–space compression' through the myriad ways in which humans have minimized spatial distances and barriers to the movement of information, people, goods and services; Beck's (1992: 23) metaphor of a 'boomerang effect', whereby 'risks of modernization sooner or later strike those who produce or profit from them'; Castells' (1996) conception of a globalized, self-organizing and adaptable 'network society', facilitated by a vast information and communications technology infrastructure; Giddens' (1999) notion of a 'runaway world'; and Bauman's (2000) theory of a rapidly changing 'liquid modernity' now replacing the preceding 'solid' and stable modernity characterized by industrial production. Declaring that the social sciences' established models and frameworks are ill equipped for analysing a contemporary social order that is more defined by networks and flows than territorial boundaries and states, while its methodologies are not well suited to the realities of global complexity, Urry (2005) argues that complexity theory offers a framework for making sense of globalization and its impact, and advocates for its wider application in the social sciences.

Echoing Urry's assertions more than a decade later, Turner and Baker (2019) bemoan the fact that complexity theory has still not yet reached many disciplines within the social sciences. To date, criminological engagement has been limited, a rare exception being an edited collection by Pycroft and Bartollas (2014) showing how it can be applied to challenges of crime and criminal justice at a variety of levels: the criminal justice system as a whole, criminal justice organizations, the delivery of specific services and even its individual clients, as well as the analysis of specific social problems that have a relationship with crime. For example, outputs from a probation or social work decision or intervention may not be proportionate to inputs and are impossible to predict, given the non-linear dynamics of the interactions and the potential variables at play within each scenario (see also Fish and Hardy, 2015). Pycroft and Bartollas argue that complexity theory can inform the development of new, innovative approaches that move beyond heavily engineered solutions on the one hand, and *laissez-faire* approaches on the other.

The perspective has gained more traction in the international relations discipline, while still remaining fairly marginal. Rosenau is credited by Bousquet and Curtis (2011) as being the pioneer of complexity thinking in international relations with his book *Turbulence in World Politics* (1990) and subsequent publications (e.g. Rosenau, 1995, 2003). Writing just before the end of the Cold War, he argued that, as profound changes were taking place on a global scale, social scientists lacked the capacity to analyse their dynamics and consequences, possibly due to the 'extraordinary pace and complexity of present-day turbulence, with events moving so swiftly that we have not had time to update our analytic equipment' as well as 'a tendency to cling to old analytic habits' (p. 22). Such habits were also seen to have a Western/**Global North** bias. The book's central concept of 'turbulence', employed as a metaphor for global life, is seen to be characterized by high complexity and high dynamism, and its study to involve the analysis of 'responses to uncertainty, to the changes wrought by technology and an ever-expanding global interdependence' (p.12). Rosenau argues that the question as to how it can be analysed in an **international relations** context can be addressed by looking at disciplines in which turbulence is already a significant analytic tool, such as physics. Surveys of complexity research within international relations (e.g. Kavalski, 2007; Bousquet and Curtis, 2011; Lehmann, 2012; Orsini et al., 2019) show that it now constitutes a substantial body of literature. Yet, despite being heralded by one influential proponent as 'the greatest opportunity for creative change in the IR paradigm' (Comfort, 2000: 289) and gaining increasing recognition in the discipline, it remains under-represented and in its infancy, which Chandler (2019) asserts may be because it offers little by way of tangible policy prescriptions beyond advocating caution, humility and lowered expectations of policy successes.

Many of the analytic features of complexity feature in other areas of scholarship. A concept that is often applied in conjunction with complexity theory is that of '**wicked problems**', in which there is no clear relationship between cause and effect and no linear solution. Invented by Rittel and Webber (1973) to describe challenges in urban planning that were difficult or impossible to solve, it has influenced research in a range of disciplines. For Rittel and Webber, wicked problems are multi-causal and connected to other problems of which they may themselves be a symptom, and have multiple explanations: crime, for example, may be attributed to moral decay, opportunity or poverty, and may be explained by inadequate laws, not enough **police** or relative deprivation. They also have multiple solutions, each of which must be sophisticated and adaptable: every attempted solution has consequences, and cannot be appraised until all of its consequences have played out. Levin, Cashore, Bernstein and Auld (2007, 2012) build on the idea with the concept of 'super-wicked problems, characterized by four key features: 'time is running out, those who cause the problem also seek to provide a solution, the central authority needed to address it is weak or non-existent, and irrational discounting occurs that pushes responses into the future' (2012: 124). The challenge of global warming, and the failure of governance institutions to address the long-term environmental consequences of climate change that are already well acknowledged, provides a key example. Peters (2017) argues that it may be helpful to consider complexity and complex problems as an overarching category, and wicked problems – and especially super-wicked problems – as a subset of complex problems.

A number of influential concepts convey the challenges of uncertainty for strategic leaders and are relevant to complexity thinking. Perrow's (1984) theory of normal accidents, based on the principle that the more complex the system and the more tightly coupled its connections, the greater the risk of catastrophic failure, so that something that affects one part of the system may cause cascading effects throughout. This informed the notion of 'high reliability organizations', which describes organizations that maintain safe and reliable operations under hazardous conditions, such as nuclear power stations and air traffic control centres (Rochlin, La Porte and Roberts, 1987; Roberts, 1989). The idea of VUCA (volatile, uncertain, complex and ambiguous) environments, first attributed to teaching at the US Army War College and now gaining traction in the business lexicon, highlights the same challenges as wicked problems as they 'render useless any efforts to understand the future and to plan responses' (Bennett and Lemoine, 2014: 311). Taleb's (2007) notion of the 'black swan' describes an unpredictable, rare and catastrophic event, while his subsequent offering, 'antifragile' (2012), offers a new benchmark for **resilience**, referring to systems that not only survive disruption but actually develop under pressure, and encapsulating Nietzsche's (1968 [1888]) maxim 'What does not kill me makes me stronger'.

Today's governments remain overly focused on old problems and are inadequately structured for the complex risks of today, which are varied, global, complex and catastrophic (Centre for the Study of Existential Risk, 2019), as exemplified by the COVID-19 pandemic. Arising from such domains as technology, environment, biology and warfare, the major contemporary risks are individually quite unlikely and may take decades to arise, falling beyond typical political time scales, so that they are not currently priorities for governments. Examples of plausible global catastrophic risks (GCRs) put forward by the Centre for the Study of Existential Risk include:

- Tipping points in the natural order due to climate change or mass biodiversity loss,
- Malicious or accidentally harmful use of artificial intelligence,
- Malicious use of, or unintended consequences from, advanced biotechnologies,
- Natural or engineered global pandemic, and
- Intentional, mis-calculated, accidental, or terrorist-related use of nuclear weapons. (p. 1)

Some such risks have multiple dimensions of complexity, relating to levels of connectivity, non-linear dynamics, rapidly changing circumstances, and emergent properties that produce frequent surprises (Young, 2017; Pegram and Kreienkamp, 2019).

The COVID-19 pandemic has illustrated states' lack of preparedness for, and resilience to, such events, its rapid spread facilitated by the intensity of global interactions, and its impact severe, due to the cascading effects of the closure of borders, lockdown of populations, disruption of supply chains and resultant economic uncertainty on national economies, businesses and individual workers. The Ministry of Defence (MoD) (2018: 11) observes that over the coming decades, 'the rate of change and level of uncertainty may outpace good governance and unity', arguing that 'the complex interaction of these trends is potentially game changing and demands a new approach that places strategic adaptability at its core'. An uncomfortable truth is that autocracies may fare better, lacking the political vulnerabilities that confront democratically elected governments when trying to balance competing priorities and make potentially unpopular decisions to plan for the future.

Governing complexity

Complexity theory is yet to gain traction in criminology or recognition as a notable paradigm within international relations, a discipline that 'remains steeped in analytical linear thinking that emphasizes centralized authority and prediction' (Le Prestre, 2017: 130). It has, however, influenced the study of security governance – another increasingly prominent yet under-acknowledged perspective within the discipline – along two lines of inquiry: the governance of complexity and the complexity of governance (Pattberg and Widerberg, 2019). In other words, it places an emphasis on the governance challenges presented by complex problems, as well as the complex interactions of institutions of governance in responding to those challenges. These trends are not particular to the international sphere, as this book has demonstrated through its multidimensional framework. Rosenau (1995: 15) declares that 'global governance knows no boundaries – geographic, social, cultural, economic, or political', since modern interdependence means that the consequences of social change in a single context – for example, 'if crime grips neighborhoods ... if racial or religious prejudices become pervasive, if the drug trade starts distributing its illicit goods through licit channels' – will 'ripple across and fan out within provincial, regional, national, and international levels as well as across and within local communities'. Consequently, 'the proliferation of organizations is pervasive at and across all levels of human activity – from neighborhood organizations, community groups, regional networks, national states, and transnational regimes to international systems' (p. 16).

Resilience thinking, introduced in Chapters 3, 4 and 5 in relation to international development, national security policies and urban design and management, and also mentioned in Chapter 8 with reference to 'organizational resilience', is an approach that recognizes the complexity and interconnectedness of security challenges and advocates 'more holistic and systemic approaches' to their mitigation (Chandler, 2016: 268). In an international development context, this has been marked by a change in emphasis away from 'top-down' poverty reduction interventions, towards promoting the 'bottom-up' development of security by promoting the self-sufficiency of recipient communities' autonomous capabilities and respecting their authority. Since the complex interconnection of infrastructure systems can only increase, resilience-based approaches are now favoured by multiple agencies and governments across the world (Heath-Kelly, 2017). Coaffee and Chandler (2017: 389) argue that resilience 'offers an antidote to the vast challenges of coping with and managing future uncertainty and a way to assess the challenges that society faces, as well as providing a potential framework by which to respond'.

Some of the strengths and limitations of the UK's approach to resilience are identified in a comparison by the Organisation for Economic Co-operation and Development (OECD) (2018) of member states' national risk assessments, and an extensive and further-reaching peer review process established by the UN Office for Disaster Risk Reduction (UNODRR), European Commission and OECD (2013). The OECD (2018) report highlights the importance of national risk assessments in informing government bodies, as well as businesses and the public when results are made publicly available, about potential risks and their impact in order to inform decisions and investments. It assesses the UK's National Risk Assessment as having helped the country adopt a better strategy for managing risks, by undertaking evidence-based planning, prioritizing investment decisions and guiding local emergency planners. The UNODRR (2013: 12) reviewers judged the UK to have achieved a 'high level of preparedness' and show 'state-of-the-art innovations', including 'the extensive use of science to support policy; attention to business-continuity issues and full partnerships with the private sector; flexible institutional mechanisms and partnerships focused on delivery through voluntary approaches; professional and dedicated co-workers in the field of DRR [disaster risk reduction] throughout the country; [and] national commitment to continue improving policy-making and pushing further implementation'.

The challenges for the UK government identified in the OECD (2018) report concern the identification of risk owners in circumstances where the risk does not fall neatly within the remit of a single department and could potentially go undetected or unassessed; striking the balance between science and policy judgement, since departments may overstate or underplay risks to influence their prioritization and funding, and the Government Office for Science plays a key role as an independent moderator and arbiter; and the difficulties of making precise risk estimates where the evidence does not support this, so that a margin of uncertainty and a possible future need for further detail are accepted. Those identified by the UNODRR (2013) relate to the need for more emphasis on prevention and vulnerability, particularly in relation to risks with potentially large impacts and high likelihoods, with the UK resilience approach identified as placing much more emphasis on emergency preparedness and response. The key recommendations give priority to measures that will help institutionalize disaster risk reduction through better monitoring of implementation progress and targeting of resources where they are most needed; bolstering measures to identify, assess and monitor disaster risks and enhance early warning; harnessing knowledge, innovation and education more effectively; extending the focus of local resilience forums to vulnerability reduction; and strengthening preparedness for disaster response, including exercising for high-impact, low-probability events.

Yet despite the UK's well-developed preparedness architecture, COVID-19 has exposed the grave weaknesses that remain within governmental preparation to manage the distinct challenges presented by GCRs. While the UK government had recognized the likelihood of a global pandemic on its *National Risk Register* (Cabinet Office, 2017), in accordance with the UNODRR (2013) observations it appears to have underestimated the nation's vulnerability. At the time of writing, the UK is reported to have the fourth highest COVID-19 death rate in the world in relation to the population size (Statista, 2020), with marked inequalities in its impact also having come to light. Just as Hurricane Katrina in New Orleans in 2005 was shown to have affected black and less economically privileged people (see Allen, 2007; Stivers, 2007) much more adversely, people living in deprived areas, members of Black and Asian ethnic groups, and frontline workers such as carers, taxi drivers and security personnel, were found by a UK government inquiry to have higher diagnosis and death rates from COVID-19 (Public Health England, 2020).

In order to become more resilient to complex challenges, Pegram and Kreienkamp (2019: 3) argue that governments and other actors in global governance must 'throw off the shackles of old ways of thinking and embrace a complexity paradigm', which requires 'both revisiting the design logics underlying how we build global governance structures, as well as adopting a complex sensibility more capable of responding adequately to instability, surprise and extraordinary change'. Since existing structures are ill equipped for mitigating GCRs, they put forward a set of recommendations for supplementing inherited governance system design and practices with design principles oriented to dealing with such risks. They argue that this requires 'evolutionary design' methods, which first emerged in programming and software design but are increasingly being applied in policy design for complex social systems, continually adapting to changing circumstances and allowing for continuous incremental changes, and term this a 'complex governance approach'.

Their recommendations begin with actions to enhance awareness and understanding of the problems faced, with better modelling and analysis tools, drawing on big and open data. Transparency of approach is advocated to prevent information hoarding (such as a nation's late disclosure of a pandemic) and increase government accountability (e.g. government commitments to Paris Agreement targets). They emphasize the importance of effective deliberative mechanisms that are collaborative and inclusive (e.g. conservation knowledge co-production with local and indigenous communities). Adaptive policy responses are recommended, which enable continuous learning, through 'coordinated experimentation, simultaneous probing of strategies, feedback loops on success and failure, rapid action to correct failure before they cascade, and incentives for scaling up success' (p. 25). Finally, they call for adaptive system design that includes 'stabilizing system dynamics through strategic intervention, responding to unintended consequences, stabilizing reciprocal expectations among participants, and rebalancing power differentials in the interests of system integrity and social cohesion' (p. 27). Pegram and Kreienkamp conclude that 'the stakes could not be higher' as global catastrophes are possible or even probable in the long run, and argue that a complex governance approach to governing GCRs offers the possibility of preventing 'calamitous failure' (p. 30).

Crime, security and complexity

The 'converged perspectives' or interdisciplinary analysis underpinning this book have demonstrated the extent to which the concept of security has permeated multiple realms of policy and scholarship and become a significant organizing concept. It was argued in the first chapter that most, if not all, topics of criminological research could be placed under a 'security' heading, a key advantage of doing so being the greater rhetorical power attached to the term than that of 'crime', so that it has become a significant focus of research funding calls due to the political support and economic resources it generates. Such calls are often interdisciplinary due to the many facets of contemporary security problems, with the need for interdisciplinary engagement only likely to increase as the world becomes more complex. The importance of such approaches is well expressed by Crawford and Hutchinson (2016: 1059), who argue, 'Disciplinary boundary crossing ... is both an essential and dynamic element of problem-solving which prompts a continual reassessment of our conventions, and critical self-reflection on questions of terminology and values', practices that are essential when confronting complexity. The field of security studies, having originated within the international relations discipline, has come to reflect this as it has grown into a more inter-disciplinary area. Equally important is an international outlook, as a means of being open to findings, ideas and voices from around the world; reducing the barriers to knowledge-sharing in a highly unequal world; and challenging ethnocentrism.

As noted in Chapter 1, Shearing (2015) associates a security-focused criminology with a concern with a broader set of 'harms' beyond simply crime, a shifting of focus beyond the state to take account of a broader range of actors, and risk-focused and forward-looking strategies. The research funding that has been made available to support COVID-19-related research across all disciplines, and the range of new criminological studies prompted by the pandemic (e.g. Miller and Blumstein, 2020; Murphy, Williamson, Sargeant and McCarthy, 2020) illustrate the relevance of Shearing's categories to the policy challenges of today and tomorrow. These dimensions are not prerequisites for criminologists engaging more actively with the concept of security, although a recognition of the challenges presented by complexity, and a willingness to move beyond state-centred analyses, are essential. The need for adaptation extends to pedagogy: 'traditional' students (i.e. those entering higher education straight from school) must prepare to enter a job market requiring the more sophisticated skill sets necessary for meeting the needs of the **fourth industrial revolution**, as discussed in Chapter 7, while mature students may be seeking to retrain for new opportunities. The professionalization of security roles is a recurring imperative, highlighted in Chapters 4 to 8 in relation to intelligence, policing and security careers, and presenting opportunities for learning providers to develop new courses catering further to the needs of those professions.

There are three aspirations for this book and its readership. First, it is hoped that this book goes some way to demystifying the meaning and nature of security for scholars and practitioners who do not routinely identify with the concept, but have interests or responsibilities that intersect with some of the many issues being presented here. Second, for those who are already engaged in security-focused work, it is hoped that the book will bring to light connections with other areas of theory and practice that may not previously have been given much consideration, and encourage thinking and collaboration across professional, policy and academic disciplines. Finally, there is a wish to inspire students to identify and consider possible career directions that may not previously have been obvious, and position them to employ some of the information and ideas presented in the book as part of the future workforce. In these ways, the book may make a small contribution to facilitating the flexible and networked approaches that are central to the governance of complexity.

Study questions

- How valid is the security governance concept as a basis for making sense of post-Cold War transformations in the delivery of security across multiple policy dimensions?
- What are the key features of complexity thinking?
- What are the main prerequisites for governing complexity?
- How well equipped is the criminology discipline to adapt to a more complex, more security-focused world?

Further reading

For a vision of a technologically driven future and the opportunities and challenges presented, *Shaping the Future of the Fourth Industrial Revolution* (Schwab, 2018b) offers a useful framework. Thorough appraisals of complexity thinking are offered in the books *Embracing Complexity: Strategic Perspectives for an Age of Turbulence* (Boulton, Allen, Bowman, 2015) and *Critical Systems Thinking and the Management of Complexity* (Jackson, 2019), and *Applying Complexity Theory: Whole Systems Approaches to Criminal Justice and Social Work* (Pycroft and Bartollas, 2014) explores its application to criminal justice. *Governing Complexity* (Pegram and Kreienkamp, 2019) presents informative proposals on how inherited governance structures and practices can be adapted to manage complex and catastrophic global risks, and publications by the Centre for the Study of Existential Risk (www.cser.ac.uk) provide further research-based perspectives on the mitigation of extreme risks. The *Handbook of Governance and Security* (edited by Sperling, 2014) is a helpful text for understanding the concept of security governance and exploring its application in multiple contexts. A holistic, sustainable and human-centred appraisal of the challenges of global insecurity and how they are best addressed is presented in *Losing Control: Global Security in the 21st Century* (Rogers, 2010), a perspective that has informed the development of the Sustainable Security Index (Oxford Research Group, 2020), which 'seeks to demonstrate the interconnectedness of the drivers of global insecurity and begin a broader conversation about how to benchmark and measure national contributions to such insecurity (p. 1). Also of potential interest to scholars and practitioners alike is the article 'Legitimate security? Understanding the contingencies of security and deliberation', which shows how such principles inform policy-making at a societal level in the Nordic countries, according to a framework informed by complexity thinking (Virta and Branders, 2016).

Glossary

Artificial intelligence   the capability of machines to perform human-like tasks such as learning, problem-solving and decision-making.

Big data analytics   the use of advanced analytic techniques to collect, organize and analyse very large volumes of data to derive insights, inform decision-making and enable process automation.

Biosecurity   the measures taken by governments, institutions and the public to protect the economy, the environment and the health of living things from the introduction or spread of disease, pests, or biological or chemical attacks.

Blue economy   an emerging concept promoting the sustainable management of ocean resources to support economic development, sustainable livelihoods and ecosystem resilience.

Border security   the measures taken by a state to protect its borders against the risks associated with cross-border travel and trade – including crime, terrorism, irregular migration and vulnerability to pandemics – while promoting the legitimate movement of people and goods.

Business continuity management   the advance planning and preparation undertaken by organizations to enable them to restore their business functions following disruption.

Cold War   a period of political tension and hostility between the Soviet-led communist world and the US-led capitalist world that ran from 1945 to 1991. The concept of 'cold war' refers to a state of geopolitical conflict between nations that falls short of direct military action.

Collective security   an approach to conflict management based on states pledging to take collective action in response to threats or aggression against any state.

Colonization   the process in which one country imposes and maintains control over other peoples or territories.

Commercial security   businesses that supply products and services for the protection of people, property or information assets to corporate, governmental and individual clients.

Community policing   a policing model that contrasts with reactive policing strategies, and focuses on building relationships with local communities to create collaborative partnerships, develop solutions to problems of crime and disorder, and increase trust in police.

Community security the human security of groups that are vulnerable to identity-based marginalization and oppression, including ethnic minorities, indigenous groups, women, children, the disabled and members of the LGBT community.

Complexity theory an interdisciplinary field focused on the study of complex systems based on dynamic networks of interactions and how they develop, adapt and evolve.

Corporate governance the framework of rules, mechanisms and practices by which a company is controlled and managed, in order to facilitate effective and responsible management and the protection of the interests of all stakeholders.

Corporate security the strategies, processes and practices for securing a business enterprise, encompassing the protection of its people, property and information assets.

Counter-terrorism the strategies, techniques and practices employed by governments, security agencies and businesses to prevent or thwart terrorism.

Critical national infrastructure those assets, services and systems that are so vital to the economic, political and social life of a nation that their disruption or failure would have a serious impact on the economy, national security and/ or public health and safety.

Cyber security the practice of defending networks, servers, systems, devices, software and data from attack, damage or unauthorized access.

Cyber security governance the frameworks, rules, standards and processes employed to mitigate the risks of operating in cyberspace.

Cybercrime criminal activity conducted online by means of electronic communications networks and information systems.

Cyberspace the virtual space that exists within the scope of the internet.

Dark web content from the World Wide Web that exists on encrypted networks and cannot be found through traditional browsers and search engines.

Decolonization the undoing of colonization, a term that normally refers to the period following the Second World War when European colonial empires, ruling over approximately 750 million people and nearly a third of the world's population at that time, were removed from Asia and Africa.

Economic security access to an assured basic income for individuals through employment or the provision of social welfare payments (when employed as a dimension of human security).

Energy security access of national economies and people to uninterrupted, affordable and sustainable energy sources.

Environmental security protection of the individual, society and the biosphere from direct and indirect threats resulting from human or natural impacts on the environment.

Flag state the state under whose laws a vessel is licensed, serving as a regulatory body for its operating standards as well as a legal jurisdiction on the high seas, applicable both within the confines of the vessel and with respect to criminal acts it may come across at sea.

Food security physical and economic access to sufficient, safe and nutritious food at all times.

Foresight studies research-based techniques employed by governments and organizations to identify long-term trends and developments and their implications.

Fourth industrial revolution the present, advanced stage of industrial development, which is driven by the fusion of technologies across the physical, digital and biological worlds, and creating dramatic change at exponential speed.

Global commons areas and resources beyond sovereign jurisdiction and the protection of governments, specifically the oceans, polar regions, air space, outer space and cyberspace.

Global governance collective action by international and transnational actors, including states, inter-governmental organizations, non-governmental organizations, multinational corporations and other actors through alliances and networks, to negotiate responses to challenges within the international system.

Global North the high income societies of Europe, North America, and the developed parts of Asia and Oceania.

Global South the low or middle income societies of Africa, Asia, Oceania, Latin America and the Caribbean.

Globalization a process of increasing global interconnectedness and interdependence between societies.

Health security access to basic health care (when employed as a dimension of human security).

Homeland security coordinated national efforts to prevent, protect against and respond to hazards within a country's borders.

Human rights the fundamental rights and freedoms to which all human beings are equally entitled without discrimination as set out in international law, including civil, cultural, economic, political and social rights.

Human security   a people-centred conception of security that places a focus on protection of the individual as opposed to the state.

Information security   a set of practices for protecting electronic, print and other information from unauthorized or unintended access, disclosure, tampering or destruction.

Intelligence   information that has gone through a systematic process of collection, evaluation, analysis and synthesis for the purpose of informing decision-making.

Intelligence agency   an organization responsible for the collection, analysis and exploitation of information in the interests of security.

Intelligence-led policing   an operational strategy for law enforcement that places an emphasis on the collection and analysis of information and collaborative, strategic solutions to the mitigation of crime.

International relations   the relations of states with each other, as well as inter-governmental organizations and other international actors, including regional organizations, multinational corporations and non-governmental organizations. The term also refers to the study of such relations as an academic discipline.

International security   measures taken by nations, inter-governmental organizations and other actors to mitigate threats to the international system and ensure mutual survival, order and peace.

Internet governance   the development and application by governments, the private sector and civil society of rules, policies, standards and practices that shape the evolution and use of the internet.

Internet of things   the extension of internet and other network technologies to smart devices and sensors, which gather and share data from their environments with other devices and networks, enabling significant advancements in the automation of processes and the merging of the digital and physical worlds.

Liberalism   a school of thought in international relations that favours cooperation and collective action over the dominance of states, underpinned by the belief that individuals' rights and freedoms are better served through cooperative patterns of behaviour.

Maritime piracy   an act of robbery or criminal violence at sea, committed for private ends and from a privately owned vessel.

Maritime security   the rules, policies, measures and operations employed to secure the maritime domain, in the interests of national and international security, the preservation and safety of the marine environment, sustainable economic development and human security.

National security the protection and defence of a state, its territories, its institutions and its people from substantial threats.

Neighbourhood policing a strategic framework for the delivery and reprioritization of community policing that was introduced early in the new millennium, with the aim of promoting closer relationships between police forces and communities in defined local geographic areas.

Neocolonialism the use of economic, political, or other indirect pressures to control or influence less-developed countries, instead of the previous colonial methods.

New public management the introduction into public service provision of private sector management methods and incentive structures such as internal markets and performance management.

Ocean governance the rules, processes, institutions, policies and actions employed to manage humans' use of the world's oceans and conserve and protect the marine environment.

Personal security the security of the individual from physical harm arising from conflict, crime, industrial or traffic accident, or threats to the self, such as suicide or drug use (when employed as a dimension of human security).

Personnel security measures employed in an organization to mitigate insider risk and enhance trust in staff, suppliers or business partners with access to its important assets.

Physical security the protection of people, premises and physical assets from actions or events that could cause damage, loss or harm.

Police a body of officers empowered by a state to maintain order, prevent and detect crime and enforce the law.

Political security the realization of citizens' fundamental civil and political rights and freedom from political oppression.

Postcolonial studies an interdisciplinary field that critically explores the cultural legacy of European colonial rule, and seeks to represent and give voice to colonized peoples.

Private security protective services provided within or on behalf of private entities.

Realism a school of thought in international relations that views states as the primary actors in the international system, motivated by self-interest and the prioritization of their own security.

Regional security collective measures taken by nations, inter-governmental organizations and other actors in a given region to mitigate regionally based threats.

Resilience   the ability of an individual, system, community or society to recover from an adverse event.

Risk   the likelihood and impact of loss, injury or other adverse outcome.

Safeguarding   actions to promote the welfare and human rights of vulnerable people and protect them from abuse, neglect or exploitation.

Securitization   a political process by which issues come to be constructed as security concerns, enabling them to receive disproportionate attention and resources.

Security   the state of being or feeling secure.

Security governance   the combined efforts of multiple actors and stakeholders to deliver security through hierarchies, networks and markets.

Security studies   an interdisciplinary field concerned with the study of security, initially established as a sub-field of the international relations discipline, which has traditionally focused on organized violence but more recently come to reflect a much wider range of issues on the security agenda.

Security–development nexus   the convergence of security and development agendas in international politics, policy and practice.

Smart city   an urban area that employs intelligent networks of physical devices connected through internet of things technologies to improve operational efficiency and sustainability.

Space security   the secure and sustainable access to and use of outer space, and the protection of space assets from natural and deliberate threats.

Surveillance   the systematic monitoring of people, activities or information.

Sustainable development   maintaining economic development and progress while protecting the long-term integrity and stability of the natural system.

Systems theory   an interdisciplinary field focused on the study of systems, investigating the arrangement of and relations between their component parts, and the interaction of systems with their environments.

Universal jurisdiction   an international law that affords to every state jurisdiction over a limited range of offences including piracy, genocide, torture and human trafficking that are generally recognized as being of universal concern, irrespective of the location of the offence, and the nationalities of the offender and victim.

Wicked problem   a complex problem with many interdependent factors that make it difficult or impossible to solve.

References

Abrahamsen, R. and Leander, A. (eds.) (2016) *Routledge Handbook of Private Security Studies*. London: Routledge.

Abrahamsen, R. and Sandor, A. (2018) 'The global south and international security', in A. Gheciu and W.C. Wohlforth (eds.), *The Oxford Handbook of International Security*. Oxford: Oxford University Press.

Abrahamsen, R. and Williams, M.C. (2011) *Security Beyond the State: Private Security in International Politics*. Cambridge: Cambridge University Press.

Acharya, A. and Buzan, B. (2019) *The Making of Global International Relations: Origins and Evolution of IR at its Centenary*. London: Routledge.

Action Fraud (2020) 'A–Z of fraud'. Available at: www.actionfraud.police.uk/a-z-of-fraud.

Africa Leadership Forum (1991) *The Kampala Document: Towards a Conference on Security, Stability, Development and Cooperation in Africa*. Kampala: Africa Leadership Forum.

African Union (2012) *2050 African Integrated Maritime Strategy*. Addis Ababa: African Union.

Age UK (2018) '1.4 million older people aren't getting the care and support they need', 9 July. Available at: www.ageuk.org.uk/latest-news/articles/2018/july/1.4-million-older-people-arent-getting-the-care-and-support-they-need–a-staggering-increase-of-almost-20-in-just-two-years/.

Agozino, B. (2003) *Counter-Colonial Criminology: A Critique of Imperialist Reason*. London: Pluto Press.

Aleem, A., Wakefield, A. and Button, M. (2013) 'Addressing the weakest link: implementing converged security', *Security Journal*, 26(3): 236–248.

Algosaibi, A.A., Albahli, S. and Melton, A. (2015) 'World Wide Web: a survey of its development and possible future trends', *16th International Conference on Internet Computing and Big Data*, 15: 79–84.

All Party Parliamentary Group on Hate Crime (2019) *How Do We Build Community Cohesion When Hate Crime is on the Rise?* London: APPG Hate Crime.

Allen, G. and Zayed, Y. (2018) *Research Briefing: Hate Crime Statistics*. London: House of Commons Library.

Allen, T.D. (2007) 'Katrina: race, class, and poverty: reflections and analysis', *Journal of Black Studies*, 37(4): 466–468.

Allum, F. and Gilmour, S. (eds.) (2019) *Handbook of Organised Crime and Politics*. Cheltenham: Edward Elgar.

Amnesty International (2018) *Amnesty International Report 2017/2018: The State of the World's Human Rights*. London: Amnesty International.

Andersen-Rodgers, D. and Crawford, K.F. (2018) *Human Security: Theory and Action*. Lanham, MD: Rowman and Littlefield.

Andrew, C. (2009) *The Defence of the Realm: The Authorized History of MI5*. London: Allen Lane.

Aradau, C. (2014) 'The promise of security: resilience, surprise and epistemic politics', *Resilience*, 2(2): 73–87.

Archibugi, D. and Pease, A. (2018) *Crime and Global Justice: The Dynamics of International Punishment*. Cambridge: Polity Press.

ASIS International (2020) 'Join Us'. Available at: www.asisonline.org/membership/join/.

ASIS International and the Institute of Finance and Management (2013) *'The United States Security Industry: Size and Scope, Insights, Trends, and Data'*. Washington, DC: ASIS International and the Institute of Finance and Management.

Association of Security Consultants (2020) *'Find a Consultant'*. Available at: https:// securityconsultants.org.uk/find-a-consultant.

Australian Government Attorney-General's Department (2018) *Protective Security Policy Framework. Securing Government Business: Protective Security Guidance for Executives*. Canberra: Commonwealth of Australia.

Avant, D.D. (2005) *The Market for Force: The Consequences of Privatizing Security*. New York: Cambridge University Press.

Axworthy, L. (2013) 'Human security in the R2P era', in M. Martin and T. Owen (eds.), *Routledge Handbook of Human Security*. London: Routledge.

Ayoob, M. (1997) 'Defining security: a subaltern realist perspective', in K. Krause and M.C. Williams (eds.), *Critical Security Studies: Concepts and Cases*. Minneapolis, MN: University of Minnesota Press.

Babuta, A. and Krasodomski-Jones, A. (2018) *The Personal Security of Individuals in British Public Life*. London: Royal United Services Institute.

Babuta, A., Oswald, M. and Janjeva, A. (2020) *Artificial Intelligence and UK National Security: Policy Considerations*. London: Royal United Services Institute.

Baldwin, R. (2018) *'If this is Globalization 4.0, what were the other three?'* Available at: www. weforum.org/agenda/2018/12/if-this-is-globalization-4-0-what-were-the-other-three/.

Baltic and International Maritime Council, International Chamber of Shipping, International Group of P&I Clubs, INTERTANKO and Oil Companies International Marine Forum (2018) *BMP 5: Best Management Practices to Deter Piracy and Enhance Maritime Security in the Red Sea, Gulf of Aden, Indian Ocean and Arabian Sea* (5th ed.). Edinburgh: Witherby Publishing Group.

Barber, B. (1992) 'Jihad vs. McWorld', *The Atlantic*, March.

Barber, B. (2001) *Jihad versus McWorld: Terrorism's Challenge to Democracy*. London: Corgi Books.

Barkawi, T. and Laffey, M. (2006) 'The postcolonial moment in security studies', *Review of International Studies*, 32(2): 329–352.

Barrow, C.W. and Keck, M. (2017) 'Globalization theory and state theory: the false antinomy', *Studies in Political Economy*, 98(2): 177–196.

Batvinis, R.J. (2010) 'The future of FBI counterintelligence through the lens of the past hundred years', in L.K. Johnson (ed.), *The Oxford Handbook of National Security Intelligence*. New York: Oxford University Press.

Bauman, Z. (1998) *Globalization: The Human Consequences*. Cambridge: Polity Press.

Bauman, Z. (2000) *Liquid Modernity*. Cambridge: Polity Press.

Bayley, D.H. and Shearing, C.D. (1996) 'The future of policing', *Law and Society Review*, 30(3): 585–606.

Bayley, D.H. and Shearing, C.D. (2001) *The New Structure of Policing: Description, Conceptualization, and Research Agenda*. Washington, DC: US Department of Justice.

BBC News (2011) *'Somali piracy: armed guards to protect UK ships'*, 30 October. Available at: www.bbc.co.uk/news/uk-15510467.

BBC News (2016) 'Last winter's flooding "most extreme on record" in UK', 5 December. Available at: www.bbc.co.uk/news/uk-38204334.

BBC News (2018) 'Two jailed for smuggling migrants across Channel to Kent', 21 November. Available at: www.bbc.co.uk/news/uk-england-46295429.

BBC News (2020) 'Grays migrant lorry deaths "tragedy on a large scale"', 19 March. Available at: www.bbc.co.uk/news/uk-england-essex-51961653.

Beck, D., Gips, M. and McFarland Pierce, B. (2019) *The State of Security Convergence in the United States, Europe and India*. Washington, DC: ASIS Foundation.

Beck, U. (1992) *Risk Society: Towards a New Modernity*. London: Sage.

Behari-Leak, K. (2019) 'Decolonial turns, postcolonial shifts, and cultural connections: Are we there yet?', *English Academy Review*, 36(1): 58–68.

Bennett, N. and Lemoine, G.J. (2014) 'What a difference a word makes: understanding threats to performance in a VUCA world', *Business Horizons*, 57(3): 311–317.

Bigo, D. (2002) 'Security and immigration: toward a critique of the governmentality of unease', *Alternatives*, 27(1): 63–92.

Bigo, D. (2016) 'Rethinking security at the crossroad of international relations and criminology', *British Journal of Criminology*, 56(6): 1049–1067.

Bilgin, P. (2012) 'Globalization and in/security', in S. Stetter (ed.), *The Middle East and Globalization*. New York: Palgrave Macmillan.

Booth, K. (1991) 'Security and emancipation', *Review of International Studies*, 17(4): 313–326.

Booth, K. (ed.) (2005) *Critical Security Studies and World Politics*. Boulder, CO: Lynne Rienner.

Booth, K. (2007) *Theory of World Security*. Cambridge: Cambridge University Press.

Borodzicz, E.P. (2005) *Risk, Crisis and Disaster Management*. Chichester: Wiley.

Bosworth, M. and Hoyle, C. (eds.) (2011) *What Is Criminology?* Oxford: Oxford University Press.

Bourbeau, P. (ed.) (2015) *Security: Dialogue across Disciplines*. Cambridge: Cambridge University Press.

Boulton, C., Allen, J.G. and Bowman, P.M. (2015) *Embracing Complexity: Strategic Perspectives for an Age of Turbulence*. Oxford: Oxford University Press.

Bousquet, A. and Curtis, S. (2011) 'Complexity theory, systems thinking and international relations', *Cambridge Review of International Affairs*, 24(1): 43–62.

Bowling, B. (2009) 'Transnational policing: the globalization thesis, a typology and a research agenda', *Policing*, 3(2): 149–160.

Bowling, B., Reiner, R. and Sheptycki, J. (2019) *The Politics of the Police* (5th ed.). Oxford: Oxford University Press.

Braes, B.M. and Brooks, D.J. (2011) 'Organisational resilience: understanding and identifying the essential concepts', in M. Guarascio, G. Reniers, C.A. Brebbia and F. Garzia (eds.), *Safety and Security Engineering IV*. Southampton: WIT Press.

Bremner, L. (2004) 'Bounded spaces: demographic anxieties in post-apartheid Johannesburg', *Social Identities*, 10(4): 455–468.

Brennen, J.S., Simon, F.M., Howard, P.N. and Nielsen, R.K. (2020) *Types, Sources, and Claims of COVID-19 Misinformation*. Oxford: Reuters Institute for the Study of Journalism.

Breslin, B., Ezickson, D. and Kocoras, J. (2010) 'The Bribery Act 2010: raising the bar above the US Foreign Corrupt Practices Act', *Company Lawyer*, 31(11): 362–369.

Briggs, R. (2003) *Doing Business in a Dangerous World*. London: The Foreign Policy Centre.

Briggs, R. and Edwards, C. (2006) *The Business of Resilience: Corporate Security for the 21st Century*. London: Demos.

Brisman, A. and South, N. (2020) *Routledge International Handbook of Green Criminology* (2nd ed.). London: Routledge.

Brodeur, J.-P. (1983) 'High and low policing: remarks about the policing of political activities', *Social Problems*, 30(5): 507–521.

Brodeur, J-P. (2003) 'Cops and spooks: the uneasy partnership', in T. Newburn (ed.) *Policing: Key Readings*. Cullompton: Willan.

Brodeur, J-P. (2010) *The Policing Web*. Oxford: Oxford University Press.

Brodeur, J.P., Walsh, W.F., Kelling, G.L., Banton, M.P. and Whetstone, T. (2020) 'Police', in *Encyclopædia Britannica*. Available at: www.britannica.com/topic/police.

Broniatowski, D.A., Jamison, A.M, Qi, S., AlKulaib, L., Chen, T., Benton, A. et al. (2018) 'Weaponized health communication: Twitter bots and Russian trolls amplify the vaccine debate', *American Journal of Public Health*, 108(10): 1378–1384.

Brooks, D.J. (2013) 'Corporate security: using knowledge construction to define a practising body of knowledge', *Asian Journal of Criminology*, 8(2): 1–13.

Brundage, M., Avin, S., Clark, J., Toner, H., Eckersley, P., Garfinkel, B. et al. (2018) *The Malicious Use of Artificial Intelligence: Forecasting, Prevention, and Mitigation*. preprint arXiv:1802.07228.

Bueger, C. (2015) 'What is maritime security?', *Marine Policy*, 53: 159–164.

Bueger, C. and Edmunds, T. (2017) 'Beyond seablindness: a new agenda for maritime security studies', *International Affairs*, 93(6): 1293–1311.

Bujun, P.D., Foucault, M. and Mérand, F. (2014) 'Regional security governance and collective action', in J. Sperling (ed.), *Handbook of Governance and Security*. Cheltenham: Edward Elgar.

Burchill, S. (2005) *The National Interest in International Relations Theory*. Basingstoke: Palgrave Macmillan.

Burrows, M.J. and Gnad, O. (2018) 'Between "muddling through" and "grand design": regaining political initiative – the role of strategic foresight', *Futures*, 97: 6–17.

Bush, G.H.W. (1991) Address before a Joint Session of the Congress on the State of the Union, 29 January. American Presidency Project. Available at: www.presidency.ucsb.edu/.

Bush, G.W. (2001) Executive Order 13228: Establishing the Office of Homeland Security and the Homeland Security Council. Washington, DC: White House.

Business Continuity Institute (2020) Benefits of Membership. Available at: www.thebci.org/membership/benefits-of-bci-membership.html.

Button, M. (2006) *Doing Security: Critical Reflections and an Agenda for Change*. Basingstoke: Palgrave Macmillan.

Button, M. (2019) *Private Policing*. London: Routledge.

Button, M., Shepherd, D. and Blackbourn, D. (2017) *Annual Fraud Indicator 2017: Identifying the Cost of Fraud to the UK Economy*. London: Crowe Clark Whitehill.

Buzan, B. (1983) *People, States and Fear: An Agenda for International Security Studies in the Post-Cold War Era*. Colchester: ECPR Press.

Buzan, B. and Hansen, L. (2009) *The Evolution of International Security Studies*. Cambridge: Cambridge University Press.

Buzan, B. and Wæver, O. (2003) *Regions and Powers: The Structure of International Security*. Cambridge: Cambridge University Press.

Buzan, B., Wæver, O. and de Wilde, J. (1998) *Security: A New Framework for Analysis*. Boulder, CO: Lynne Rienner.

Cabinet Office (2013) *The Role of Local Resilience Forums: A Reference Document*. London: Cabinet Office.

Cabinet Office (2017) *National Risk Register of Civil Emergencies*. London: Cabinet Office.

Cabinet Office (2018) *HMG Security Policy Framework*. London: Cabinet Office.

Caldeira, T.P.R. (1996) 'Fortified enclaves: the new urban segregation', *Public Culture*, 8(2): 303–328.

Care Quality Commission (2020) *The State of Health Care and Adult Social Care in England 2018/19*. Newcastle: Care Quality Commission.

Carrington, K., Hogg, R., Scott, J., Sozzo, M. and Walters, R. (2018) *Southern Criminology*. London: Routledge.

Castells, M. (1996) *The Rise of the Network Society. The Information Age: Economy, Society and Culture*, vol. I. Oxford: Blackwell.

Cavalty, M.D. and Mauer, V. (eds.) (2010) *The Routledge Handbook of Security Studies*. Abingdon: Routledge.

Centre for the Protection of National Infrastructure (2013) *CPNI Insider Data Collection Study*. London: Centre for the Protection of National Infrastructure.

Centre for the Study of Existential Risk (2019) *Managing Global Catastrophic Risks: Part 1: Understand*. Cambridge: CSER.

Centrex (2006) *Practice Advice on Professionalising the Business of Neighbourhood Policing*. Wyboston: Centrex.

Cha, V.D. (2000): 'Globalization and the study of international security', *Journal of Peace Research*, 37(3): 391–403.

Chalk, P. (2008) *Maritime Dimension of International Security: Terrorism, Piracy, and Challenges for the United States*. Santa Monica, CA: RAND.

Chandler, D. (2007) 'The security–development nexus and the rise of "anti-foreign policy"', *Journal of International Relations and Development*, 10(4): 362–386.

Chandler, D. (2008) 'The human security paradox: how nation states grew to love cosmopolitan ethics', paper presented at *Globalization, Difference, and Human Securities* conference, Graduate School of Human Sciences, Osaka University, Japan, 12–14 March.

Chandler, D. (2014) *Resilience: The Governance of Complexity*. London: Routledge.

Chandler, D. (2016) 'New narratives of international security governance: the shift from global interventionism to global self-policing', *Global Crime*, 17(3–4): 264–280.

Chandler, D. (2019) 'Conclusion', in A. Orsini, P. Le Prestre, M. Brosig, P. Pattberg, L. Gomez-Mera, J-F. Morin, N. Harrison, R. Geyer and D. Chandler (eds.), 'Forum: complex systems and international governance', *International Studies Review*, 70: 1–31.

Chandler, D. and Coaffee, J. (2017) 'Introduction: contested paradigms of international resilience', in D. Chandler and J. Coaffee (eds.), *The Routledge Handbook of International Resilience*. London: Routledge.

Charman, S. (2017) *Police Socialisation, Identity and Culture: Becoming Blue*. Basingstoke: Palgrave Macmillan.

Chartered Management Institute (2013) *Weathering the Storm: The 2013 Business Continuity Management Survey*. London: Chartered Management Institute.

Choudhury, N. (2014) 'World Wide Web and its journey from Web 1.0 to Web 4.0', *International Journal of Computer Science and Information Technologies*, 5(6): 8096–8100.

Cillizza, C. (2016) 'The remarkable parallels between the Brexit vote and the rise of Donald Trump', *Washington Post*, 24 June. Available at: www.washingtonpost.com/news/the-fix/wp/2016/06/24/the-remarkable-parallels-between-the-brexit-vote-and-the-rise-of-donald-trump/.

Clarke, R.V. (1997) *Situational Crime Prevention: Successful Case Studies* (2nd ed.). Albany, NY: Harrow and Heston.

Clarke, R.V. and Felson, M. (eds.) (1993) *Routine Activity and Rational Choice*. London: Transaction.

Coaffee, J. and Chandler, D. (2017) 'Conclusion: the future of resilience', in D. Chandler and J. Coaffee (eds.), *The Routledge Handbook of International Resilience*. London: Routledge.

Coaffee, J. and Fussey, P. (2017) 'The politics, practices and tensions of security-driven resilience', in D. Chandler and J. Coaffee (eds.), *The Routledge Handbook for International Resilience*. London: Routledge.

Cohen, S. (1982) 'Western crime control models in the Third World: benign or malignant?', *Research in Law, Deviance and Social Control*, 4: 85–119.

Coles, T.J. (2019) 'The world's oldest democracy and the Universal Declaration of Human Rights at 70', *Peace Review*, 30(4): 537–546.

College of Policing (2015) *College of Policing Analysis: Estimating Demand on the Police Service*. London: College of Policing.

Comfort, L.K. (2000) 'Disaster: agent of diplomacy or change in international affairs?', *Cambridge Review of International Affairs*, 14(1): 277–294.

Commission on the Roles and Capabilities of the United States Intelligence Community (1996) *Preparing for the 21st Century: An Appraisal of U.S. Intelligence*. Washington, DC: US Government Printing Office.

Committee on Standards in Public Life (2017) *Artificial Intelligence and Public Standards*. London: Committee on Standards in Public Life.

Conservative and Unionist Party (2019) *Conservative and Unionist Party Manifesto*. London: Conservative and Unionist Party.

Contact Group on Piracy off the Coast of Somalia (2019) *FAQ*. Available at: www.lessonsfrompiracy.net/faq/.

Cook, I.R. (2009) 'Private sector involvement in urban governance: the case of Business Improvement Districts and Town Centre Management partnerships in England', *Geoforum*, 40(5): 930–940.

Cook, I.R. and Ward, K. (2012) 'Conferences, informational infrastructures and mobile policies: the process of getting Sweden "BID ready"', *European Urban and Regional Studies*, 19(2): 137–152.

Coole, M.P., Brooks, D.J. and Minnaar, A. (2017) 'The physical security professional: mapping a body of knowledge', *Security Journal*, 30(4): 1169–1197.

Coole, M., Corkill, J. and Woodward, A. (2012) 'Defence in depth, protection in depth and security in depth: a comparative analysis towards a common usage language', *Proceedings of the 5th Australian Security and Intelligence Conference*, Perth, Western Australia, 3–5 December.

Cooper, R.N. (1968) *The Economics of Interdependence: Economic Policy in the Atlantic Community*. New York: McGraw–Hill/Council on Foreign Relations.

Cornish, D. and Clarke, R.V. (eds.) (1986) *The Reasoning Criminal: Rational Choice Perspectives on Offending*. New York: Springer-Verlag.

Cornish, P.N. (2005) *Homeland Security and Resilience in the United Kingdom*. London: Chatham House.

Cornish, P.N. (2007) *Domestic Security, Civil Contingencies and Resilience in the United Kingdom: A Guide to Policy*. London: Chatham House.

Cornwall, A. (2007) 'Buzzwords and fuzzwords: deconstructing development discourse', *Development in Practice*, 17(4–5): 471–484.

Council of the European Union (2005) *The European Union Counter-Terrorism Strategy*, 14469/4/05. Brussels: Council of the European Union.

Coughlan, S. (2020) 'Oxford college wants to remove Cecil Rhodes statue', *BBC News*, 18 June. Available at: www.bbc.co.uk/news/education-53082545.

Council of the European Union (2014) *European Union Maritime Security Strategy*, 11205/14. Brussels: Council of the European Union.

Cox, M. (2017) 'The rise of populism and the crisis of globalisation: Brexit, Trump and beyond', *Irish Studies in International Affairs*, 28, 9–17.

Crawford, A. and Hutchinson, S. (2016) 'The future(s) of security studies', *British Journal of Criminology*, 56(6): 1049–1067.

Crawford, A., Lister, S., Blackburn, S. and Burnett, J. (2004) *Plural Policing: The Mixed Economy of Visible Patrols in England and Wales*. Bristol: Policy Press.

Cunneen, C. (2011) 'Postcolonial perspectives for criminology', in M. Bosworth and C. Hoyle (eds.), *What Is Criminology?* Oxford: Oxford University Press.

Curran, J., Fenton, N. and Freedman, D. (2016) *Misunderstanding the Internet*. London: Routledge.

Czerniawska, F. (1999) *Management Consultancy in the 21st Century*. Basingstoke: Palgrave.

Dalton, D. (2003) *Rethinking Corporate Security in the Post-9/11 Era: Issues and Strategies for Today's Global Business Community*. Burlington, MA: Butterworth–Heinemann.

Davis, M. (1990) *City of Quartz: Excavating the Future in Los Angeles*. New York: Verso.

de Boer, J. and Bosetti, L. (2015) *The Crime–Conflict 'Nexus': State of the Evidence*. New York: United Nations University Centre for Policy Research.

Department for Environment, Food and Rural Affairs (2018) *A Green Future: Our 25 Year Plan to Improve the Environment*. London: DEFRA.

Department for International Development (2011) *Saving Lives, Preventing Suffering and Building Resilience: The UK Government's Humanitarian Policy*. London: DfID.

Department for Media, Culture and Sport (2020) *Cyber Security Breaches Survey 2020*. London: DMCS.

Department of Energy and Climate Change (2012) *Energy Security Strategy*. London: DECC.

Department of Homeland Security (2020) About DHS. Available at: www.dhs.gov/about-dhs.

Dholakia, N., Dholakia, R.R. and Kshetri, N. (2004) 'Global diffusion of the internet', in H. Bidgoli (ed.), *The Internet Encyclopedia*. New York: Wiley.

Dodd, V. (2020) 'Levels of child criminal exploitation "almost back to Victorian times"', *The Guardian*, 2 January. Available at: www.theguardian.com/society/2020/jan/02/levels-child-criminal-exploitation-almost-back-to-victorian-times.

Dolata, P. (2017) 'Energy security', in R. Dover, H. Dylan and M. Goodman (eds.), *Palgrave Handbook of Security, Risk and Intelligence*. Basingstoke: Palgrave Macmillan.

Dover, R., Goodman, M.S. and Hillebrand, C. (eds.) (2015) *The Routledge Companion to Intelligence Studies*. London: Routledge.

Downes, D. (1988) 'The sociology of crime and social control in Britain, 1960–1987', in P. Rock (ed.), *A History of British Criminology*. Oxford: Clarendon.

Dreyer, I. and Stang, G. (2013) 'Foresight in governments – practices and trends around the world', in European Union Institute for Security Studies (ed.), *YES 2013: EUISS Yearbook of European Security*: Paris: EUISS.

Duffield, M. (2012) 'Challenging environments: danger, resilience and the aid industry', *Security Dialogue*, 43(5): 475–492.

Duffield, M. (2014) *Global Governance and the New Wars: The Merging of Development and Security*. London: Zed Books.

Duffield, M. (2016) 'How did we become unprepared? Emergency and resilience in an uncertain world', *British Academy Review*, 21: 55–58.

Dunne, T. and Wheeler, N.J. (2004) '"We the peoples": contending discourses of security in human rights theory and practice', *International Relations*, 18(1): 9–23.

Economist (2019) 'China's "social credit" scheme involves cajolery and sanctions', 28 March. Available at: www.economist.com/china/2019/03/28/chinas-social-credit-scheme-involves-cajolery-and-sanctions.

Economist Intelligence Unit (2018) *Risk 2018: Planning for an Unpredictable Decade*. London: EIU.

Economist Intelligence Unit (2020) *Democracy Index 2019: A Year of Democratic Setbacks and Popular Protest*. London: EIU.

Edwards, S. and Edmunds, T. (2020) 'Why are more small boats crossing the English Channel – and why are border forces struggling to stop them?', *The Conversation*, 14 August. Available at: https://theconversation.com/why-are-more-small-boats-crossing-the-english-channel-and-why-are-border-forces-struggling-to-stop-them-144466.

Electoral Commission (2018) 'Digital campaigning: increasing transparency for voters'. Available at: www.electoralcommission.org.uk/who-we-are-and-what-we-do/changing-electoral-law/transparent-digital-campaigning/report-digital-campaigning-increasing-transparency-voters.

Electric Infrastructure Security Council (2018) *The London Black Sky Seminar 2018: Infrastructure and Societal Resilience to Black Sky Hazards*. EIS Council: Washington, DC.

Elliott, J.A. (2012) *An Introduction to Sustainable Development* (4th ed.). London: Routledge.

Emsley, C. (1999) 'A typology of nineteenth-century sociétés', *Crime, History and Societies*, 3(1): 19–24.

Emsley, C. (2009) 'History', in A. Wakefield and J. Fleming (eds.), *The Sage Dictionary of Policing*. London: Sage.

Emsley, C. (2014) *The English Police: A Political and Social History* (2nd ed.). London: Routledge.

Equality Trust (2020) 'The scale of economic inequality in the UK'. Available at: www.equalitytrust.org.uk/scale-economic-inequality-uk.

Ericson, R. (1994) 'The division of expert knowledge in policing and security', *British Journal of Sociology*, 42(2): 149–176.

European Agency for Safety and Health at Work (2011) *Workplace Violence and Harassment: A European Picture*. Bilbao: European Agency for Safety and Health at Work.

Evans, B. and Reid, J. (2014) *Resilient Life: The Art of Living Dangerously*. Chichester: John Wiley and Sons.

Evans, M.D. and Galani, S. (2020) *Maritime Security and the Law of the Sea: Help or Hindrance?* Cheltenham: Edward Elgar.

Facebook (2020) *Community Standards Enforcement Report*. Available at: https://transparency.facebook.com/community-standards-enforcement#dangerous-organizations.

Fawcett, L. (2018) 'Regional organizations', in P.D. Williams and M. McDonald (eds.), *Security Studies: An Introduction* (3rd ed.). London: Routledge.

Felson, M. and Boba, R.L. (2010) *Crime and Everyday Life* (4th ed.). Thousand Oaks, CA: Sage.

Fieldhouse, D.K. (1989) *The Colonial Empires*. London: Macmillan.

Finkelstein, L. (1995) 'What is global governance?', *Global Governance*, 1(3): 367–372.

Finnemore, M. (1996) *National Interests in International Society*. Ithaca, NY: Cornell University Press.

Fischer, R.J., Halibozek, E. and Green, G. (2018) *Introduction to Security* (10th ed.). Burlington, MA: Butterworth–Heinemann.

Fish, S. and Hardy, M. (2015) 'Complex issues, complex solutions: applying complexity theory in social work practice', *Nordic Social Work Research*, 5(Suppl. 1): 98–114.

Fleming, J. (2009) 'Managerialism', in A. Wakefield and J. Fleming (eds.) *The Sage Dictionary of Policing*. London: Sage.

Food and Agriculture Organization of the United Nations (2019) *The Future of Food and Agriculture: Alternative Pathways to 2050*. Rome: FAO.

Food and Agriculture Organization of the United Nations, International Fund for Agricultural Development, UN Children's Fund, World Food Programme and World Health Organization (2019) *The State of Food Security and Nutrition in the World*. Rome: FAO.

Fortune (2020) Global 500. Available at https://fortune.com/global500/.

Foster, P. (2013) '"Bogus" AP tweet about explosion at the White House wipes billions off US markets', *The Telegraph*, 23 April. Available at: www.telegraph.co.uk/finance/markets/10013768/Bogus-AP-tweet-about-explosion-at-the-White-House-wipes-billions-off-US-markets.html.

Foucault, M. (1991 [1978]) 'On governmentality', in G. Burchell, C. Gordon and P. Miller (eds.), *The Foucault Effect: Studies in Governmental Rationality*. Hemel Hempstead, Harvester–Wheatsheaf.

Fox, A.C. and Rossow, A.J. (2017) *Making Sense of Russian Hybrid Warfare: A Brief Assessment of the Russo–Ukrainian War*. Arlington, VA: Institute of Land Warfare.

Franko, K. (2020) *Globalization and Crime* (3rd ed.). London: Sage.

Freedonia Group (2020) *Global Security Services*. Cleveland, OH: Freedonia.

Fridman, O. (2018) *Russian 'Hybrid Warfare': Resurgence and Politicization*. London: Hurst and Company.

Froestad, J. and Shearing, C. (2012) *Security Governance, Policing, and Local Capacity*. Boca Raton, FL: CRC Press.

Froestad, J., Shearing, C. and van der Merwe, M. (2015) 'Criminology: re-imagining security and risk', in P. Bourbeau (ed.), *Security: Dialogue across Disciplines*. Cambridge: Cambridge University Press.

Fukuyama, F. (1989) 'The end of history?', *The National Interest*, Summer: 3–18.

Fukuyama, F. (1992) *The End of History and the Last Man*. Harmondsworth: Penguin.

Fukuyama, F. (2016) 'US against the world? Trump's America and the new global order', *Financial Times*, 12 November. Available at: www.ft.com/content/6a43cf54–a75d-11e6-8b69-02899e8bd9d1.

Furnell, S. (2002) *Cybercrime: Vandalizing the Information Society*. London: Addison–Wesley.

G4S (2020) Our Employees. Available at: www.g4s.com/who-we-are/our-people/our-employees.

Garland, D. (1996) 'The limits of the sovereign state: strategies of crime control in contemporary society', *British Journal of Criminology*, 36(4): 445–471.

Garland, D. (2001) *The Culture of Control: Crime and Social Order in Contemporary Society*. Oxford: Oxford University Press.

Gasper, D. (2010) 'The idea of human security', in K. O'Brien, A. St Clair and B. Kristoffersen (eds.), *Climate Change, Ethics and Human Security*. Cambridge: Cambridge University Press.

Gee, J. and Button, M. (2019) *The Financial Cost of Fraud 2019*. London: Crowe.

Gerber, J. (2000) 'On the relationship between organized and white-collar crime: government, business, and criminal enterprise in post-communist Russia', *European Journal of Crime, Criminal Law and Criminal Justice*, 8(4): 327–342.

Germond, B. (2015) 'The geopolitical dimension of maritime security', *Marine Policy*, 54: 137–142.

Gibson, W. (1984) *Neuromancer*. New York: Ace.

Gidda, M. (2020) 'Police forces in England and Wales up to seven times more likely to fine BAME people in lockdown', 17 June. Available at: https://libertyinvestigates.org.uk/articles/police-forces-in-england-and-wales-up-to-seven-times-more-likely-to-fine-bame-people-in-lockdown/.

Giddens, A. (1991) *Modernity and Self-Identity: Self and Society in the Late Modern Age*. Cambridge: Polity Press.

Giddens, A. (1999) *Runaway World: How Globalisation is Reshaping Our Lives*. London: Profile.

Giddens, A. (2005) 'Scaring people may be the only way to avoid the risks of new-style terrorism', *New Statesman*, 18(840): 29–31.

Gilbert, M. (2004) *The First World War: A Complete History* (2nd ed.). New York: Henry Holt and Company.

Gilbert, M. (2009) *The Second World War: A Complete History*. New York: Henry Holt and Company.

Gill, M. (ed.) (2014) *The Handbook of Security* (2nd ed.). Basingstoke: Palgrave Macmillan.

Gill, M. and Hart, J. (1997) 'Exploring investigative policing: a study of private detectives in Britain', *British Journal of Criminology*, 37(4): 549–567.

Gill, M., Owen, K. and Lawson, C. (2010) *Private Security, the Corporate Sector and the Police: Opportunities and Barriers to Partnership Working*. Leicester: Perpetuity Research and Consultancy International.

Gill, P. (2009) 'Intelligence agency', in A. Wakefield and J. Fleming (eds.), *The Sage Dictionary of Policing*. London: Sage.

Gill, P. and Phythian, M. (2018) *Intelligence in an Insecure World*. Cambridge: Polity Press.

Global Centre for the Responsibility to Protect (2019) *About Us*. Available at: www.globalr2p.org/about.

Goodhart, D. (2017) *The Road to Somewhere: The New Tribes Shaping British Politics*. London: Penguin.

Goodman, M.S. (2014) 'The United Kingdom', in R. Dover, M.S. Goodman and C. Hillebrand (eds.) *Routledge Companion to Intelligence Studies*. London: Routledge.

Goodman, P.S. (2020) 'A global outbreak is fueling the backlash to globalization', *New York Times*, 5 March. Available at: www.nytimes.com/2020/03/05/business/coronavirus-globalism.html.

Goold, B.J. and Lazarus, L. (2019) *Security and Human Rights* (2nd ed.). Oxford: Hart Publishing.

Gorbachev, M. (1987) *Perestroika: New Thinking for Our Country and the World*. New York: Harper and Row.

Gorbachev, M. (1988) *Perestroika*. Fontana: London.

Gordine, E. (2020) 'Petition launched to shut down PornHub after reported abuse cases', *DW*, 11 March. Available at: www.dw.com/en/pornhub-petition/a-52692766.

Gordon, S. and Ford, R. (2006) *Cyberterrorism?* Cupertino, CA: Symantec.

Government Commercial Function (2019) *Tackling Modern Slavery in Government Supply Chains*. London: Civil Service.

Graham, L. (2018) 'The new face of piracy: cyber crime is threatening the shipping industry', *City AM*, 26 November. Available at: www.cityam.com/new-face-piracy-cyber-crime-threatening-shipping-industry/.

Graham-Harrison, E., Giuffrida, A., Smith, H. and Ford, L. (2020) 'Lockdowns around the world bring rise in domestic violence', *Guardian*, 28 March. Available at: www.theguardian.com/society/2020/mar/28/lockdowns-world-rise-domestic-violence.

Gray, H.P. (1993) 'Globalization versus nationhood', *Development and International Cooperation*, 9(16): 35–49.

Greenfield, P. and Marsh, S. (2019) 'Rising number of councils issuing fines for rough sleeping', *The Guardian*, 7 March. Available at: www.theguardian.com/society/2019/mar/07/rising-number-of-councils-issuing-fines-for-rough-sleeping.

Gregory, F. (2007) 'National governance structures to manage the response to terrorist threats and attacks: a cross-national comparative analysis with special reference to the UK "lead department" response structure and UK counter-terrorism strategy', in P. Wilkinson (ed.), *Homeland Security in the UK: Future Preparedness for Terrorist Attack Since 9/11*. London: Routledge.

Grierson, J. (2020) 'Domestic abuse killings "more than double" amid Covid-19 lockdown', *The Guardian*, 15 April. Available at: www.theguardian.com/society/2020/apr/15/domestic-abuse-killings-more-than-double-amid-covid-19-lockdown.

Grimshaw, R. and Ford, M. (2018) *Young People, Violence and Knives: Revisiting the Evidence and Policy Discussions*. London: Centre for Crime and Justice Studies.

Grother, P., Ngan, M. and Hanaoka, K. (2019) *Face Recognition Vendor Test (FRVT) Part 3: Demographic Effects*. Gaithersburg, MD: National Institute of Standards and Technology.

Guinness World Records (2020) 'Busiest shipping lane'. Available at: www.guinnessworldrecords.com/world-records/busiest-shipping-lane.

Habib, H. (1995) 'Defining the "Asia–Pacific Region"', *Indonesian Quarterly*, 23(4): 302–312.

Hadjimatheou, K. (2019) 'Citizen-led digital policing and democratic norms: The case of self-styled paedophile hunters', *Criminology and Criminal Justice*. Epub ahead of print 16 October. https://doi.org/10.1177/1748895819880956.

Haglund, D.G. (2011) '"Let's call the whole thing off"? Security culture as strategic culture', *Contemporary Security Policy*, 32(3): 494–516.

Hall, S. (1992) 'West and the rest: discourse and power', in B. Gieben and S. Hall (eds.), *The Formations of Modernity*. Cambridge: Polity Press.

Hamann, R., Makaula, L., Ziervogel, G., Shearing, C. and Zhang, A. (2019) 'Strategic responses to grand challenges: why and how corporations build community resilience', *Journal of Business Ethics*, 161(4): 835–853.

Hampson, F.O. (2004) 'Can the UN still mediate?', R. Price and M. Zacher (eds.), *The United Nations and Global Security*. New York: Palgrave Macmillan.

Harding, S. (2020) *County Lines: Exploitation and Drug Dealing among Urban Street Gangs*. Bristol: Bristol University Press.

Hardy, S-J. and Chakraborti, N. (2020) *Blood, Threats and Fears: The Hidden Worlds of Hate Crime Victims*. Basingstoke: Palgrave Macmillan.

Harrington, C. and Shearing, C. (2017) *Security in the Anthropocene: Reflections on Safety and Care*. New York: Columbia University Press.

Harris, T. (2016) *An Independent Review of London's Preparedness to Respond to a Major Terrorist Incident*. London: Greater London Authority.

Harvey, D. (1989) *The Condition of Postmodernity: An Enquiry into the Origins of Cultural Change*. Oxford: Blackwell.

Heath-Kelly, C. (2017) 'Resilience and disaster sites: the disastrous temporality of the 'recovery-to-come', in J. Coaffee and D. Chandler (eds.), *The Routledge Handbook of International Resilience: Policies, Theories and Practices*. London: Routledge.

Henig, R. (2019) *The Peace That Never Was: A History of the League of Nations*. London: Haus Publishing.

Her Majesty's Inspectorate of Constabulary (2015) *PEEL: Police Efficiency 2015*. London: HMIC.

Hillyard, P. and Tombs, S. (2007) 'From "crime" to social harm?', *Crime, Law and Social Change*, 48(1): 9–25.

Hillyard, P., Pantazis, C., Tombs, S. and Gordon, D. (eds.) (2004) *Beyond Criminology: Taking Harm Seriously*. London: Pluto Press.

HM Government (2014a) *National Space Security Policy*. London: HM Government.

HM Government (2014b) *The UK National Strategy for Maritime Security*. London: HM Government.

HM Government (2015) *National Security Strategy and Strategic Defence and Security Review 2015*. London: The Cabinet Office.

HM Government (2016) *National Cyber Security Strategy 2016–2021*. London: The Cabinet Office.

HM Government (2017) *UK Climate Change Risk Assessment 2017*. London: HM Government.

HM Government (2018a) *Initial National Cyber Security Skills Strategy*. London: HM Government.

HM Government (2018b) *National Security Capability Review*. London: The Cabinet Office.

HM Government (2018c) *UK Biological Security Strategy*. London: The Home Office.

HM Government (2019) *Online Harms White Paper*. London: HM Government.

Holling, C.S. (1973) 'Resilience and stability of ecological systems', *Annual Review of Ecology and Systematics*, 4(1): 1–23.

Home Office (1999) *The Stephen Lawrence Inquiry: Report of an Inquiry by Sir William Macpherson of Cluny*. Cm 4262-I. London: Home Office.

Home Office (2001) *Policing: A Blueprint for Reform*. London: Home Office.

Home Office (2002) *Secure Borders, Safe Haven: Integration with Diversity in Modern Britain*. London: The Stationery Office.

Home Office (2012a) 'Definition of policing by consent', 10 December. Available at: www.gov.uk/government/publications/policing-by-consent/definition-of-policing-by-consent.

Home Office (2012b) *The Strategic Policing Requirement*. London: Home Office.

Home Office (2018a) *CONTEST: The United Kingdom's Strategy for Countering Terrorism*. London: Home Office.

Home Office (2018b) *Hate Crime, England and Wales, 2017/18*. London: Home Office.

Home Office (2018c) *Understanding the Costs of Cyber Crime*. London: Home Office.

Homeland Security Council (2007) *National Strategy for Homeland Security*. Washington, DC: Executive Office of the President, Homeland Security Council.

Horner, H., Schindler, S., Haberly, D. and Aoyama, Y. (2018) 'Globalisation, uneven development and the North–South "big switch"', *Cambridge Journal of Regions, Economy and Society*, 11(1): 17–33.

Hough, P. (2005) 'Who's securing whom? The need for international relations to embrace human security', *St Antony's International Review*, 1(2): 72–87.

Hough, P. (2014) *Environmental Security: An Introduction*. London: Routledge.

Hough, P. (2018) *Understanding Global Security* (4th ed.). London: Routledge.

Hough, P. (2020a) 'Food security', in P. Hough, A. Moran, B. Pilbeam and W. Stokes (eds.), *International Security Studies: Theory and Practice* (2nd ed.). London: Routledge.

Hough, P. (2020b) 'Health security', in P. Hough, A. Moran, B. Pilbeam and W. Stokes (eds.), *International Security Studies: Theory and Practice* (2nd ed.). London: Routledge.

Hough, P. (2020c) 'Regional security organizations', in P. Hough, A. Moran, B. Pilbeam and W. Stokes (eds.), *International Security Studies: Theory and Practice* (2nd ed.). London: Routledge.

Hough, P. (2020d) 'Security in Africa', in P. Hough, A. Moran, B. Pilbeam and W. Stokes (eds.), *International Security Studies: Theory and Practice* (2nd ed.). London: Routledge.

Hough, P., Moran, A., Pilbeam, B. and Stokes, W. (eds.) (2020) *International Security Studies: Theory and Practice* (2nd ed.). London: Routledge.

House of Commons Defence Committee (2009) *The Defence Contribution to UK National Security and Resilience*. London: The Stationery Office.

House of Commons Foreign Affairs Committee (2011) *Piracy off the Coast of Somalia*. London: The Stationery Office.

House of Commons Home Affairs Committee (2018a) *Immigration Policy: Basis for Building Consensus*. London: House of Commons.

House of Commons Home Affairs Committee (2018b) *Policing for the Future*. London: House of Commons.

Huntington, S. (1993) 'Clash of civilisations?', *Foreign Affairs*, 72(3): 22–49.

Huntington, S. (1996) *The Clash of Civilizations and the Remaking of World Order*. London: Free Press.

Ilyushina, M., Hodge, N. and Gold, H. (2019) 'Russia rolls out its "sovereign internet". Is it building a digital Iron Curtain?', *CNN*, 1 November. Available at: https://edition.cnn.com/2019/11/01/tech/russia-internet-law/index.html.

Imlay, T. (2007) 'Total war', *Journal of Strategic Studies*, 30(3):, 547–570.

Independent Commission on International Development Issues (1980) *North–South: A Programme for Survival*. Washington, DC: World Bank.

Indian Navy (2015) *Ensuring Secure Seas: Indian Maritime Security Strategy*. New Delhi: Integrated Headquarters, Ministry of Defence (Navy).

Inoue, T. (2018) *Public Relations in Hyper-Globalization: Essential Relationship Management – A Japan Perspective*. London: Routledge.

Institute for Economics and Peace (2019) *Global Terrorism Index 2019*. Sydney: Institute for Economics and Peace.

Institute for Economics and Peace (2020) *Global Peace Index 2020*. Sydney: Institute for Economics and Peace.

Intellectual Property Office and IP Crime Group 2019 (2019) *IP Crime and Enforcement Report 2018 to 2019*. Newport: IP Crime Group 2019.

International Labour Organization (2020) *'Safety and health at work'*. Available at: www.ilo.org/global/topics/safety-and-health-at-work/lang–en/index.htm.

International Labour Organization and Walk Free Foundation (2017) *Global Estimates of Modern Slavery: Forced Labour and Forced Marriage*. Geneva: ILO.

International Maritime Organization (2020a) *'Marine environment'*. Available at: www.imo.org/en/OurWork/Environment.

International Maritime Organization (2020b) *Reports on Acts of Piracy and Armed Robbery Against Ships: Annual Report – 2019*. London: IMO.

International Maritime Organization Assembly (2009) Resolution A.1025(26): Code of Practice for the Investigation of the Crimes of Piracy and Armed Robbery Against Ships (2 December). A 26/Res.1025. Available at: wwwcdn.imo.org/localresources/en/KnowledgeCentre/IndexofIMOResolutions/AssemblyDocuments/A.1025(26).pdf.

International Organization for Migration (2020) 'Mediterranean arrivals reach 110,699 in 2019; deaths reach 1,283. World deaths Fall', 1 March. Available at: www.iom.int/news/iom-mediterranean-arrivals-reach-110699-2019-deaths-reach-1283-world-deaths-fall.

International Standards Organization (2018) *ISO 31000 Risk Management*. Geneva: ISO.

International Standards Organization and the International Electrotechnical Commission (2013) *ISO/IEC 27001 Information Security Management*. Geneva: ISO.

Internet Telecommunications Union (2003) *World Communication Development Report: Access Indicators for the Information Society*. Geneva: ITU.

International Telecommunications Union (2018) *Measuring the Information Society Report*, Volume 1. Geneva: ITU.

Internet Telecommunications Union (2019) *Measuring Digital Development Facts and Figures 2019*. Geneva: ITU.

Internet Watch Foundation (2020) *Annual Report 2019*. Cambridge: IWF.

Internet World Stats (2020) *World Internet Users and 2020 Population Stats*. Available at: https://internetworldstats.com/stats.htm.

Interpol (2018) 'Marine pollution crime: first global multi-agency operation', 13 November. Available at: www.interpol.int/News-and-Events/News/2018/Marine-pollution-crime-first-global-multi-agency-operation.

ISACA and RSA (2020) *State of Cyber Security 2020*. Schaumburg, IL: ISACA.

Jackson, M.C. (2019) *Critical Systems Thinking and the Management of Complexity*. Chichester: Wiley.

Jackson, R., Jarvis, L., Gunning, J. and Breen-Smyth, M. (2011) *Terrorism: A Critical Introduction*. London: Red Globe Press.

James, A. (2011) 'The influence of intelligence-led policing models on investigative policy and practice in mainstream policing 1993–2007: Division, resistance and investigative orthodoxy'. PhD Thesis, London School of Economics.

Jansen, J.C. and Osterhammel, J. (2017) *Decolonization: A Short History*. Princeton, NJ: Princeton University Press.

Jasper, S. (2014) 'Cyberspace', in J. Sperling (ed.), *Handbook of Governance and Security*. Cheltenham: Edward Elgar.

Jayawardene, S., Larik, J. and Jackson, E. (2015) *Cyber Governance: Challenges, Solutions, and Lessons for Effective Global Governance*. The Hague: The Hague Institute.

Jeffery, C.R. (1971) *Crime Prevention Through Environmental Design*. Beverly Hills, CA: Sage.

Johnson, L.K. (2004) 'The Aspin–Brown intelligence inquiry: behind the closed doors of a blue ribbon commission', *Studies in Intelligence*, 48(3): 1–20.

Johnson, L.K. (ed.) (2010) *The Oxford Handbook of National Security Intelligence*. New York: Oxford University Press.

Johnston, L. (1992) *The Rebirth of Private Policing*. London: Routledge.

Johnston, L. and Shearing, C. (2003) *Governing Security: Explorations in Policing and Justice*. London: Routledge.

Jones, R. and Johnson, C. (2016) 'Border militarisation and the re-articulation of sovereignty', *Transactions of the Institute of British Geographers*, 41(2): 187–200.

Jones, T. and Newburn, T. (1998) *Private Security and Public Policing*. Oxford: Clarendon.

Jones, T. and Newburn, T. (2002) 'The transformation of policing? Understanding current trends in policing systems', *British Journal of Criminology*, 42(1): 129–146.

Jones, T. and Newburn, T. (eds.) (2006) *Plural Policing: A Comparative Perspective*. London: Routledge.

Jordan, J. (2017) 'Political and social trends in the future of global security. A meta-study on official perspectives in Europe and North America', *European Journal of Futures Research*, 5(11): 1–11.

Joseph Rowntree Foundation (2018) *Destitution in the UK 2018*. York: Joseph Rowntree Foundation.

Kagan, J. (1975) 'Resilience in cognitive development', *Ethos,* 3(2): 231–247.

Kahan, J.H. (2015) 'Resilience redux: buzzword or basis for homeland security', *Homeland Security Affairs*, 11: 1–19.

Kahan, J.H., Allen, A.C. and George, J.K. (2009) 'An operational framework for resilience', *Journal of Homeland Security and Emergency Management*, 6(1): 1–48.

Kaldor, M. (2012) *New and Old Wars* (2nd ed.). Cambridge: Polity Press.

Kambil, A. (2008) 'What is your Web 5.0 strategy?', *Journal of Business Strategy*, 29(6): 56–58.

Kanno-Youngs, Z. (2020) 'Trump administration adds six countries to travel ban', *New York Times*, 31 January. Available at: www.nytimes.com/2020/01/31/us/politics/trump-travel-ban.html.

Katzenstein, P. (1996) *Cultural Norms and National Security*. Ithaca, NY: Cornell University Press.

Kavalski, E. (2007) 'The fifth debate and the emergence of complex international relations theory: notes on the application of complexity theory to the study of international life', *Cambridge Review of International Affairs*, 20(3): 435–454.

Kavalski, E. (2008) 'The complexity of global security governance: an analytical overview', *Global Society*, 22(4): 423–443.

Kempa, M., Carrier, C., Wood, J. and Shearing, C. (1999) 'Reflections on the evolving concept of "private policing"', *European Journal on Criminal Policy and Research*, 7(2): 197–223.

Keohane, R.O. and Nye, J.S. (1972) *Transnational Relations and World Politics*. Cambridge, MA: Harvard University Press.

Keohane, R.O. and Nye, J.S. (2011) *Power and Interdependence* (4th ed.), Upper Saddle River, NJ: Pearson.

Kirchner, E.J. and Sperling, J. (eds.) (2010) *National Security Cultures: Patterns of Global Governance*. Abingdon: Routledge.

Kirkup, J. and Winnett, R. (2012) 'Theresa May: "We're going to give illegal migrants a really hostile reception"', *The Telegraph*, 26 May. Available at: www.telegraph.co.uk/news/0/theresa-may-interview-going-give-illegal-migrants-really-hostile/.

Klein, N. (2003) 'The rise of the fortress continent', *The Nation*, 3 February. Available at: www.thenation.com/article/archive/rise-fortress-continent/.

Klein, N. (2011) *Introduction to Maritime Security and the Law of the Sea*. Oxford: Oxford University Press.

Klein, R.A. (2016) 'Crime at sea: a comparison of crime on Carnival Cruise Lines, 2007–2011', in A. Papathanassis (ed.), *Cruise Business Development: Safety, Product Design and Human Capital*. Heidelberg: Springer.

Koopmans, M. (2017) 'Perspectives on complexity, its definition and applications in the field', *Complicity: An International Journal of Complexity and Education*, 14(1): 16–35.

Kostka, G. (2019) 'What do people in China think about "social credit" monitoring?', *Washington Post*, 21 March. Available at: www.washingtonpost.com/politics/2019/03/21/what-do-people-china-think-about-social-credit-monitoring/.

Krahmann, E. (2003a) 'Conceptualizing security governance', *Cooperation and Conflict*, 38(1): 5–26.

Krahmann, E. (2003b) 'National, regional, and global governance: one phenomenon or many?', *Global Governance*, 9(3): 323–346.

Kraska, J. (2011) *Maritime Power and the Law of the Sea: Expeditionary Operations in World Politics*. Oxford: Oxford University Press.

Kraska, J. and Pedrozo, R. (2013) *International Maritime Security Law*. Leiden: Martinus Nijhoff.

Krause, K. (1994) 'Is human security more than just a good idea?', in M. Brzoska and P.J. Croll (eds.), *Promoting Security: But How and for Whom?* Bonn International Center for Conversion: Geneva.

Krause, K. and Williams, M.C. (eds.) (1997) *Critical Security Studies: Concepts and Cases*. Minneapolis, MN: University of Minnesota Press.

Krishna, S. (2008) *Globalization and Postcolonialism: Hegemony and Resistance in the Twenty-First Century*. Lanham, MD: Rowman and Littlefield.

Kuehl, D.T. (2009) 'From cyberspace to cyberpower: defining the problem', in F.D. Kramer, S. Starr and L.K. Wentz (eds.), *Cyberpower and National Security*. Washington, DC: National Defense.

Kuerbis, B. and Badiei, F. (2017) 'Mapping the cybersecurity institutional landscape', *Digital Policy, Regulation and Governance*, 19(6): 466–492.

Kumar, S., Kumar, N. and Vivekadhish, S. (2016) 'Millennium Development Goals (MDGs) to Sustainable Development Goals (SDGs): addressing unfinished agenda and strengthening sustainable development and partnership', *Indian Journal of Community Medicine*, 41(1): 1–4.

Kupchan, C.A. and Kuchan, C.A. (1991) 'Concerts, collective security, and the future of Europe', *International Security*, 16(1): 114–161.

Lancet (2018) *Global Burden of Disease Study 2017*. London: The Lancet.

Lanoszka, A. (2016) 'Russian hybrid warfare and extended deterrence in eastern Europe', *International Affairs*, 92(1): 175–195.

Lasswell, H.D. (1950) *National Security and Individual Freedom*. New York: McGraw–Hill.

Le Prestre, P. (2017) *Global Ecopolitics Revisited: Towards a Complex Governance of Global Environmental Problems*. Abingdon: Routledge.

Lehmann, K.E. (2012) 'Unfinished transformation: the three phases of complexity's emergence into international relations and foreign policy', *Cooperation and Conflict*, 47(3): 404–413.

Leman-Langlois, S. and Shearing, C. (2009) 'Human rights implications of new developments in policing', in International Council on Human Rights Policy (ed.), *Modes and Patterns of Social Control: Implications for Human Rights Policy*. Geneva: International Council on Human Rights Policy.

Levin, K., Cashore, B., Bernstein, S. and Auld, G. (2007) 'Playing it forward: path dependency, progressive incrementalism, and the "super wicked" problem of global climate change', paper presented at *International Studies Association Convention*, Chicago, 28 February to 3 March.

Levin, K., Cashore, B., Bernstein, S. and Auld, G. (2012) 'Overcoming the tragedy of super wicked problems: constraining our future selves to ameliorate global climate change', *Policy Sciences*, 45(2): 123–152.

Levy, D. and Newell, P. (2006) 'Multinationals in global governance', in S. Vachani (ed.), *Transformations in Global Governance: Implications for Multinationals and Other Stakeholders*. Cheltenham: Edward Elgar.

Levy, S. (1993) *Artificial Life: A Report from the Frontier Where Computers Meet Biology*. New York: Random House Inc.

Leys, C. (1996) 'The crisis in "development theory"', *New Political Economy*, 1(1): 41–58.

Lilley, P. (2002) *Hacked, Attacked and Abused: Digital Crime Exposed*. London: Kogan Page.

Liotta, P.H. and Owen, T. (2006) 'Why human security?', *Whitehead Journal of Diplomacy and International Relations*, 7(1): 37–54.

Lippert, R.K. and Walby, K. (2014) 'Critiques of corporate security: cost, camouflage, and creep', in M. Gill (ed.), *The Handbook of Security* (2nd ed.). Basingstoke: Palgrave Macmillan.

Lippmann, W. (1943) *US Foreign Policy*. London: Hamish Hamilton.

Liu, J. (2009) 'Asian criminology – challenges, opportunities, and directions', *Asian Journal of Criminology*, 4(1): 1–9.

Lloyd's List (2019) 'Top 10 Flag States 2019', 3 December. Available at: https://lloydslist.maritimeintelligence.informa.com/LL1129840/Top-10-flag-states-2019.

Loader, I. (1999) 'Consumer culture and the commodification of policing and security', *Sociology*, 33(2): 373–392.

Loader, I. (2000) 'Plural policing and democratic governance', *Social and Legal Studies*, 9(3): 323–345.

Loader, I. and Percy, S. (2012) 'Bringing the "outside" in and the "inside" out: crossing the criminology/IR divide', *Global Crime*, 13(4): 213–218.

Loomba, A. (2015) *Colonialism/Postcolonialism: The New Critical Idiom* (3rd ed.). London: Routledge.

Loopstra, R. and Lalor, D. (2017) *Financial Insecurity, Food Insecurity, and Disability: The Profile of People Receiving Emergency Food Assistance from the Trussell Trust Foodbank Network in Britain*. Salisbury: Trussell Trust.

Lorenz, E. (1972) 'The butterfly effect: does the flap of a butterfly's wing in Brazil set off a tornado in Texas?', 139th Meeting of the American Association for the Advancement of Science, Washington, DC, 29 December.

Loveday, B. (2017) 'Still plodding along? The police response to the changing profile of crime in England and Wales', *International Journal of Police Science and Management*, 19(2): 101–109.

Lucas, E.R. (2013) 'Somalia's pirate cycle – the three phases of Somali piracy', *Journal of Strategic Security*, 6(1): 55–63.

Lucas, E. and Pomerantsev, P. (2016) *Winning the Information War: Techniques and Counter-strategies to Russian Propaganda in Central and Eastern Europe*. Washington, DC: Centre for European Policy Analysis.

Lyon, D. (2001) *Surveillance Society: Monitoring Everyday Life*. Buckingham: Open University Press.

Macaskill, E. and Dance, G. (2013) 'NSA files decoded', *The Guardian*, 1 November. Available at: www.theguardian.com/world/interactive/2013/nov/01/snowden-nsa-files-surveillance-revelations-decoded#section/1.

Macedo, S. (ed.) (2004) *Universal Jurisdiction: National Courts and the Prosecution of Serious Crimes Under International Law*. Philadelphia: University of Pennsylvania Press.

Maguire, M. (2008) 'Criminal investigation and crime control', in T. Newburn (ed.), *Handbook of Policing* (2nd ed.). Cullompton: Willan.

Makarenko, T. (2004) 'The crime–terror continuum: tracing the interplay between transnational organised crime and terrorism', *Global Crime*, 6(1): 129–145.

Malik, S. (2020) 'Human security', in P. Hough, A. Moran, B. Pilbeam and W. Stokes (eds.), *International Security Studies: Theory and Practice* (2nd ed.). London: Routledge.

Mancusi-Ungaro, G. (2016) 'Fake news stories present real threats to businesses', *Security Info Watch*, 30 November. Available at: www.securityinfowatch.com/security-executives/article/12283638/fake-news-stories-present-real-threats-to-businesses.

Marrin, S. (2014) 'The United States', in R. Dover, M.S. Goodman and C. Hillebrand, C. (eds.) *Routledge Companion to Intelligence Studies*. London: Routledge.

Martin, G. (1985) 'The historical, economic, and political bases of France's African policy', *Journal of Modern African Studies*, 23(2): 189–208.

Martin, M. (2014) 'A road still to be travelled: human security and a continuing search for meaning', in S. Takahashi (ed.), *Human Rights, Human Security and State Security*, Volume 2. Santa Barbara CA: Praeger.

Martin, P. (2019) *The Rules of Security*. Oxford: Oxford University Press.

Maslow, A.H. (1970) *Motivation and Personality* (2nd ed.). Harper and Row: New York.

Mawby, R.I. (1999) *Policing Across the World: Issues for the Twenty-First Century*. London: Routledge.

Mayhew, P.M., Clarke, R.V., Sturman, A. and Hough, J.M. (eds.) (1976) *Crime as Opportunity*. Home Office Research Study No. 34. London: HMSO.

McGuire, M. (2018) *Into The Web of Profit: An In-Depth Study of Cybercrime, Criminals and Money*. Cupertino, CA: Bromium, Inc.

McGuire, M. and Dowling, S. (2013) *Cyber Crime: A Review of the Evidence*. London: Home Office.

McGuire, M.R. and Holt, T.J. (eds.) (2017) *The Routledge Handbook of Technology, Crime and Justice*. London: Routledge.

McKenzie, R. and Lee, D. (1991) *Quicksilver Capital: How the Rapid Movement of Wealth Has Changed the World*. New York: Free Press.

McLaughlin, E. (2019) 'State crime', in E. McLaughlin and J. Muncie (eds.), *The Sage Dictionary of Criminology*. London: Sage.

McLeish, C. (2017) 'Emerging biosecurity frameworks', in R. Dover, H. Dylan and M. Goodman (eds.), *Palgrave Handbook of Security, Risk and Intelligence*. Basingstoke: Palgrave Macmillan.

McSweeney, B. (1999) *Security, Identity and Interests: A Sociology of International Relations*. Cambridge: Cambridge University Press.

Mead, W.R. (2017) 'The Jacksonian revolt: American populism and the liberal order', *Foreign Affairs*, March/April.

Mentan, T. (2018) *Africa in the Colonial Ages of Empire: Slavery, Capitalism, Racism, Colonialism, Decolonization, Independence as Recolonization, and Beyond*. Mankon, Bamenda, Cameroon: Langaa Research and Publishing Common Initiative Group.

Miller, J.M. and Blumstein, A. (eds.) (2020) 'Crime, justice and the COVID-19 pandemic: toward a national research agenda', special issue of the *American Journal of Criminal Justice*, 45(4): 515–524.

Ministry of Defence (1998) *Strategic Defence Review*. London: The Stationery Office.

Ministry of Defence (2008) *Defence Plan 2008–2012*. London: The Stationery Office.

Ministry of Defence (2018) *Global Strategic Trends: The Future Starts Today*. London: Ministry of Defence.

Mohdin, A. and Swann, G. (2020) 'How George Floyd's death sparked a wave of UK anti-racism protests', *The Guardian*, 29 July. Available at: www.theguardian.com/ uk-news/2020/jul/29/george-floyd-death-fuelled-anti-racism-protests-britain.

Moore, D. and Rid, T. (2015) 'Cryptopolitik and the darknet', *Survival*, 58(1): 7–38.

Moosavi, L. (2020) 'The decolonial bandwagon and the dangers of intellectual decolonisation', *International Review of Sociology*, 30(2): 332–354.

Moran, A. (2020) 'Cybersecurity', in P. Hough, A. Moran, B. Pilbeam and W. Stokes (eds.), *International Security Studies: Theory and Practice* (2nd ed.). London: Routledge.

Morgenthau, H.J. (1948) *Politics Among Nations: The Struggle for Power and Peace*. New York: A.A. Knopf.

Moynihan, D.P. (1991) 'Do we still need the C.I.A? The State Dept. can do the job', *New York Times*, 19 May.

Mueller, M. (2017) 'Is cybersecurity eating internet governance? Causes and consequences of alternative framings', *Digital Policy, Regulation and Governance*, 19(6): 415–428.

Murphy, K., Williamson, H., Sargeant, E. and McCarthy. M. (2020) 'Why people comply with COVID-19 social distancing restrictions: Self-interest or duty?', *Australian and New Zealand Journal of Criminology*, 53(4): 477–496.

Murphy, K.M. and Topel, R.H. (2013) 'Some basic economics of national security', *American Economic Review*, 103(3): 508–511.

Mutongwizo, T., Holley, C., Shearing, C.D. and Simpson, N.P. (2019) 'Resilience policing: an emerging response to shifting harm landscapes', *Policing: A Journal of Policy and Practice*, Epub ahead of print 10 June. https://doi.org/10.1093/police/paz033.

Nalla, M.K. (2001) 'Designing an introductory survey course in private security', *Journal of Criminal Justice Education*, 12(1): 35–52.

Nalla, M. and Morash, M. (2002) 'Assessing the scope of corporate security: common practices and relationships with other business functions', *Security Journal*, 15: 7–19.

Nalla, M. and Wakefield, A. (2014) 'The security officer', in M. Gill (ed.), *The Handbook of Security* (2nd ed.). Basingstoke: Palgrave Macmillan.

Nasu, H. (2013) 'The place of human security in collective security', *Journal of Conflict and Security Law*, 18(1): 95–129.

Natarajan, M. (2019) *International and Transnational Crime and Justice* (2nd ed.). Cambridge: Cambridge University Press.

National Center for Missing and Exploited Children (NCMEC) (2020) *2019 CyberTipline Reports by Country*. Available at: www.missingkids.org/gethelpnow/cybertipline.

National Commission on Terrorist Attacks upon the United States (2004) *The 9/11 Commission Report: Final Report of the National Commission on Terrorist Attacks upon the United States*. New York: Norton.

National Consortium for the Study of Terrorism and Responses to Terrorism (2019) *Global Terrorism Database*. College Park, MD: University of Maryland.

National Intelligence Council (2017) *Global Trends: Paradox of Progress*. Washington, DC: National Intelligence Council.

National Institute of Standards and Technology (2014) *Framework for Improving Critical Infrastructure Cybersecurity*, Version 1.0. Gaithersburg, MD: National Institute of Standards and Technology, US Department of Commerce.

National Oceanic Atmospheric Administration (2018a) 'How much of the ocean have we explored?' Available at: https://oceanservice.noaa.gov/facts/exploration.html.

National Oceanic Atmospheric Administration (2018b) 'How much water is in the ocean?' Available at: https://oceanservice.noaa.gov/facts/oceanwater.html.

Nay, O. (2013) 'Fragile and failed states: critical perspectives on conceptual hybrids', *International Political Science Review*, 34(3): 326–341.

Nederveen Pieterse, J. (1995) *Globalization and Culture: Global Mélange*. Lanham, MD: Rowman and Littlefield.

Nederveen Pieterse, J. (2019) *Globalization and Culture: Global Mélange* (4th ed.). Lanham, MD: Rowman and Littlefield.

Neocleous, N. (2007) 'Security, commodity, fetishism', *Critique*, 35(3): 339–355.

Neumann, P. (2009) *Old and New Terrorism: Late Modernity, Globalization and the Transformation of Political Violence*. Cambridge: Polity Press.

Newburn, T. (2017) *Handbook of Criminology* (3rd ed.). London: Routledge.

Nietzsche, F. (1968 [1888]) *Twilight of the Idols and the Anti-Christ*. Harmondsworth: Penguin.

Nkrumah, K. (1965) *Neo-Colonialism, the Last Stage of Imperialism*. London: Thomas Nelson and Sons.

North Atlantic Treaty Organization (2011) *Alliance Maritime Strategy*. Brussels: NATO.

Nye, J.S. (1968) *International Regionalism*. Boston, MA: Little, Brown and Company.

Nye, J.S. (2010) *Cyber Power*. Cambridge, MA: Harvard Kennedy School.

O'Malley, P. (1992) 'Risk, power and crime prevention', *Economy and Society*, 21(3): 252–275.

O'Malley, P. (2009) 'Responsibilization', in A. Wakefield and J. Fleming (eds.) *The Sage Dictionary of Policing*. London: Sage.

O'Reilly, C. (2010) 'The transnational security consultancy industry: a case of state–corporate symbiosis', *Theoretical Criminology*, 14(2): 183–210.

Office for National Statistics (2020) *Crime in England and Wales: Year Ending March 2020*. London: ONS.

Office of the United Nations High Commissioner for Human Rights (2017) 'Human Rights Council opens special session on the situation of human rights of the Rohingya and other minorities in Rakhine State in Myanmar', 15 December. Available at: www.ohchr.org/EN/NewsEvents/Pages/DisplayNews.aspx?NewsID=22491.

Oman, C. (1994) *Globalisation and Regionalisation: The Challenge for Developing Countries*. Paris: Organisation for Economic Co-operation and Development.

Omand, D. (2010) *Securing the State*. London: Hurst.

Omeje, K. (ed.) (2021) *The Governance, Security and Development Nexus: Africa Rising*. Basingstoke: Palgrave Macmillan.

O'Neill, J. (2001) *Building Better Global Economic BRICs*, Global Economics Paper No. 66. New York: Goldman Sachs and Co.

Onuf, N.G. (1989) *World of Our Making*. Columbia: University of South California Press.

Organisation for Economic Co-operation and Development (2007) *Principles for Good International Engagement in Fragile States and Situations*. Paris: OECD.

Organisation for Economic Co-operation and Development (2016) *The Ocean Economy in 2030*. Paris: OECD.

Organisation for Economic Co-operation and Development (2018) *National Risk Assessments: A Cross Country Perspective*. Paris: OECD.

Organisation for Economic Co-operation and Development (2019) *ITF Transport Outlook 2019*. Paris: OECD.

Organisation for Economic Co-operation and Development (2020) *OECD Economic Outlook*, Volume 2020, Issue 1. Paris: OECD.

Organisation for Economic Co-operation and Development and European Union Intellectual Property Office (2019) *Trends in Trade in Counterfeit and Pirated Goods*. Paris: OECD.

Organization for Security and Co-operation in Europe (2020) *Annual Report 2019*. Vienna: OSCE.

Orsini, A., Le Prestre, P., Brosig, M., Pattberg, P., Gomez-Mera, L., Morin, J-F., Harrison, N., Geyer, R. and Chandler, D. (2019) 'Forum: complex systems and international governance', *International Studies Review*, 70: 1–31.

Owen, G. and Savage, N. (2015) *The Tor Dark Net*. Waterloo, ON: Centre for International Governance Innovation and the Royal Institute of International Affairs.

Oxford English Dictionary (3rd ed.) (2011) 'Security', *n*. Available at: www.oed.com.

Oxford Research Group (2020) *Sustainable Security Index: 2020 Edition*. London: Oxford Research Group.

Patel, K. (2013) 'Incremental journey for World Wide Web: introduced with Web 1.0 to recent Web 5.0: a survey paper', *International Journal of Advanced Research in Computer Science and Software Engineering*, 3(10): 410–417.

Pattberg, P. and Widerberg, O. (2019) 'Studying global governance as a complex system: a network perspective', in A. Orsini, P. Le Prestre, M. Brosig, P. Pattberg, L. Gomez-Mera, J-F. Morin, N. Harrison, R. Geyer and D. Chandler (eds.), 'Forum: complex systems and international governance', *International Studies Review*, 70: 1–31.

Pauli, G. (2010) *The Blue Economy: 10 Years, 100 Innovations, 100 Million Jobs*. Taos, NM: Paradigm Publications.

Pegram, T. and Kreienkamp, J. (2019) *Governing Complexity: Design Principles for Improving the Governance of Global Catastrophic Risks*. London: University College London.

Percy, S. (2016) 'Maritime crime and naval response', *Survival*, 58(3): 155–186.

Percy, S. (2018) 'Maritime security', in A. Gheciu and W.C. Wohlforth (eds.), *The Oxford Handbook of International Security*. Oxford: Oxford University Press.

Perrow, C. (1984) *Normal Accidents: Living with High-Risk Technologies*. Princeton, NJ: Princeton University Press.

Perry, J., Williams, M., Sefton, T. and Haddad, M. (2014) *Emergency Use Only: Understanding and Reducing the Use of Food Banks in the UK*. Oxford: Child Poverty Action Group, Church of England, Oxfam GB and the Trussell Trust.

Peters, B.G. (2017) 'What is so wicked about wicked problems? A conceptual analysis and a research program', *Policy and Society*, 36(3): 385–396.

Pettersson, T., Högbladh, S. and Öberg, M. (2019) 'Organized violence, 1989–2018 and peace agreements', *Journal of Peace Research*, 56(4): 589–603.

Pickering, S. and Ham, J. (2014) *The Routledge Handbook on Crime and International Migration*. London: Routledge.

Planet Retail RNG (2018) *The Sensormatic Global Shrink Index: Results and Executive Summary*. London: Planet Retail Limited.

Police Foundation (2020) *Public Safety and Security in the 21st Century: The First Report of the Strategic Review of Policing in England and Wales*. London: Police Foundation.

Ponemon Institute (2016) *Security Beyond the Traditional Perimeter*. Traverse City, MI: Ponemon Institute.

Portland (2019) *The Soft Power 30: A Global Ranking of Soft Power 2019*. London: Portland.

Premier Ministre de la République Française (2015) *National Strategy for the Security of Maritime Areas*. Paris: Premier Ministre de la République Française.

Provost, C. (2017) 'The industry of inequality: why the world is obsessed with private security', *The Guardian*, 12 May. Available at: www.theguardian.com/inequality/2017/may/12/industry-of-inequality-why-world-is-obsessed-with-private-security.

Public Health England (2020) *Beyond the Data: Understanding the Impact of COVID-19 on BAME Groups*. London: Public Health England.

Pycroft, A. and Bartollas, C. (2014) *Applying Complexity Theory: Whole Systems Approaches to Criminal Justice and Social Work*. Bristol: Policy Press.

Raadschelders, J.C.N., Larrison, J. and Thapar, A.V. (2019) 'Refugee migration as a "wicked problem": American controlling, palliative, and governance policies in global context', *World Affairs*, 182(3): 228–255.

Radzinowicz, L. (1968) *History of English Criminal Law and Its Administration From 1750. Vol. 4: Grappling for Control*. London: Stevens and Sons.

RAND (2020) RAND Database of Worldwide Terrorism Incidents. Available at: www.rand.org/nsrd/projects/terrorism-incidents.html.

Ratcliffe, J.H. (2009) 'Intelligence-led policing', in A. Wakefield and J. Fleming (eds.), *The Sage Dictionary of Policing*. London: Sage.

Reagan, R. (1983) Statement on United States Oceans Policy, 10 March.

Reuters (2016) 'Rana Plaza collapse: 38 charged with murder over garment factory disaster', *The Guardian*, 18 July. Available at: www.theguardian.com/world/2016/jul/18/rana-plaza-collapse-murder-charges-garment-factory.

Rhodes, R.A.W. (1996) 'The new governance: governing without government', *Political Studies*, 44(4): 652–657.

Rhodes, R.A.W. (1997) *Understanding Governance*. Buckingham: Open University Press.

Ripsman, N.M. and Paul, T.V. (2005) 'Globalization and the national security state: a framework for analysis', *International Studies Review*, 7(2): 199–227.

Ripsman, N.M. and Paul, T.V. (2010) *Globalization and the National Security State*. New York: Oxford University Press.

Rittel, H.W.J. and Webber, M.M. (1973) 'Dilemmas in a general theory of planning', *Policy Sciences*, 4(2): 155–169.

Roberts, K.H. (1989) 'New challenges in organizational research: high reliability organizations', *Industrial Crisis Quarterly*, 3(2): 111–125.

Robertson, N., Cruickshank, P. and Lister, T. (2012) 'Documents reveal al Qaeda's plans for seizing cruise ships, carnage in Europe', *CNN*, 1 May. Available at: https://edition.cnn.com/2012/04/30/world/al-qaeda-documents-future/index.html.

Robertson, R. (1992) *Globalization: Social Theory and Global Culture*. London: Sage.

Rochlin, G.I., La Porte, T.R. and Roberts, K.H. (1987) 'The self-designing high-reliability organization: aircraft carrier flight operations at sea', *Naval War College Review*, 40(4): 76–92.

Rodrik, D. (1997) *Has Globalization Gone Too Far?* Washington, DC: Peterson Institute of International Economics.

Rodrik, D. (2011) *The Globalization Paradox: Democracy and the Future of the World Economy*. New York: W. W. Norton and Co.

Rogers, C. (2017) *Plural Policing: Theory and Practice*. Bristol: Policy Press.

Rogers, P. [Paul] (2010) *Losing Control: Global Security in the 21st Century* (3rd ed.). London: Pluto Press.

Rogers, P. [Paul] (2018) 'Sustainable security: global ideas for a greater Britain', Global Security Briefing. Oxford Research Group, July.

Rogers, P. [Peter] (2016) *Resilience and the City: Change, (Dis)Order and Disaster*. London: Routledge.

Rojko, A. (2017) 'Industry 4.0 concept: background and overview', *International Journal of Interactive Mobile Technologies*, 11(5): 77–90.

Roosevelt, F.D. (1941) Annual Message to Congress on the State of the Union. American Presidency Project. Available at: www.presidency.ucsb.edu/node/209473.

Rosemont, H. (2015) 'A UK "security–industrial complex"? A reassessment of the origins, characteristics, and consequences of private sector involvement in the counter-terrorism aspects of contemporary UK national security strategy'. PhD Thesis, Kings College London.

Rosenau, J. (1990) *Turbulence in World Politics: A Theory of Change and Continuity*. Princeton, NJ: Princeton University Press.

Rosenau, J.N. (1992) 'Governance, order, and change in world politics', in J.N. Rosenau and E-O. Czempiel (eds.), *Governance Without Government: Order and Change in World Politics*. Cambridge: Cambridge University Press.

Rosenau, J.N. (1995) 'Governance in the twenty-first century', *Global Governance*, 1(1): 13–43.

Rosenau, J. N. (2003) *Distant Proximities: Dynamics Beyond Globalization*. Princeton, NJ: Princeton University Press.

Rosenau, J.N. and Czempiel, E-O. (eds.) (1992) *Governance Without Government: Order and Change in World Politics*. Cambridge: Cambridge University Press.

Rosenberg, M., Confessore, N. and Cadwalladr, C. (2018) 'How Trump consultants exploited the Facebook data of millions', *New York Times*, 17 March. Available at: www.nytimes.com/2018/03/17/us/politics/cambridge-analytica-trump-campaign.html.

Roser, M. (2020) 'War and peace', Our World in Data. Available at: https://ourworldindata.org/war-and-peace.

Ruggie, J.G. (1998) *Constructing the World Polity: Essays on International Institutionalization*. New York: Routledge.

Russell, S. and Norvig, P. (2020) *Artificial Intelligence: A Modern Approach* (4th ed.). Upper Saddle River, NJ: Pearson.

Said, E. (1978) *Orientalism*. New York: Pantheon.

Said, E.W. (2004) *From Oslo to Iraq and the Road Map*. New York: Pantheon.

Saurin, J. (2006) 'International relations as the imperial illusion; or, the need to decolonize IR', in B.G. Jones (ed.), *Decolonizing International Relations*. Lanham, MD: Rowman and Littlefield.

Sauvy, A. (1952) 'Trois mondes, une planète', *L'Observateur*, 118, 14 August.

Scarman, Lord L. (1981) *The Brixton Disorders 10–12 April 1981: Report of an Inquiry*. London: HMSO.

Schwab, K. (2017) *The Fourth Industrial Revolution*. London: Portfolio Penguin.

Schwab, K. (2018a) 'Globalization 4.0 – what does it mean?' *World Economic Forum*, 5 November. Available at: https://www.weforum.org/agenda/2018/11/globalization-4-what-does-it-mean-how-it-will-benefit-everyone/.

Schwab, K. (2018b) *Shaping the Future of the Fourth Industrial Revolution: A Guide to Building a Better World*. London: Portfolio Penguin.

Scott, J. (2017) *Metadata: The Most Potent Weapon in This Cyberwar: The New Cyber-Kinetic-Meta War*. Washington, DC: Institute for Critical Infrastructure Technology.

Securitas (2019) *Top Security Threats and Management Issues Facing Corporate America: 2019 Survey of Fortune 1000 Companies*. Parsippany, NJ: Securitas Security Services USA.

Securitas (2020) Brief Facts About the Securitas Group. Available at www.securitas.com/about-us/brief-facts.

Security Institute (2020) About. Available at https://security-institute.org.

Shackleford, S.J. (2020) *Governing New Frontiers in the Information Age: Toward Cyber Peace*. Cambridge: Cambridge University Press.

Shearing, C. (2015) 'Criminology and the Anthropocene', *Criminology and Criminal Justice*, 15(3): 255–269.

Shearing, C.D. and Stenning, P.C. (1981) 'Modern private security: its growth and implications', in M. Tonry and N. Morris (eds.) *Crime and Justice: An Annual Review of Research*, Vol. 3. Chicago: University of Chicago Press.

Shearing, C.D. and Stenning, P.C. (1983) 'Private security: implications for social control', *Social Problems*, 30(5): 498–505.

Shearing, C.D. and Stenning, P.C. (1985) 'From the panopticon to Disney World: the development of discipline', in A.N. Doob and E.L. Greenspan (eds.), *Perspectives in Criminal Law: Essays in Honour of John J. Edwards*. Toronto: Canada Law Book.

Shemella, P. (ed.) (2016) *Global Responses to Maritime Violence: Cooperation and Collective Action*. Stanford, CA: Stanford University Press.

Sherman, J. and Raymond, M. (2019) 'The U.N. passed a Russia-backed cybercrime resolution. That's not good news for Internet freedom', *Washington Post*, 4 December. Available at: www.washingtonpost.com/politics/2019/12/04/un-passed-russia-backed-cybercrime-resolution-thats-not-good-news-internet-freedom/.

Shields, I. (2020) 'Space and security', in P. Hough, A. Moran, B. Pilbeam and W. Stokes (eds.), *International Security Studies: Theory and Practice* (2nd ed.). London: Routledge.

Siitonen, L. (2010) 'The role of development assistance in fragile situations', in H. Alvaa (ed.), *Exploring the Security–Development Nexus: Perspectives from Nepal, Northern Uganda and 'Sugango'*. Helskinki: Ministry for Foreign Affairs of Finland.

Simpson, N.P., Simpson, K.J., Shearing, C.D. and Cirolia, L.R. (2019) 'Municipal finance and resilience lessons for urban infrastructure management: a case study from the Cape Town drought', *International Journal of Urban Sustainable Development*, 11(3): 257–276.

Smart, W. (2018) *Lessons Learned Review of the WannaCry Ransomware Cyber Attack*. London: Department of Health and Social Care, NHS Improvement and NHS England.

Smith, B. (2017) 'The need for a Digital Geneva Convention', *Microsoft*, 14 February. Available at: https://blogs.microsoft.com/on-the-issues/2017/02/14/need-digital-geneva-convention/#bAiKWlyybLBRAp40.99.

Smith, C. L. (2003) *Understanding Concepts in the Defence in Depth Strategy*. School of Engineering and Mathematics, Edith Cowan University, Perth, Australia.

Smith, D. (2006) 'Modelling the crisis management process: approaches and limitations', in D. Smith and D. Elliott (eds.), *Key Readings in Crisis Management: Systems and Structures for Prevention and Recovery*. London: Routledge.

Smith, M. (2016) *International Survey: Globalisation is Still Seen as a Force for Good in the World*. London: YouGov.

Smith, M.A. (2010) 'United Kingdom: how much continuity? How much change?', in E.J. Kirchner and J. Sperling (eds.), *National Security Cultures: Patterns of Global Governance*. Abingdon: Routledge.

Smith, R., Grabosky, P. and Urbas, G. (2004) *Cyber Criminals on Trial*. Cambridge: Cambridge University Press.

Smith, S. (2005) 'The contested concept of security', in K. Booth (ed.), *Critical Security Studies and World Politics*. Boulder, CO: Lynne Rienner.

Social Metrics Commission (2019) *Measuring Poverty 2019: A Report of the Social Metrics Commission*. London: Social Metrics Commission.

Sperling, J. (2010a) 'National security cultures, technologies of public goods supply and security governance', in E.J. Kirchner and J. Sperling (eds.), *National Security Cultures: Patterns of Global Governance*. Abingdon: Routledge.

Sperling, J. (2010b) 'Permanent allies or friends with benefits? The Anglo-American security relationship', in D. Brown (ed.), *The Development of British Defence Policy: Blair, Brown and Beyond*. Farnham: Ashgate.

Sperling, J. (2010c) 'United States: a full spectrum contributor to governance?', in E.J. Kirchner and J. Sperling (eds.), *National Security Cultures: Patterns of Global Governance*. Abingdon: Routledge.

Sperling, J. (ed.) (2014) *Handbook of Governance and Security*. Cheltenham: Edward Elgar.

Sperling, J. and Webber, M. (2014) 'Security governance in Europe: a return to system', *European Security*, 23(2): 126–144.

Spitzer, S. (1987) 'Security and control in capitalist societies: the fetishism of security and the secret thereof', in J. Lowman, R.J. Menzies and T.S. Plays (eds.), *Transcarceration*. Aldershot: Gower.

Stanko. E. (1988) 'Hidden violence against women', in M. Maguire and J. Ponting (eds.), *Victims of Crime: A New Deal?* Milton Keynes: Open University Press.

Statista (2019) 'Number of pirate attacks against ships worldwide from 2010 to 2019'. Available at: www.statista.com/statistics/266292/number-of-pirate-attacks-world wide-since-2006/.

Statista (2020) 'Coronavirus (COVID-19) deaths worldwide per one million population as of September 4, 2020, by country'. Available at: www.statista.com/statistics/1104709/coronavirus-deaths-worldwide-per-million-inhabitants/.

Stern, M. and Öjendal, J. (2010) 'Mapping the security–development nexus: conflict, complexity, cacophony, convergence?' *Security Dialogue*, 41(1): 5–29.

Stevens, D. and Vaughan-Williams, N. (2017) *Everyday Security Threats: Perceptions, Experiences, and Consequences*. Manchester: Manchester University Press.

Stiglitz, J. (2017) *Globalization and Its Discontents Revisited: Anti-Globalization in the Era of Trump*. New York: W.W. Norton.

Stivers, C. (2007) '"So poor and so black": Hurricane Katrina, public administration, and the issue of race', *Public Administration Review*, 67(1): 48–56.

Stockholm International Peace Research Institute (2019) *SIPRI Yearbook 2019: Armaments, Disarmament and International Security*. Stockholm: SIPRI.

Strickland, P. and Dent, J. (2017) *Online Harassment and Cyber Bullying*. London: House of Commons Library.

Subramanian, A. and Kessler, M. (2013) *The Hyperglobalization of Trade and Its Future*. Washington, DC: Peterson Institute for International Economics.

Sutton, R.M. and Farrall, S. (2005) 'Gender, socially desirable responding and the fear of crime: are women really more anxious about crime?', *British Journal of Criminology*, 45(2): 212–224.

Tadjbakhsh, S. (2013) 'In defense of the broad view of human security', in M. Martin, T. Owen (eds.), *Routledge Handbook of Human Security*. London: Routledge.

Tadjbakhsh, S. and Chenoy, A. (2007) *Human Security: Concepts and Implications*. London: Routledge.

Taleb, N.N. (2007) *The Black Swan: The Impact of the Highly Improbable*. London: Penguin.

Taleb, N.N. (2012) *Antifragile: How to Live in a World We Don't Understand*. New York: Random House.

Tavares, R. (2009) *Regional Security: The Capacity of International Organizations*. London: Routledge.

Taylor R. (2018) *Impact of 'Hostile Environment' Policy*. London: House of Lords Library.

Temperley, H.W.V. (ed.) (1920) *A History of the Peace Conference of Paris*, Vol. I. London: Oxford University Press and Hodder and Stoughton.

The Smart Cube and Ernie Deyle (2015) *Global Retail Theft Barometer 2014–15*. Thorofare, NJ: Checkpoint Systems, Inc.

The Times (1829) 'Instructions to the New Police', 25 September.

Thomas, D. and Loader, B. (2000) *Cybercrime: Law Enforcement, Security and Surveillance in the Information Age*. London: Routledge.

Thomas, M. (2019) 'The millennium bug was real – and 20 years later we face the same threats', *The Guardian*, 31 December. Available at: www.theguardian.com/commentisfree/2019/dec/31/millennium-bug-face-fears-y2k-it-systems.

Thomas, N. and Tow, W.T (2002) 'The utility of human security: sovereignty and humanitarian intervention', *Security Dialogue*, 33(2): 177–192.

Timberlake, F. (2020) 'Confined to the border: Covid-19 and the UK–France border controls', *Border Criminologies blog*, 1 July. Available at: www.law.ox.ac.uk/research-subject-groups/centre-criminology/centreborder-criminologies/blog/2020/07/confined-border.

Toft, M.D. and Duursma, A. (2018) 'Globalization and security', in M. Juergensmeyer, S. Sassen, M.B. Steger and V. Faessel (eds.), *The Oxford Handbook of Global Studies*. Oxford: Oxford University Press.

Topping, A. (2020) 'UK firms face up to threat of domestic abuse as more staff work from home', *Guardian*, 13 August. Available at: www.theguardian.com/society/2020/aug/13/uk-firms-face-up-to-threat-of-domestic-abuse-as-more-staff-work-from-home.

Tor Project (2020) History. Available at: www.torproject.org/about/history/.

Trussell Trust (2020a) About. Available at: www.trusselltrust.org/about/.

Trussell Trust (2020b) Latest Stats. Available at: www.trusselltrust.org/news-and-blog/latest-stats/end-year-stats/.

Turner, J.R. and Baker, R.M. (2019) 'Complexity theory: an overview with potential applications for the social sciences', *Systems*, 7(1): 1–23.

Ullman, R.J. (1983) 'Redefining security', *International Security*, 8(1): 129–153.

UN News (2017) *Human security approach "central" to achieving sustainable development – UN officials*', 7 July. Available at: https://news.un.org/en/story/2017/07/561142-human-security-approach-central-achieving-sustainable-development-un-officials.

United Nations (2015a) *The Millennium Development Goals Report 2015*. New York: United Nations.

United Nations (2015b) The Sendai Framework for Disaster Risk Reduction 2015–30, A/CONF.224/CRP.1, 18 March.

United Nations (2021) Growth in United Nations membership, 1945–present. Available at: https://www.un.org/en/sections/member-states/growth-united-nations-membership-1945-present/index.html.

United Nations Conference on Trade and Development (2014) *Maritime Piracy: Part I: An Overview of Trends, Costs and Trade-Related Implications*. Geneva: United Nations.

United Nations Department of Economic and Social Affairs (2019) *World Population Prospects 2019: Highlights*. New York: UN.

United Nations Development Programme (1994) *Human Development Report 1994: New Dimensions of Human Security*. New York: UNDP.

United Nations Development Programme (2009) *Community Security and Social Cohesion*. New York: UNDP.

United Nations Educational, Scientific and Cultural Organization (2020) 'Ocean Governance and Institutional Challenges'. Available at: www.unesco.org/new/en/natural-sciences/ioc-oceans/focus-areas/rio-20-ocean/ocean-governance/.

United Nations Environment Programme (2019) *Global Environment Outlook 6*. Available at: www.unenvironment.org/resources/global-environment-outlook-6.

United Nations General Assembly (1948) Resolution 217 (III) A: Universal Declaration of Human Rights (10 December). A/RES/217 (III) A.

United Nations General Assembly (1960) Resolution 1514 (XV): Declaration on the Granting of Independence to Colonial Countries and Peoples (14 December). A/RES/1514(XV).

United Nations General Assembly (1970) Resolution 2626 (XXV): International Development Strategy for the Second United Nations Development Decade (24 October). A/RES/2626(XXV).

United Nations General Assembly (2000) Resolution 55/2: United Nations Millennium Declaration (18 September). A/RES/55/2.

United Nations General Assembly (2004) *A More Secure World: Our Shared Responsibility, Report of the High-Level Panel on Threats, Challenges and Change*. New York: United Nations.

United Nations General Assembly (2008) Oceans and the Law of the Sea: Report of the Secretary-General (10 March). A/63/63.

United Nations General Assembly (2012) Resolution 66/290: Follow-up to paragraph 143 on human security of the 2005 World Summit Outcome (10 September). A/RES/66/290.

United Nations General Assembly (2015) Resolution 70/1: Transforming our world: the 2030 Agenda for Sustainable Development (25 September). A/RES/70/1.

United Nations General Assembly (2017) Resolution 71/256: New Urban Agenda (23 December). A/RES/71/256.

United Nations General Assembly (2019) Resolution 74/247: Countering the use of information and communications technologies for criminal purposes (27 December). A/RES/74/247.

United Nations High Commissioner for Refugees (2019) *Europe Situation*. Available at: https://www.unhcr.org/pages/561cc0696.html.

United Nations High Commissioner for Refugees and the International Organization for Migration (2015) 'A million refugees and migrants flee to Europe in 2015', 22 December. Available at: www.unhcr.org/uk/news/press/2015/12/567918556/million-refugees-migrants-flee-europe-2015.html.

United Nations International Strategy for Disaster Reduction (2005) *Hyogo Framework for Action 2005–2015: Building the Resilience of Nations and Communities to Disasters*. Geneva: UNISDR.

United Nations International Strategy for Disaster Reduction (2009) *2009 UNISDR Terminology on Disaster Risk Reduction*. Geneva: UNISDR.

United Nations Office for Disaster Risk Reduction, European Commission and Organisation for Economic Co-operation and Development (2013) *United Kingdom Peer Review – Building Resilience to Disasters: Implementation of the Hyogo Framework for Action (2005–2015)*. Geneva: UNODRR, EC and OECD.

United Nations Office for the Coordination of Humanitarian Affairs (2009) *Human Security in Theory and Practice*. New York, NY: UNOCHA.

United Nations Office on Drugs and Crime (2010) *Handbook on Effective Police Responses to Violence Against Women*. Vienna: UNODC.

United Nations Peacekeeping (2020) Our History. Available at: https://peacekeeping.un.org/en/our-history.

United Nations Security Council (1992) Note by the President of the Security Council: The Council's Responsibility in the Maintenance of International Peace and Security (31 January). S/23500.

United Nations Security Council (2001) Resolution 1377: Threats to international peace and security caused by terrorist acts (12 November). S/RES/1377.

United Nations Security Council (2008) Resolution 1816: On acts of piracy and armed robbery against vessels in territorial waters and the high seas off the coast of Somalia (2 June). S/RES/1816.

Urry, J. (2005) 'The complexities of the global', *Theory, Culture and Society*, 22(5): 235–254.

US Government (2005) *The National Strategy for Maritime Security*. Washington DC: US Government.

US Senate Committee on Commerce, Science, and Transportation (2013) *Cruise Industry Oversight: Recent Incidents Show Need for Stronger Focus on Consumer Protection*. Washington, DC: US Government Publishing Office.

Valverde, M. (2001) 'Governing security, governing through security', in R. Daniels, P. Macklem and K. Roach (eds.), *The Security of Freedom: Essays on Canada's Anti-Terrorism Bill*. Toronto: University of Toronto Press.

Valverde, M. (2013) 'Time and space in the governance of crime and security', Criminology and Criminal Justice Journal Lecture for 2013, University of Leeds, 16 October.

Valverde M. (2014) 'Studying the governance of crime and security: space, time and jurisdiction', *Criminology and Criminal Justice*, 14(4): 379–391.

van der Linden, S., Leiserowitz, A., Rosenthal, S. and Maibach, E. (2017) 'Inoculating the public against misinformation about climate change', *Global Challenges*, 1(2): 1–7.

van Dijk, J. (1991) *The Network Society*. London: Sage.

van Eeten, M. (2017) 'Patching security governance: an empirical view of emergent governance mechanisms for cybersecurity', *Digital Policy, Regulation and Governance*, 19(6): 429–448.

Vaughan-Williams, N. (2010) 'The UK border security continuum: virtual biopolitics and the simulation of the sovereign ban', *Environment and Planning D: Society and Space*, 28(6): 1071–1083.

Virta, S. and Branders, M. (2016) 'Legitimate security? Understanding the contingencies of security and deliberation', *British Journal of Criminology*, 56(6): 1146–1164.

Vlek, C. (2013) 'How solid is the Dutch (and the British) national risk assessment? Overview and decision-theoretic evaluation', *Risk Analysis*, 33(6): 948–971.

Volkov, V. (1999) 'Violent entrepreneurship in post-communist Russia', *Europe–Asia Studies*, 51(5): 741–754.

von Dyck, C. (2016) *DDR and SSR in War-to-Peace Transition*. Geneva: Geneva Centre for the Democratic Control of Armed Forces.

Vreÿ, F. (2013) 'Turning the tide: revisiting African maritime security', *Scientia Militaria: South African Journal of Military Studies*, 41(2): 1–23.

Wæver, O. (1995) 'Securitization and desecuritization', in R. Lipschutz (ed.), *On Security*. New York: Colombia University Press.

Wæver, O., Buzan, B., Kelstrup, M. and Lemaitre, P. (1993) *Identity, Migration and the New Security Agenda in Europe*. New York: St Martin's Press.

Wakefield, A. (2003) *Selling Security: The Private Policing of Public Space*. Cullompton: Willan Publishing.

Wakefield, A. (2009) 'Pluralization', in A. Wakefield and J. Fleming (eds.) *The Sage Dictionary of Policing*, London: Sage.

Wakefield, A. (2014) 'Corporate security and enterprise risk management', in K. Walby and R.K. Lippert (eds.), *Corporate Security in the 21st Century: Theory and Practice in International Perspective*, Basingstoke: Palgrave Macmillan.

Wakefield, A. and Button, M. (2014) 'Private policing in public spaces', in M. Reisig and R. Kane (eds.), *The Oxford Handbook of Police and Policing*. New York: Oxford University Press.

Wakefield, J. (2019) 'China is getting smarter – but at what cost?', *BBC News*, 24 December. Available at: www.bbc.co.uk/news/technology-50658538.

Walby, K. and Lippert, R.K. (2014) 'Introduction: governing every person, place and thing – critical studies of corporate security', in K. Walby and R.K. Lippert (eds.), *Corporate Security in the 21st Century: Theory and Practice in International Perspective*. Basingstoke: Palgrave-MacMillan.

Walby, K. and Lippert, R.K. (2015) 'Ford first? Corporate security and the US Department of War's Plant Protection Service's interior organization unit 1917–1918', *Labor History*, 56(2): 117–135.

Walk Free Foundation (2019) *Measurement, Action, Freedom: An independent assessment of government progress towards achieving Sustainable Development Goal 8.7*. Nedlands, Western Australia: Minderoo Foundation.

Wall, D.S. (2001) 'Cybercrimes and the internet', in D.S. Wall (ed.), *Crime and the Internet*. London: Routledge.

Wall, D.S. (2007) *Cybercrime: The Transformation of Crime in the Information Age*. Cambridge: Polity Press.

Wall, D.S. (2009) 'Cybercrime', in A. Wakefield and J. Fleming (eds.), *The Sage Dictionary of Policing*. London: Sage.

Walt, S. (1991) 'The Renaissance of Security Studies,' *International Studies Quarterly* 35(2): 211–239.

Waltz, K. (1979) *Theory of International Politics*. New York: McGraw–Hill.

Warner, M. (2002) *The Office of Strategic Services: America's First Intelligence Agency*. Washington, DC: Central Intelligence Agency.

Warner, M. (2010) 'The rise of the U.S. intelligence system, 1917–1977', in L.K. Johnson (ed.), *The Oxford Handbook of National Security Intelligence*. New York: Oxford University Press.

Waters, M. (1995) *Globalization*. London: Routledge.

Weatheritt, M. (1983) 'Community policing: does it work and how do we know?', in T. Bennett (ed.), *The Future of Policing*. Cambridge: Institute of Criminology.

Webber, M. (2014) 'Security governance', in J. Sperling (ed.), *Handbook of Governance and Security*. Cheltenham: Edward Elgar.

Weber, L. and Pickering, S. (2011) *Globalization and Borders: Death at the Global Frontier*. Basingstoke: Palgrave Macmillan.

Webster, F. (2014) *Theories of the Information Society*. (4th ed.). London: Routledge.

Weiss, R.P. (1978) 'The emergence and transformation of private detective and industrial policing in the United States, 1850–1940', *Crime and Social Justice*, 1: 35–48.

Weiss, R.P. (2014) 'Corporate security at Ford Motor Company: from the Great War to the Cold War', in K. Walby and R.K. Lippert (eds.), *Corporate Security in the 21st Century: Theory and Practice in International Perspective*. Basingstoke: Palgrave Macmillan.

Wendt, A. (1999) *Social Theory of International Politics*. Cambridge: Cambridge University Press.

White, A. (2010) *The Politics of Private Security: Regulation, Reform and Re-Legitimation*. Basingstoke: Palgrave Macmillan.

White, A. and Gill, M. (2013) 'The transformation of policing: from ratios to rationalities', *British Journal of Criminology*, 53(1): 74–93.

White, R. and Heckenberg, D. (2014) *Green Criminology: An Introduction to the Study of Environmental Harm*. London: Routledge.

White House (1991) *Intelligence Capabilities 1992–2005*. National Security Review 29. White House: Washington, DC.

White House (1999) *A National Security Strategy for a New Century*. Washington, DC: White House.

White House (2002) *National Security Strategy of the United States of America*. Washington, DC: White House.

White House (2010) *National Security Strategy of the United States of America*. White House: Washington, DC.

White House (2015) *National Security Strategy of the United States of America*. White House: Washington, DC.

White House (2017) *National Security Strategy of the United States of America*. White House: Washington, DC.

Whitfield, J. (2004) *Unhappy Dialogue: The Metropolitan Police and London's West Indian Community*. London: Routledge.

Whitman, R.G. (2015) 'Brexit or Bremain: what future for the UK's European diplomatic strategy?' *International Affairs*, 92(3): 509–529.

Williams, W. (2020) *Windrush Lessons Learned Review: Independent Review by Wendy Williams*. London: House of Commons.

Williamson, J. (2009) 'A short history of the Washington Consensus', *Law and Business Review of the Americas*, 15(1): 7–23.

Williamson, O.E. (1996) *The Mechanisms of Governance*. New York: Oxford University Press.

Willis, K.S. and Aurigi, A. (eds.) (2020) *The Routledge Companion to Smart Cities*. London: Routledge.

Wilner, A.S. (2018) 'Cybersecurity and its discontents: artificial intelligence, the internet of things, and digital misinformation', *International Journal*, 73(2): 308–316.

Wing, M.J. (2003) 'Rethinking the easy way out: flags of convenience in the post-September 11th era', *Tulane Maritime Law Journal*, 28(1): 173–190.

Wolfers, A. (1962) 'National security as an ambiguous symbol', in A. Wolfers (ed.), *Discord and Collaboration: Essays on International Politics*. Baltimore, MD: John Hopkins University Press.

Wood, J. and Shearing, C. (2007) *Imagining Security*. Cullompton: Willan.

World Bank (2016) 'Cause of Death, by non-communicable diseases (% of total)'. Available at: https://data.worldbank.org/indicator/SH.DTH.NCOM.ZS.

World Bank (2018) *Poverty and Shared Prosperity 2018: Piecing Together the Poverty Puzzle*. Washington, DC: World Bank.

World Bank (2020) 'What is the blue economy?' Available at: www.worldbank.org/en/news/infographic/2017/06/06/blue-economy.

World Economic Forum (2018) *Future of Jobs Report 2018*. Geneva: WEF.

World Economic Forum (2020) *The Global Risks Report 2020*. Geneva: WEF.

World Health Organization (2020) 'UN Tackles "Infodemic" of Misinformation and Cybercrime in COVID-19 Crisis'. Available at: www.un.org/en/un-coronavirus-communications-team/un-tackling-%E2%80%98infodemic%E2%80%99-misinformation-and-cybercrime-covid-19.

Wyn-Jones, R. (1999) *Security, Strategy and Critical Theory*. Boulder, CO: Lynne Rienner.

Yar, M. and Steinmetz, K.F. (2019) *Cybercrime and Society* (3rd ed.). London: Sage.

Young, O.R. (2017) *Governing Complex Systems: Social Capital for the Anthropocene*. Cambridge, MA: MIT Press.

Young, R.O. (1999) *Governance in World Affairs*. Ithaca, NY: Cornell University Press.

Zedner, L. (2006) 'Policing before and after the police: the historical antecedents of contemporary crime control', *British Journal of Criminology*, 46(1): 78–96.

Zedner, L. (2009) *Security*. London: Routledge.

Index